YOU DESERVE IT

YOU

DESERVE

IT

*The Definitive Guide to
Getting the Veteran Benefits
You've Earned*

REVISED AND EXPANDED **SECOND EDITION**

BRIAN REESE

LIONCREST
PUBLISHING

YOU DESERVE IT
The Definitive Guide to Getting the Veteran Benefits You've Earned
Second Edition

ISBN	978-1-5445-4014-6	*Hardcover*
	978-1-5445-4015-3	*Paperback*
	978-1-5445-4016-0	*Ebook*

*This revised and expanded second edition book is dedicated
to you. Us. Veterans. So here's to the brave ones who raised
their right hand and took the oath to support and defend the
Constitution of the United States against all enemies, foreign and
domestic. For that, I salute you and stand alongside you forever.*

CONTENTS

Introduction   **xiii**

PART I: VA BENEFITS

1. VA Disability Compensation Benefits   **3**
2. VA Pension   **43**
3. VA Healthcare   **51**
4. VA Education   **57**
5. VA Housing and Home Loan Guarantees   **65**
6. VA Job Training and Employment   **71**
7. VA Burials and Memorials   **77**
8. VA Mental Health Resources   **81**

PART II: STATE BENEFITS

9. The Midwest Region   **95**
10. The North-East Region   **143**
11. The Southern Region   **187**
12. The West Region   **241**

PART III: OTHER BENEFITS

13. Nonprofit Resource List   **297**
14. For-Profit Veterans Discounts   **321**

PART IV: BONUS RESOURCES

15. Bonus Resources   **377**

Conclusion   **387**
Acknowledgments   **389**
About the Author   **391**

INTRODUCTION

Dear veteran, what you're about to discover in this book could change your life. You'll uncover a variety of federal and state benefits that may provide you with hundreds of thousands—maybe millions—of dollars' worth of tax-free compensation and benefits. Currently, according to our data at VA Claims Insider, eight out of ten veterans are *not* receiving the benefits they know they deserve by law.[1] Truth bomb: that means 80% of you reading this now are missing out on FREE money. And that's if you have a Department of Veterans Affairs (VA) disability rating at all. Did you know that of the roughly 18 million veterans alive today,[2] about 5.2 million veterans[3]—or less than 29% of you reading this book right now (yep, around one in four veterans)—receive *any* VA disability benefits at all? That's shameful, and I'm on a mission to change it.

---

1 Statistics adapted from a survey performed by VA Claims Insider of more than 1,000 veterans with disability ratings; 87% of respondents reported that their ratings did not represent their disabilities.

2 US Census Bureau, *Those Who Served: America's Veterans from World War II to the War on Terror* (Washington, DC: US Census Bureau, 2020), 1.

3 US Department of Veterans Affairs, *VBA Annual Benefits Report: Fiscal Year 2021*, "Compensation" section, 5. https://www.benefits.va.gov/REPORTS/abr/docs/2021_compensation.pdf.

How is this situation possible? First, there's a lack of awareness, due in part to inadequate education. I didn't even know the VA—the US Department of Veterans Affairs—existed until the day I took off the uniform. And even then, I didn't know about disability benefits. It would be *years* before I learned I could receive help from the government for my service-related disabilities. Heck, it was years before I figured out the pain I suffered from even was a disability.

Maybe you were ahead of me. You might have even started an application...but then gotten so confused by the complexity of the system, the convoluted process, and the seemingly endless addendums and amendments to eligibility rules that you just gave up.

Or maybe you *did* apply. Except the response you received was either a denial or an "underrating" (meaning the VA acknowledged some kind of disability but disagreed about its severity or origin). If that's you, you are understandably frustrated. You probably spent dozens of hours searching on Google, combing the VA website, collecting the documents you needed, and navigating the system—only to feel unseen or, worse, like you've been called a liar.

You're not a liar. The problem isn't you. Nor is it the VA, honestly! The VA is not trying to keep money from you. It wants to help you. *The problem is the system.* That's where I come in. This book is a comprehensive guide to hundreds of benefits at the federal and state levels, plus information about even more benefits and discounts you can get from nonprofit organizations and businesses. And I'll tell you how to actually get those benefits.

But even if you don't have a VA disability, there are still loads of benefits available to you as a veteran—and this book is the most comprehensive resource ever published on the topic. It's an encyclopedia of veterans' benefits. It's your North Star to guide you on your veterans' benefits journey.

But first, I need to change your mind about something.

YOU SERVED. YOU DESERVE.

A lot of veterans think the word "disabled" only applies to people who have it much worse than they do. They think, "I haven't been in combat. I haven't lost a limb. I don't have cancer from Agent Orange. Heck, I'm lucky to have a job! I shouldn't apply for benefits because those are for veterans who actually deserve them." Frankly, that is complete bullshit. It's one of the LIES we tell ourselves. First of all, there are enough benefits to go around. Your benefits do not affect any other veterans' benefits! But more importantly, if you have any kind of disability as a result of your service, then guess what? You *deserve* benefits. Yes, you read that correctly: you deserve benefits for your honorable service.

Allow me to give you permission to be disabled. You don't have to pretend you're fine or suffer alone in silence. The notion of *service before self* may have served you well while you wore the uniform. But afterward, it causes pain and suffering. Truth is, you're no good to your family, friends, or work unless you take care of yourself first.

Further, not all disabilities are visible. Most—yes, most—veterans struggle with undiagnosed mental health issues such as post-traumatic stress disorder, anxiety, and depression. Often, these lead to substance abuse, and almost always, they lead to isolation and loneliness. I want to tell you right now that you are important and you matter. My colleagues and I have been where you are. I can be in a room full of people and feel alone, completely detached.

When you wear the uniform, you're connected with other people who've experienced the same stuff. Then you take the uniform off and are surrounded by people who can't possibly comprehend what you've gone through. You feel separate from the reality everybody else lives in. I hear stories like this *all* the time. People come to us not only for help applying for financial benefits but also because they crave identity, community, and purpose in life. They want to feel important again. Our fellow veterans tell us they feel lost after service. They feel like people hear the word "veteran" and immediately think they're broken or crazy. This stigma leads them to try and pretend like everything's fine, ignoring whatever struggles they face.

But you might not be fine, and that's okay. It's okay not to be okay! You experienced tough stuff while you served and now you're processing it. This is exactly why there are resources to help you. The VA exists to help you. And my company, VA Claims Insider, exists to make sure you *get* that help.

★ ★ ★

Need Immediate Help?

I will cover mental health resources in depth later, but if you need help right now or are thinking about taking your own life, I am directing you to call 988 and then press 1, or chat with someone online at *VeteransCrisisLine.net*. America loses roughly twenty-two veterans to suicide every day. Please don't be one of them.

★ ★ ★

Getting your benefits is about more than money. Tuition benefits help veterans find a career that gives them purpose. Home loan benefits help provide a more stable environment for their families. Healthcare benefits improve their physical and psychological health and well-being. Veterans tell us that getting the benefits they deserve has improved their relationships with their loved ones, helped them secure better futures for their kids, and made them exponentially happier and healthier.

At VA Claims Insider, we celebrate life change. People tell us our services have saved their marriages and even their lives. We serve veterans virtually, in community, and with purpose. And yes, we can help you get the benefits you deserve. You could spend a tiny amount of time and money on this book and two weeks later have saved $200,000 on student loans.

Would that change your life? I think so.

★　★　★

History of the VA

Taking care of veterans goes back to the earliest days of our nation, when a Plymouth Colony law in 1636 provided pensions for soldiers wounded in battle. Then, shortly after the start of the Revolutionary War, to encourage enlistments and reduce desertions, the fledgling nation promised financial aid to any soldier or sailor injured in the service of the colonies who couldn't earn a living *as a result*. Later, during the Civil War, the General Pension Act expanded the idea by providing payments to Union soldiers based on their degree of disability.

Over the years, even as progress led to the development of better care for veterans and their families, federal veterans' programs still lacked a unified governing body to oversee and standardize operations. The first comprehensive consolidation effort of federal veterans' programs wouldn't happen until after World War I, when Congress created the Veterans Bureau, which Herbert Hoover later made a federal administration and renamed the Veterans Administration. The VA finally became a cabinet-level executive department under President Ronald Reagan. President George H. W. Bush hailed the creation of the new department, saying, "There is only one place for the Veterans of America: in the Cabinet Room, at the table with the President of the United States of America."

Today's VA is responsible for serving the needs of those injured in our nation's defense, as well as the families of those injured or killed in service, by providing healthcare, disability compensation and rehabilitation, education assistance, home loans, and national cemetery services, among other services and benefits. The VA is the largest healthcare system in the world and the largest provider and supporter of telehealth services in the world! As we stand in the present and look toward the future, the very existence of the VA helps us remember our storied past, all who have served or are serving, and all who honor America's veterans.

MY PATH TO PURPOSE

I left the United States Air Force in 2012 with a variety of physical and mental ailments, some of which I was willing to be honest about and some of which I wasn't. When I attended my Transition Assistance Program, a representative from the VA in Boston gave a one-hour presentation that basically said, "If you have some stuff going on, you may be eligible for benefits." That was the first time I'd ever heard about the VA, and it was *way* too late. I had multiple undiagnosed mental health conditions from a combat deployment to Afghanistan.

Still, generally speaking, I was lucky. I was put in touch with a Veterans Service Organization called AMVETS, and a quality officer helped me navigate the disability application process, which allowed me to get a VA disability rating for my service-connected disabilities. But it would be *six years* before I got the benefits I deserved. I didn't even know you could be underrated! There was no comprehensive resource to help me educate myself on the topic. If you do the math, over those six years, I lost almost $100,000 of tax-free benefits that I deserved by law—simply because I didn't know any better.

Meanwhile, even with my VA rating, I wasn't getting the mental health care I needed because I wasn't fully honest with myself. As a former officer in the US Air Force, I believed it wasn't possible for me to have a mental health condition. *I'm too strong*, I thought. *As the commander, I take care of our troops and their well-being*, I told myself. But what I have since realized is that I can't take care of anybody else unless I care for myself first.

At the time, I coped by turning to alcohol and drugs. It was a way to hide. But then I became addicted, and that led to all kinds of destruction. I ended a relationship in divorce. I struggled at work and eventually resigned. I lost most of my friendships. I pushed loved ones away. And I thought I was the only veteran suffering from a mental health condition, which in retrospect is bonkers, but that's how it **feels**. So I suffered alone in silence.

I eventually hit rock bottom, too broken to stand on my own two feet. And then, through prayer and by being open and vulnerable, I finally got help. Part of that help came from a coach who forced me to answer really tough questions about who I am and what my purpose is. I realized that God put me on earth to serve fellow veterans and give them *hope*. There can be beauty in the brokenness.

Then I thought, *Well, I know a lot about the VA disability system...and most veterans know very little about it, yet we all desperately need this information.* So I started VA Claims Insider, which is now the largest community of Veterans Helping Veterans Worldwide. That's how I regained a sense of purpose. Being in community with other veterans has been hugely therapeutic for me. I got my identity back—you helped save my life—and that's what we want to do for you.

WHAT YOU WILL LEARN IN THIS BOOK

In these pages, you will uncover the federal and state benefits you deserve by law and what you need to do to secure them. This book is not a series of tricks to help you file false claims or get what you don't deserve. That's wrong and illegal. Remember at the beginning of this chapter, when I told you that you will probably walk away from this book with hundreds of thousands of dollars? The crazy thing about that statement is that it is absolutely *legal*. The reason it sounds too good to be true is simply because almost nobody knows this money is available to them, just sitting out there waiting.

I've also provided a list of some of the best services and discounts available from both nonprofit and for-profit organizations. I've organized all the information in short chapters and tried to make simple what can otherwise be a very confusing process. The result is a guide—a clear, straightforward, no-nonsense guide.

To that point, this resource is definitely not exhaustive. There's so much information out there that trying to tell you everything would only confuse you and hamstring your motivation. If there's one thing I want to do, it is to motivate you. So I've stuck to what I believe are the best and most accessible benefits. This is your action plan to get them.

The sole purpose of this book is to educate and inspire veterans to take action. Only through action can you finally get the federal and state benefits you deserve by law. I can't emphasize the word "action" enough.

If you simply read this book as a passive observer and don't act on its contents, you will not get anything. Think about this brilliant quote by George Bernard Shaw: "If you teach a man anything, he will never learn." Knowledge is not power. Knowledge is knowledge, and power is power. But knowledge can become power through action. And this is your action moment!

Yes, I said that this book will make the process of getting your benefits as simple as possible, but simple is not always easy. Still, I'm here to help you get back up off the ground, get into the ring, and throw a few more punches. I will never let you quit, nor will I let you fail.

✶ ✶ ✶

Seven Tips to Get the Most Out of This Book

- **Tip #1:** Before you skip a section completely, stop to ask, "How does this concept fit into the bigger picture?" Although there may be sections that don't pertain to your specific needs, most of the content is intertwined and sometimes builds on what comes before.

- **Tip #2:** Highlight, underline, and dog-ear the most important pages of this book. Some of the content is complex, although I've done my best to keep it simple. Mark whatever parts you know you'll need to find again later.

- **Tip #3:** Look for ways to teach these concepts to other veterans. The best way to master a concept is by teaching it. And what a great way to serve other veterans in the process!

- **Tip #4:** Set a clear goal for when you will finally get the benefits you deserve, and mark it on the calendar. Will it happen exactly on that timeline? Maybe, maybe not. But if you don't set a goal, you may never start working toward it at all. Hold yourself accountable for your own results. Nobody should care more about your benefits than you do.

- **Tip #5:** Don't be afraid to fail! There are so many factors involved in the rating process that even if you do everything "right," you still might not get the rating you deserve the first time around. It'll feel like a gut punch. That's when you get back up off the ground and punch back. The VA disability process never ends, unless you quit. But we won't let you quit.

- **Tip #6:** Keep a journal of the most important concepts in this book that apply to you. Writing forces clear thinking. In the meantime, you'll create your own personal tip sheet of helpful strategies and lessons learned.

- **Tip #7:** Stay up to date and educate yourself! Laws and rules change often. The concepts in this book are evergreen, but some of the specifics may change. Scan the QR codes throughout this book for direct links to expert-level educational resources. The bonus resources at the end of this book list some websites where you can find additional great information.

Now take a moment to stop what you're doing.

Close your eyes and breathe.

Imagine how the mastery of the core concepts taught in this book will help you lead a richer, happier, and healthier life.

Imagine having more tax-free benefits for you and your family.

Imagine being able to give more back to society.

Imagine going to the doctor, being vulnerable about your disability conditions, and finally getting the help and treatment you need.

You *can* have all these things and more, but you must will them into existence through your actions.

Nobody will do this work for you.

You must do it for yourself, and we will lead you through the maze of veterans' benefits.

Herbert Spencer once remarked, "For the great aim of education is not knowledge but action."

Fellow veterans, this is an action book.

BOOM!

PART 1

VA BENEFITS

In this section, you'll find out how to secure disability compensation, healthcare, pensions, burial benefits, mental health attention, and a variety of loans, including student, home, and business. This discussion will not be exhaustive—there's already too much information out there, and much of it applies to only a small number of people. My goal is to simplify the process by focusing on VA benefits that are either the most helpful or the most commonly needed.

First and foremost, I'll demystify disability compensation: how to get the rating you deserve and how that rating affects *every* other benefit available from the VA. Most of the chapters in this book are short and sweet, but not Chapter 1. Understanding disability compensation is the difference between thousands of dollars and millions of dollars. Strap in! This is life-changing work.

I can tell you about a gentleman by the name of Gabe, who went from a 40% rating to a 100%

permanent-and-total rating in seventy-six days, which qualified his entire family for free healthcare and dropped his property taxes to zero. In just a few months, he secured the kind of status that will provide him with more than $1 million over the rest of his life.

How to Approach Part 1

- First, in Chapter 1, learn how to achieve the highest possible VA disability rating allowed to you by law.

- Then in Chapters 2 through 8—which are all much shorter than Chapter 1—learn how to use that new, higher VA disability rating to apply for a whole slew of other federal benefits.

★ ★ ★

CHAPTER ONE

VA DISABILITY COMPENSATION BENEFITS

The Department of Veteran Affairs exists to take care of veterans who served. You served, so you're a veteran—therefore, the VA exists both for you and because of you! *You Served. You Deserve.* I'm going to *keep* reminding you of that throughout this book. If you are eligible for disability compensation—a tax-free monetary benefit that can be paid to you every month for the rest of your life—then you deserve it. That's right, VA disability compensation benefits are tax-free at both the state and federal levels. And I want to help you learn how to get them.

By law, the VA disability process is not supposed to be adversarial, but it certainly feels that way! After you apply, the Compensation and Pension (C&P) examiner and VA rater determine the validity of your claim. That's just the way the process works, but it doesn't mean the VA is trying to get out of helping you. It *wants* to take care of you. Heck, that is its main function.

If you have an injury or disease that was incurred or aggravated during active military service and it negatively impacts your work or life, VA disability compensation benefits can provide you with tax-free monetary relief. You may also receive compensation for disabilities that arose before or after service. For instance, you might have had a preexisting condition that your active duty service made worse ("aggravated"), or a disability that began during your active duty military service may not have been properly documented in your Service Treatment Records (STRs) at the time.

In the following pages, I'll tell you everything you'll need to know (and have) in order to file a strong and verifiable claim, and I'll prepare you for every part of the process afterward, including how long each step takes and how to share your "uncomfortable truths" during the independent medical exam (aka the "C&P exam").

The amount of VA disability compensation you'll receive will depend on the final combined VA disability rating. Therefore, I'll also explain how the VA's rating process works and how to make sure you get the highest possible rating you deserve by law, because that final number will, in turn, determine your eligibility for every other federal and state benefit available (basically, all of Part 1 and Part 2 of this book).

Thus, this chapter is foundational and critically important!

ELIGIBILITY

If you were separated or discharged under dishonorable conditions, that's a nonstarter. You must upgrade your discharge first, which you can do right on the VA's website. But you probably already knew that, so let's move on to the nitty-gritty. If (1) you suffer from any of the 834-plus disability conditions recognized by the VA, (2) your active duty service caused those disability conditions or made them worse, and (3) your disability conditions are limiting or affecting your work or life in a negative way, then *boom*, you're eligible!

But, of course, that's not the end of the story. You must prove it. If you ask the VA to do that work for you, it's a recipe for disaster. They don't have the time! It's much better to advocate for yourself or work with an accredited representative.

When the VA denies disability compensation claims, it's almost always because there isn't enough proof, meaning you failed to prove your case on an "at least as likely as not" basis. That means you need a minimum of 50% positive evidence. (If there's a tie between positive and negative evidence, the benefit of the doubt passes to the veteran.)

Later in this chapter, we will discuss exactly how to prove eligibility in your application. But first, you'll need to understand the three elements required to get your claim approved. Let's jump into the nuts and bolts of "evidence" so you can win, connect with services, and get rated at the appropriate level under the law.

1. A Medical Diagnosis

The number one thing you can do to improve the chances of a VA disability compensation claim approval is to have your condition(s) diagnosed and documented in a military, VA, or private medical record. If you think you have a disability but don't yet have it diagnosed, please consider going to see a doctor or other healthcare professional right away. If you've never seen a doctor for the conditions you're claiming, you're wasting your time. You've got no evidence!

Say, for example, you're tired all the time, you wake up gasping for air, and you snore loudly, so you think you might have sleep apnea. A recent study found that 69% of Iraq and Afghanistan veterans had a high risk for sleep apnea and that this risk increased in those who also suffered from PTSD,[4] so you're probably right—and eligible for benefits. But you won't get them just by telling the VA, "Hey, I've got sleep apnea, and it's due to my military service, so you connect the dots." Only a sleep study can confirm the presence of sleep apnea. Furthermore, if you weren't diagnosed on active duty, chances are you'll have a tough time connecting your sleep apnea directly to service (more on that in a bit).

In an ideal world, you wouldn't have to see a VA doctor or private doctor now to get a diagnosis because you saw a military doctor while you were active, and therefore your condition was diagnosed—and documented—during service. If your diagnosis came from a military doctor while you were in service, your claim will almost certainly be approved (as long as you can also prove that the condition is negatively affecting your work or livelihood and generally that it is a chronic disability). *Pro Tip*: It is very helpful to get a *current* medical diagnosis of a disability condition even if it's documented in your STRs. Doing so provides evidence in establishing that you are currently suffering from a disabling condition or disease that could be a result of the illness, injury, exposure, or aggravation that occurred in service, and generally this condition or disease must be chronic.

Unfortunately, however, many veterans never went to the doctor while they were in the military. Maybe they didn't want to seem or feel vulnerable. Maybe, in their unit, being sick carried a stigma. Maybe they didn't realize they had a medical condition. Or maybe they were just lazy. Whatever the reason, they don't have a record of their condition. Fortunately, it's never too late to get your butt to a doctor. My humble

---

4   Peter J. Colvonen, Tonya Masino, Sean P. A. Drummond, Ursula S. Myers, Abigail C. Angkaw, and Sonya B. Norman, "Obstructive Sleep Apnea and Posttraumatic Stress Disorder among OEF/OIF/OND Veterans," *Journal of Clinical Sleep Medicine* 11, no. 5 (May 15, 2015): 513–18, doi: 10.5664/jcsm.4692.

advice is not to even try applying for VA disability compensation benefits until you've had that appointment. And make darn sure your disability condition is medically diagnosed in a medical record.

2. Proof of Service Connection (aka "Nexus")

VA disability compensation benefits require that your disability condition be "service-connected," which the VA calls a "Nexus." It's nothing more than a fancy word for a logical link or connection between A and B. For example, Event A happened, and now I have Condition B as a result. In other words, your disability must be the result of an injury or disease that was incurred or aggravated while on active duty or active duty for training or that was caused or aggravated by another service-connected disability (we call those situations "secondary claims").

Therefore, in addition to having a medical diagnosis from the doctor, you also need to have a powerful argument that the disability is related to service or another service-connected disability and not caused by something else. Ideally, this support comes in the form of a Medical Nexus Letter, which is an evidence-based document prepared by a qualified medical professional, such as a PA-C or an MD, that helps to establish a connection between the claimed in-service disease or injury and your current disability.

Pro Tip: You must ensure your independent medical opinion (aka Medical Nexus Letter) has high probative value, meaning it reaches a high level of proof. For a credible Medical Nexus Letter to have *high* probative value in support of your claim for VA disability benefits, it should be thorough, factual, and include a convincing evidence-based rationale based in scholarly research. The letter should also include all records reviewed as well as relevant medical research reports, including Board of Veterans' Appeals (BVA) decisions, to help support the doctor's independent medical opinion. The strongest Nexus Letters include a Nexus statement with the words "at least as likely as not," assuming the independent medical provider believes your disability condition was caused or aggravated by your active duty military service or another service-connected disability.

★ ★ ★

Five Types of Service Connection

- **Direct Service Connection:** This is the most common method of service connection for VA disability compensation benefits. You're telling the VA that your current disability condition is the direct result of your active duty military service. Perhaps it was a training incident, car accident, combat deployment, stress from the job, or other in-service incident, injury, event, or disease that directly caused or made your current disability condition worse. An example is combat PTSD due to constant rocket and mortar attacks in Afghanistan. The PTSD is due to your combat deployment, which is directly related to your military service.

- **Secondary Service Connection:** In accordance with 38 CFR § 3.310, a current disability condition that is proximately due to or the result of a service-connected disease or injury is also service connected. Let's say, for example, you contracted tinnitus while serving. Today, even though you are no longer serving, that service-connected tinnitus might be causing or aggravating your migraine headaches, anxiety, and/or depression. Service connection on a secondary basis requires a "showing of causation or aggravation." Instead of proving that your disability is directly service connected, you'll need to prove that it's caused or made worse by a different disability (which is service connected). In this example, you could file a VA disability claim for migraine headaches secondary to your service-connected tinnitus. *Pro Tip:* A Medical Nexus Letter is highly recommended to help you prove secondary service connection under the law.

- **Presumptive Service Connection:** If your disability condition meets certain criteria set forth by Congress, then your disability condition will be presumed to have been caused by service. Examples include certain chronic debilitating diseases, diseases specific to radiation exposure, and diseases associated with herbicide agents. Blue Water Navy, Persian Gulf War, and Camp Lejeune veterans are included under this provision. (38 CFR § 3.309 discusses diseases subject to presumptive service connection in more detail.) *Pro Tip:* Although you are not required to provide a Nexus to establish presumptive service connection, it's highly recommended that you at least write a personal statement as to *why* you think your disability meets the legal requirements for presumptive service connection. You might want to obtain a Medical Nexus Letter as well.

- **Service Connection by Aggravation:** Sometimes military service worsens a preexisting condition. For example, a veteran may have had flat feet prior to entering service, but wearing military boots and prolonged standing worsened the condition, leading to a painful disability called plantar fasciitis, which is eligible for compensation under the law. Additionally, if a veteran has a service-connected knee condition that aggravates a nonservice-connected back condition, they could get service connection for their back based on aggravation—provided they can prove that their condition was worsened beyond its natural progression by military service or the service-connected disability it is secondary to.

- **Service Connection by 38 USC 1151:** This refers to disabilities or death that result from "hospital care, medical or surgical treatment, or examination" by a VA medical professional or facility or due to participation in a program of vocational rehabilitation. In my experience, this type of service connection is uncommon and hard to prove, and it typically requires an accredited VA attorney to pursue.

★ ★ ★

3. *"Severity of Symptoms," Plus Negative Work/Life Impacts*

To receive VA disability compensation benefits, you must prove not only that you have a disability and that it is connected to your military service but *also* that your disability is negatively affecting your work, life, and/or social functioning. In other words, they're not going to provide you with monthly compensation just because you were injured. But they will compensate you if that injury continues to negatively affect you. You'll need to have a powerful argument that there are persistent and recurring symptoms that impact you, known as "Severity of Symptoms." Maybe you've had to take all your sick days at work because of your migraine headaches. Maybe your PTSD is creating anger issues that have put your job in jeopardy.

The severity of your symptoms has a direct correlation to the rating you receive, and it's up to you to argue their severity in a compelling and effective way. You'll want to write a strong personal statement for each disability condition you're claiming, using VA Form 21-4138, Statement in Support of a Claim. *Pro Tip:* Search CFR Title 38 Part 4, "Schedule for Rating Disabilities," for the name of your disability and your approximate symptoms. You'll want to tell the C&P examiner your current symptoms and how your disability negatively impacts your work, life, or social functioning. Be descriptive and use specific examples.

Further, some disabilities automatically qualify for higher ratings than others, which brings us to the next section.

VA Special Monthly Compensation (SMC) is an additional tax-free benefit that can be paid to veterans, their spouses, surviving spouses, and parents. For veterans, SMC is a higher rate of compensation paid due to special circumstances, such as the need for aid and attendance by another person or a specific disability, such as loss of use of a hand or leg. For spouses and surviving spouses, this benefit is commonly referred to as "aid and attendance" and is paid based on the need of aid and attendance by another person.

A Permanent and Total (P&T) rating requires your disabilities to have two qualities: the impairment is reasonably certain to continue throughout the life of the disabled person (it's permanent), and the impairment of the mind or body is sufficient to render it impossible for the average person to substantially hold gainful occupation (it's total). Although the VA can technically remove a P&T rating for a variety of reasons, it's unlikely to happen unless you've taken an action that would cause a VA rater to review your file, like filing for a new claim. *Pro Tip:* If you're rated at 100% or trying to upgrade to 100%, you can also apply for P&T status on the VA.gov website. You'll want to open a new claim and add a disability called "Request for P&T Status." It's recommended to have your doctor write a letter on your behalf explaining why your disabilities render you permanently and totally disabled and why all of your rated disabilities are Static. Static means they will not show material improvement over time.

★

The SEM Method

Okay, we've covered a lot already, and I want to make this information super simple and easy to remember. At VA Claims Insider, we use a formula called the SEM Method. The SEM Method should serve as a quick reminder for how to get the VA disability compensation benefits you've earned.

- If you have the right VA disability claim **Strategy**, the tactics become simple and easy.

- If you're **Educated** about the process, you're more likely to prepare, take action, and succeed.

- If you have the proper **Medical Evidence** to prove your disabilities, you're more likely to get the VA rating you deserve by law.

Here's the SEM Method formula:

Strategy + Education + Medical Evidence =
VA Rating You Deserve!

★ ★ ★

HOW THE VA RATING SYSTEM WORKS

Your combined VA disability rating number is incredibly important. It could be the difference between receiving thousands of dollars and millions of dollars. Every service-connected disability will receive a rating of 0%, 10%, 20%, 30%, 40%, 50%, 60%, 70%, 80%, 90%, or 100%. The higher your rating, the more benefits you'll receive. For example, a 10% VA rating is worth just over $160 per month, while a 100% VA rating can be worth more than $3,500 per month. Your final rating depends on the severity of your disability: the impact it has on your work, life, and social functioning. However, some disabilities by nature impact you more than others and therefore might garner higher ratings.

★ ★ ★

Pro Tip: High-Value versus Low-Value Disability Claims

A high-value VA disability claim refers to specific disability conditions that have a high likelihood of being rated at 30% or higher on their own. I've outlined the top ten high-value disability conditions here.

Logically, then, a low-value VA disability claim refers to specific disability conditions that have a low likelihood of being rated at 30% or higher on their own. These include most musculoskeletal conditions as well as conditions such as tinnitus, hearing loss, and scars, among others.

The conditions listed here are considered "high-value" claims. If you suffer from ANY of these conditions, they should become part of your VA disability claim strategy:

- mental health conditions (thirty-one ratable disability conditions)
- sleep apnea syndromes
- migraines (headaches)
- plantar fasciitis
- chronic fatigue syndrome (CFS)
- irritable bowel syndrome (IBS)

- gastroesophageal reflux disease (GERD)
- radiculopathy
- peripheral neuropathy
- Gulf War syndrome presumptive conditions
- Ménière's syndrome

Top Ten High-Value VA Disability Claims Explained

We don't have enough space in this book to explain all the high-value VA disability claims in detail, but I don't want to leave you hanging. If you want to learn how to *increase* your VA rating in *less* time (legally and ethically), please scan this QR code for your instant download of my number one most downloaded e-book. It's *free*!

Top Fifty Most Common VA Disability Claims Revealed

This is a new high-value resource for you. Many veterans want to know about the most common VA disability claims (and how to get them service connected). So we put together a "Top Fifty" list just for you. Simply scan this QR code for instant access to this *free* guide!

★ ★ ★

THE "FUZZY MATH" BEHIND YOUR RATING

If you have one disability, then the rating for that disability and the rating for your total disability will be one and the same. However, most of us have more than one service-connected disability. So how does the VA consider all of them and wind up with one combined VA rating percentage?

If you receive several ratings for corresponding disabilities, they will not just be added together in a cumulative nature. If I am rated at 70% for PTSD and 50% for sleep apnea, I won't be 120% disabled. It's physically impossible to be more than 100% disabled. Instead, the VA starts with your highest overall rating, multiplies the next highest rating into the previous one, adds it on, and so on.

In the example I just gave, the VA would take the highest rating first, the 70% for PTSD. According to that number, they would assume that 100% – 70% = 30% of me is still "healthy." Then they multiply that remaining 30% by the rating for my sleep apnea disability, which is 50%. Take 50% of 30% and you wind up with 15%. Add that 15% on to the original 70%, and you wind up with an 85% total disability rating, which would be rounded up to a 90% combined VA disability rating. The process continues for each disability remaining from highest to lowest.

Is that clear? Clear as mud! Still, it's the system we have. Now that you understand it, you can see how someone could have five or six disabilities, but if they're all low value, the rating won't reach anywhere close to 100%. You'd have to layer in some 70s, 60s, 50s, 30s, and so forth. *Fact*: It takes *twenty-seven* 10% disability ratings to reach a 100% combined VA rating.

But rather than trying to run your own calculations, just use a Combined VA Rating Calculator! We have an awesome *free* VA calculator on our website at *VAClaimsInsider.com*.

★ ★ ★

Pro Tip: Top Six Ways to Increase Your VA Rating

Wondering how to increase your VA disability rating? In this guide, I reveal and explain the six proven paths to getting a VA disability increase this year. Generally, to increase an existing VA disability rating, you need to provide the VA with medical evidence showing your symptoms are worse in terms of frequency, severity, and duration. If your disabilities have become worse, there's a significant difference in the benefits available to veterans with a higher VA rating—one such benefit is a larger monthly tax-free compensation payment. Scan the QR code below to learn how to increase your VA disability rating with my guide "Six Best Ways to Get a VA Disability Increase This Year."

Three Ways to Reach 100%

There are three main paths to a 100% combined VA rating:

- If the fuzzy math calculation puts you at or above 95% or higher, the VA will round you up to 100%.

- One of your conditions might be rated at 100% out of the gate. (For example, your PTSD is rated at 100%, so your six other rated disabilities might not come into play.)

- If your disability renders you unable to maintain substantial gainful employment, you may receive the pay and benefits of a 100% VA rating—even if your combined VA rating is below 100%. For example, a Vietnam veteran might have a 70% rating because they suffer from cancer due to Agent Orange. But if chemotherapy treatments and hospitalizations make substantial gainful employment impossible, they may instead be deemed Unemployable, which is also known as "Total Disability Individual Unemployability" (TDIU). A VA-accredited Veteran Service Officer (VSO), claims agent, or attorney can be useful in helping you secure TDIU benefits.

★ ★ ★

HOW TO AVOID GETTING DENIED

In my experience, there are two primary reasons why VA disability claims get denied.

The first reason is many veterans do not have enough medical evidence to show that they have a disability condition (for example, there may be no diagnosis in a medical record, especially STRs) or that they have symptoms severe enough to warrant a VA disability rating under the law.

The second reason is many veterans are unable to prove service connection, the Nexus.

Usually, these situations occur because when they were in the military, they never went to the freaking doctor to say, "My hand hurts...my foot hurts...I have sleep apnea...I have a mental health condition." Heck, they might not have even known what those conditions *were* while on active duty. Now they're stuck trying to prove they have service-connected disabilities after the fact. It's the ultimate catch-22.

Let's say ten years after you leave the service, you're diagnosed with sleep apnea by your primary care physician. You believe the condition was due to service, but you never got it diagnosed while in service. If you file a claim for it with the VA, you'll likely be denied unless you provide additional evidence. But they don't tell you this when you apply! Believe it or not, many veterans file disability claims without even providing a diagnosis. You also need to prove that your disability is "at least as likely as not" due to your service or another service-connected disability. The Nexus gets harder to prove the longer you've been out of the military. *No wonder* so many of us get denied or underrated!

Fortunately, the "at least as likely as not" Nexus standard is a very low burden of proof for service connection. That means all else being equal (50% positive evidence and 50% negative evidence), the benefit of the doubt goes to the veteran. You know how in baseball, if the first baseman catches the ball at the exact moment the runner touches the base, then the umpire will shout "safe," meaning the tie goes to the runner? The same concept is true with the VA disability system. If the evidence is equally weighted on both sides, for and against, you should win the claim. You can reach that threshold even if you've been previously denied! And I'll teach you how.

TESTIMONIAL: GOOD-BYE STUDENT LOANS

"When I left the army in 1993, I began looking for a way to educate and support myself. But when you're suffering from PTSD— although you're not aware of it at the time—your mind doesn't work the way you expect it to. As a result, it took me years to complete my degree(s). All my education was financed by federal loans and even some signature loans. By the time I got my MBA in 2012, my student loan debt had accumulated to just under $300,000, and my income was not sufficient to make payments. I resigned myself to dying with this debt. But in 2019, after working with VA Claims Insider, the VA granted me a disability rating of 100%. Approximately two months after applying, I was granted permanent discharge of all my student loans, removing the weight of that impossible debt from my shoulders."

—Brian L.

COMPENSATION AND PENSION
EXAMS (AND HOW TO ACE THEM)

Regardless of how much information you provide in your claim, the VA will still likely order a separate medical examination from a medical provider who is contracted to work for the VA. This is the Compensation and Pension (C&P) exam. You'll likely get a phone call and a packet in the mail with instructions. Some exams happen over the phone or via video teleconference, while others are required to be conducted in person. Some might even happen based on a records review alone, which is known as an Acceptable Clinical Evidence (ACE) exam. The C&P exam is understandably scary for veterans. Somebody you don't know, who's *never* treated you, might conduct an examination, and then whatever they write in their notes will likely determine your VA disability benefits. Yeah, that's scary.

One of the questions I get asked all the time is, "Brian, do you have any C&P exam tips?" Yes, I do! I underwent ten C&P exams over the last eight years because I have multiple disabilities and because I (successfully) reapplied for benefits. Not *one* of these exams made me feel comfortable. The examiner holds so much power! I have trouble trusting people in general, especially the gatekeeper of benefits I deserve for myself and my family.

In my opinion, the C&P exam is the number one most important day in the entire VA claim process. You can do everything else right, but if you miss your C&P exam or, worse, have a bad C&P exam, the results can *ruin* your final VA rating. It's shameful, I know; however, the sad reality is that the VA rater, also known as the Rating Veterans Service Representative (RVSR), will rely almost solely on the notes from the C&P examiner. Don't worry, though. Even if you have a terrible C&P exam, there is still hope, and you can fight it! But first, use these ten expert tips to overprepare for your C&P exam.

1. Read Through Your Military, VA, and Private Medical Records

Do this in detail prior to your C&P exam.

There is no substitute for knowing what's in your Service Treatment Records (STRs), VA medical records, or any private medical records.

Be prepared to discuss the medical diagnosis of your disability, any subjective symptoms of your disability that are in your STRs, as well as the logical link or connection between your current disability and your active duty military service—the Nexus.

When did the symptoms of the disability begin?

Did they start on active duty or after you left the service?

Do you have current symptoms of the disability into the present day?

If yes, how severe are those symptoms?

Know the answers to all these questions.

2. Review CFR, Title 38, Part 4,
"Schedule for Rating Disabilities"

The law that governs all VA disability claims is CFR, Title 38, Part 4, Schedule for Rating Disabilities (also known as the "VASRD").

The complete VA disability claims list contains 834 ratable disabilities under the law.

You should review the general schedule prior to your C&P exam, which will help you understand your disability and how your current symptoms and keywords are tied to a specific rating under the law.

You should also review the condition specific Disability Benefits Questionnaire (DBQ) for your claimed disability; this is what the C&P examiner will complete online at your exam.

Did you know one of our websites, *Military DisabilityMadeEasy.com*, has categorized the entire

VASRD with "simple" and "made easy" answers? Scan the QR code below to start your *free* 14-day trial of the Military Disability Made Easy all-access.

3. Do Not *Describe Your Best Day*

This means that you need to tell the C&P examiner how you are on your very worst days.

Remember that the VA C&P exam is a snapshot in time of how you're doing on one particular day.

If you're having a good day, but this is unusual for you, make sure to explain to the examiner how you normally are on your worst days.

For example, if your back pain is so severe that you often can't get out of bed in the morning without help, or you wear a back brace, make sure to *tell* the C&P examiner in detail.

Mission Critical: Don't ever lie or stretch the truth when it comes to your VA disability claim.

That's illegal.

At your C&P exam, you should think, look, act, and speak as you would on a normal day.

What does this mean?

Here's a few examples:

- If you don't require the daily use of braces or a walker, don't just pull them out for your C&P exam. Do what you would normally do.

- If you usually shower and dress decently, do so the-day-of your exam. We recommend you wear comfortable clothing such as sweatpants and a t-shirt. If you're reporting to the exam from work, wear what you normally wear for work.

- If you're able to lift weights and workout, tell the examiner the truth. Don't say you can't lift more than 10 pounds if you're at the gym using 40 pound dumbbells.

Pro Tip: A C&P examiner might write that you're malingering if you attempt to falsify or exaggerate your disability symptoms/impairment. Malingering is defined as "the intentional production of false or grossly exaggerated physical or psychological symptoms motivated by external incentives such as avoiding military duty, avoiding work, obtaining financial compensation, etc."

Important: According to federal law, there are criminal penalties, including a fine and/or imprisonment for up to 5 years for withholding information or for knowingly providing incorrect information in support of your VA disability compensation claim for VA benefits (See 18 U.S. Code § 1001).

4. Be "Uncomfortably Vulnerable"

If it feels uncomfortable for you to say something to a C&P examiner you just met, that means you need to say it!

For example, nobody wants to talk about their sexual dysfunction, and that's exactly why you need to talk about it.

Tell the C&P examiner about the severity of your VA erectile dysfunction (ED) and how it's hurting your relationship with your spouse.

If you're abusing alcohol as a coping mechanism because of your severe anxiety and insomnia, you should tell the examiner, because you're helping explain the severity of your mental health symptoms: *"I'm abusing alcohol and drugs to numb the pain and escape my anxiety and depression."*

5. Explain How Your Disabilities Are Limiting Your Work, Life, and Social Functioning

VA claims for all mental health conditions come down to your current level of "Occupational and Social Impairment" as well as the severity of your mental health symptoms and circumstances.

How is your severe PTSD affecting your work, life, and social functioning?

VA claims for other conditions (non-mental health) are all about three things:

- Limitation of range of motion
- Pain level
- Loss of Use

Make the examiner stop as soon as you feel any pain or discomfort.

If you can't bend over to touch your toes, don't do it! If you're unable to move your knee to your chest, don't let the examiner move you!

Be prepared to discuss how your disability is limiting and affecting your work, life, and social functioning.

For example, you can say things like, *"My PTSD is so severe that I had an angry outburst at my boss last week and got written up for it."*

Another example is, *"My plantar fasciitis is causing me so much heel pain that I can no longer run or work out, and I've gained twenty pounds in the past three months. In fact, it's difficult to walk, and shoe inserts don't help."*

6. Know Your True Story Completely, Plus Any In-Service Incidents or Stressor Events

Be prepared to discuss the many related incidents in detail with the examiner.

Most veterans don't have specific incidents well documented, so make sure to discuss the approximate month and year of when your disability symptoms began.

You may want to include a VA buddy letter to help explain and corroborate your story, which will help prove the Nexus requirement for service connection.

For example, *"I was sexually assaulted by my boss on a Navy ship in October 1987. I never told anyone about this incident, as I feared for my life and career."*

7. Give the C&P Examiner a Detailed Picture of Your Life Before, During, and After Service

You must be prepared to talk about your life in detail.

Where did you grow up and what was your life like before joining the military?

What did you do on active duty, and did you have any specific job requirements?

Did you deploy to a combat zone or other austere location?

What happened after you left active-duty service?

Make sure you've given the C&P examiner a detailed picture of your life and how the military either caused or made your disability condition worse, or how your service-connected disability caused or aggravated your currently claimed disability.

If you can make the C&P examiner feel something, they'll be able to *relate* to your story, which will help them make the proper analysis regarding the severity of your disability.

8. The C&P Examiner Is Not Your Friend; Your Exam Starts in the Parking Lot

Keep in mind that the C&P examiner is *not* your friend.

The examiner is there to do a job they're being paid for, which is to conduct an adequate examination of your claimed disability and to document the record for the VA Rater.

You are also there to do a job, which is to be open, honest, truthful, and uncomfortably vulnerable.

Be polite and courteous but stay away from small talk.

And remember this: *Your VA C&P exam begins when you pull into the parking lot!*

Yes, there are plenty of stories of cameras and front-desk personnel relaying information to the examiner from the parking lot.

9. Bring Hard-Copy Documents with You to the C&P Exam

I get asked this all the time: "Brian, I have trouble remembering things, can I bring my medical records, Nexus Letters, DBQs, and personal statements to the C&P Exam?"

The answer is: YES!

Put them in a folder and carry them with you to the exam.

It's also okay to offer them to the C&P examiner, but don't force it.

The C&P examiner should have already reviewed all your submitted evidence (digitally) before your C&P exam, but sometimes they're lazy, aren't prepared, and haven't reviewed your VA claims file.

So, yes, it's a good idea to have your hard-copy evidence with you and to offer it to the examiner.

After your exam is over, you can also leave copies of your evidence with the examiner for further review and analysis.

10. *After Your Exam, Ask Your Accredited VSO to Download Your C&P Exam Results from VBMS*

This final tip is critical, especially if you think you might have had a bad C&P exam.

You can challenge the accuracy and validity of your C&P exam, to include requesting a new exam BEFORE your final VA rating decision by calling 1-800-827-1000.

If your C&P exam was performed by a VA doctor at a VA facility, the results of your C&P exam will be in your VA medical records on *MyHealtheVet* in 48–72 hours.

If your C&P exam was performed by a contracted doctor at a private facility, the results of your C&P exam will be uploaded to the Veteran Benefits Management System (VBMS).

The fastest and easiest way to get your C&P exam results from a contracted provider is to have your accredited VSO download a copy for you from VBMS.

Finally, you can get a copy of your C&P exam results (and entire VA claims file) by filing an online FOIA request for a copy of your VA C File.

★ ★ ★

Pro Tip: Notice of Intent to File

Stand up, carry this book over to your computer, and start your claim *now*—even if you don't have all your paperwork yet. What you're going to do is start your disability compensation claim on the *VA.gov* website, and when you do, it will automatically open what's called a Notice of Intent to File. Basically, it's to save the date; you're putting the VA on notice that you're about to file a claim, and then you'll have a year to complete it.

But crucially, your claim—and the effective date for disability compensation—will be calculated based on the date of your Notice of Intent to File, *not* when you finish it (as long as you are diagnosed for the claimed disability in most situations). This means when all's said and done, the compensation you receive will be backdated to today (or the date of your Notice of Intent to File) rather than when you actually file however many months from now. The intent to file will literally take you minutes. The online application is very intuitive and easy—even if you had all your documents prepared and wanted to finish filing today, you could still do it all in less than an hour!

Action Moment!

Let's open a Notice of Intent to File and get your VA disability compensation claim started. Scan the QR code below to join me on-screen and learn *how* to prepare and file your own VA disability online at *VA.gov*.

How to Apply for Disability Compensation

- You can apply online yourself at *VA.gov*—it's *very* straightforward. (Watch the tutorial from the previous box!) Or you can do it by mail via a form available on the VA website, by calling the VBA at 1-800-827-1000 and asking them to open an intent to file for you, by showing up to a regional VA office near you, or by working with an accredited representative who can help you prepare and file your claim for free, such as the DAV, AMVETS, VFW, American Legion, or other accredited VSO organizations.

- If you've never filed a VA disability claim before, you'll need your DD 214 (discharge papers) and Social Security number, along with other basic personal information. Your Social Security number becomes your VA file number. Regardless of whether you've filed a VA disability claim before, make sure your personal profile information is correct. This includes your full name, mailing address, email address, and phone number, among other details. Accuracy is very important because the VA and contracted C&P examiners will need to contact you throughout the VA claim process.

- Choose to submit a Fully Developed Claim (FDC) instead of a Standard Claim. A Standard Claim is one with limited supporting evidence attached to it—you're relying on the VA to track down important personnel and medical records for you, which is a recipe for denial. I *always* recommend filing an FDC so that you maintain control of your own VA claim to include all supporting evidence necessary for the VA to make a rating decision.

- Upload or attach any supporting evidence. Your FDC package can and should include the following:
  - You'll need a medical diagnosis of the disability condition in a medical record. This can be in your Service Treatment Records (STRs), VA medical records, and/or private medical records. It's NOT enough to say you have a condition. You must have a current medical diagnosis (within the last twelve months or documented continuation of treatment). If you have a disability condition but don't have it diagnosed yet, get your butt to the doctor!
  - If you've been out of active duty service for more than twelve months, you'll likely want to get a

Medical Nexus Letter (an independent medical opinion) from a private provider explaining the likely cause of your disability condition, whether a connection to your service or another disability exists on an "at least as likely as not" basis, and the severity of your symptoms.

- Complete a Statement in Support of Claim (VA Form 21-4138), a written personal statement about your symptoms and how those symptoms are negatively impacting your work, life, and social functioning.
- Get a buddy letter, a firsthand witness testimony from someone eighteen years of age or older, preferably who witnessed the in-service event or injury and can shed light on the condition affecting you. (Visit the VA Claims Insider blog for more tips on how to write a buddy letter.)

The mind-boggling thing is none of these items are techni-cally "required to file a claim" In fact, some of them won't even be suggested. Just because the VA doesn't ask for it, however, doesn't mean you shouldn't include it. Heck, this is part of why I wrote this book for you. We make VA claims easy!

★

Pro Tip: The Best VSOs for VA Disability Claims

Selecting the appropriate level of representation for your VA claim is critical to getting the VA rating you deserve. But how do you pick the best VSO for disability claims? The short answer is, very carefully. The long answer is, it depends on your disability claim situation and the level of expertise required (e.g., first-time filer, increase claims, secondary claims, denied claims, or extra-scheduler claims). The truth is not all VSOs are good—some are better trained than others, and different VSOs have varying levels of staff available to assist veterans. So you need to be careful who you trust to lead you through the maze of VA disability claims. Scan the QR code below to learn how to select the best VSO for disability claims.

★

Pro Tip: Medical Nexus Letters

Even though we encourage veterans to ask their own private or VA doctors to write an evidence-based letter explaining the severity of their symptoms and why the disability is likely due to service, in our experience, most doctors are either reluctant to do so or don't know how to do it right. This leads to the veteran getting denied or "not service connected." In my experience, the *best* way to prove service connection under the law, especially if you've previously been denied VA disability compensation benefits, is to obtain an Independent Medical Opinion (IMO) from a private healthcare provider. We can help with that process. One of the services we provide is connecting veterans with private medical professionals who have experience and expertise in medical etiology of disability conditions as well as proper evidence-based documentation of symptomatology. If they agree that your condition is likely service related, they can write a convincing argument in support of that narrative, which the C&P examiner and VA rater will take seriously, because the evidence should have high probative value.

★ ★ ★

THE EIGHT-STEP VA CLAIM REVIEW PROCESS

What happens after you've filed your VA claim? And how long does it take to get the decision?

In general, the VA's Veteran Service Representative (VSR) and Rating Veteran Service Representative (RVSR) follow an eight-step process. If you submit a Fully Developed Claim (FDC)—which we highly recommend at VA Claims Insider—you'll likely get a VA rating decision within an average of 90–120 days, from start to finish.

And the best news? The VA is getting faster every day—a lot faster. Between 2018 and 2020, VA claim adjudicators shaved an average of fifty days off the processing time! Remember that at any point during the process, you can call 1-800-827-1000 and ask to speak to a VA representative about your VA disability claim status. Here's a breakdown of their process and how long each step typically takes.

Step #1: Claim Received

If you file your disability claim online, you'll get an on-screen message from the VA after you submit the application. A week or so later, the VA will send you a letter to let you know they've received your claim. You should get this letter in one to two weeks. It should show up in VA.gov, the web portal through which you manage your VA benefits, within seven to fourteen days.

If you have any questions, call the VA hotline phone number at 1-800-827-1000 and speak to a VA representative.

Step #2: Under Review

The second step in the VA claim process involves a Veterans Service Representative (VSR) reviewing your claim. If the VA doesn't need any more evidence from you, which can only happen if you submit a Fully Developed Claim, your application will proceed. This step normally takes seven to twenty-one business days.

Step #3: Gathering of Evidence

In the third step, the VSR may ask for evidence from you, healthcare providers, government agencies, or others before moving the claim to an RVSR for a decision. This is also the step where a Compensation and Pension (C&P) examination is ordered, if you meet the requirements for one. This step normally takes thirty to sixty business days and is typically the longest step in the VA claim process.

Step #4: Review of Evidence

In this step, the VA has received all required evidence, which the VSR assigned to your claim will review. If upon further review, additional evidence is required, the VSR will send the claim back to Step 3, which can happen more than once. VA claims very commonly move back and forth between phases, so if you see it happens with yours, *don't worry—* it's normal! You may also see some confusing back-and-forth messages inside your application, but they're typically for internal use only. If the VA needs something from you, you'll know. This step typically takes seven to fourteen business days.

Step #5: Preparation for Decision

In this step, your entire VA disability claim file is sent to the RVSR, who will review your application, medical records, supporting documents, personal statements, buddy letters, other supporting information, and C&P exam results to make a rating decision on your VA disability claim.

The RVSR then recommends a decision and begins the process of preparing the necessary documents to explain the reasoning in detail. This step normally takes seven to fourteen business days.

Step #6: Pending Decision Approval

Once the RVSR's decision recommendation documents are in order, your claim will receive a final award approval, which usually involves a second-tier reviewing authority. This step typically takes seven to fourteen business days.

Step #7: Preparation for Notification

The VA will prepare your Disability Claim Decision Letter and the supporting documentation used to make the rating decision, in its entirety, to be mailed to you. This step usually takes seven to fourteen business days.

Step #8: Decision Notification Sent

In the final step of the VA claim process, the VA will send you a packet by US mail that includes details of the decision on your claim. You should receive this in seven to fourteen business days. If you don't want to wait for the packet to arrive by mail, you can log in to your VA.gov account and click on the link right below your full name, "Your Disability Rating," to see if anything has been added or changed. *Pro Tip:* When you get your VA rating decision letter, read it in detail! If you disagree with some or all of the decision, you'll want to understand what you're going to challenge and why. In our experience, the VA Higher Level Review (HLR) is a great first start under the new appeals process if you disagree with the VA's decision. If the HLR doesn't work, you'll want to try a supplemental claim using new and relevant evidence not previously considered. Examples include a new independent medical opinion (IMO), a new buddy letter, a new personal statement, new medical records or reports, and so on. You can now complete the HLR online at *VA.gov*, or you can complete the HLR or a supplemental claim's paperwork and then upload and submit it online via the VA's QuickSubmit tool.

TOP TWENTY VA CLAIM MYTHS DEBUNKED

Now it's time to do some myth-busting. For some reason, people have perpetuated these VA claim myths for many years, and I'm going to set the record straight once and for all. Let's begin.

Myth #1: VA disability is only for those veterans who are more 'disabled' than I am. Other veterans deserve benefits, but not me.

Fact: This is a lie we tell ourselves as veterans. *You Served. You Deserve.* Almost all veterans are eligible for VA disability benefits, except for those with a dishonorable discharge that hasn't been upgraded. I give you permission to get what you deserve. You can be rated from 0% to 100% in increments of 10%, depending on whether your disabilities are "service connected," as well as the frequency, severity, and duration of your symptoms and circumstances.

Myth #2: If I get VA disability benefits, it will take away from another veteran's benefits.

Fact: Your VA disability benefits do not affect any other veterans' benefits. They are completely independent of one another. If you choose not to get your benefits, the only ones you're hurting are yourself and your family. Apply online now for free!

Myth #3: I've been out of the service too long to apply for VA disability benefits.

Fact: There is no statute of limitations on VA disability benefits. You can apply for benefits at any time. There are no restrictions.

Myth #4: My conditions weren't diagnosed in my military medical records, so I'll just get denied.

Fact: You don't need your condition(s) diagnosed in your STRs. But they do need to be diagnosed and documented in a medical record, such as VA medical records or private medical records. If you think you have a disability but haven't yet been diagnosed, please consider going to see a doctor or other healthcare professional.

Myth #5: The VA already gave me a VA disability rating, so I can't apply again.

Fact: The VA disability process is never over unless you quit. You can apply as many times as you'd like. Maybe your conditions have worsened, so you want to file for an increase. Perhaps you realize you're eligible for secondary service connection and want to file a secondary claim. DO IT! Just make sure you have medical evidence to back up your assertions.

Myth #6: My VSO said I should be happy with my VA disability rating percentage and not rock the boat.

Fact: The only time you should be happy with your VA disability rating percentage is if you believe you're getting everything you're legally, morally, ethically, and medically eligible for. If you think you deserve an increase, open a new claim on the VA.gov website and file for it!

Myth #7: I already got denied before, so there's nothing else I can do about it. If I apply again, the VA will just deny me.

Fact: Previous denials don't necessarily impact future claims. There are plenty of options if the VA previously denied your claim. You can file a Higher Level Review (HLR) or a supplemental claim. If those get denied, you can file a records-only Board Appeal or request a video teleconference with a BVA judge. There is always another path, but you must stay in the process and never quit!

Myth #8: If I apply for a VA rating increase, the VA will reduce my current rating.

Fact: This is highly unlikely. The VA generally only reviews the specific disability condition(s) you've filed for, and nothing else.

Myth #9: The VA has it out for veterans and intentionally denies their disability claims.

Fact: The VA does not intentionally deny claims. They're following law and regulation when reviewing your VA disability claim. Help them help you by submitting a strong claim with the appropriate medical evidence!

Myth #10: My disabilities aren't severe enough to get a VA rating.

Fact: Regardless of the severity of your symptoms, you can still get service connected at the minimum rating of 0% (noncompensable). This is important because if your condition worsens over time, it's easier to file for an increase on a disability that's already service connected.

Myth #11: If I get seen for mental health or have a VA rating for PTSD, the VA will take away my guns.

Fact: Your VA rating for mental health, including PTSD, has nothing to do with your guns. By law, the VA can't take away your guns. It would be an unlawful seizure without a warrant. However, even though the VA does not have the authority to take away your guns or impose any other limitations based on ratings, VA ratings can potentially impact other aspects of a veteran's life, and I encourage you to consider your own individual circumstances.

Myth #12: If I get a VA rating for mental health or have a VA rating for PTSD, I'll lose my security clearance.

Fact: Your VA rating for mental health, including PTSD, has nothing to do with your security clearance. If you do have a mental health condition and are seeking treatment and taking medications, you do need to notify your program security official to update your SF-86. However, doing so won't impact your security clearance. Please note that although a rating alone may not impact a security clearance, failure to disclose it may be considered a lack of integrity and honesty and *can* impact a security clearance.

Myth #13: My VA rating for mental health should be higher because I was a [insert your MOS here].

Fact: Your VA rating for mental health has nothing to do with your job in the military. It has everything to do with the current frequency, severity, and duration of your symptoms and your individual circumstances.

Myth #14: If I get a VA disability rating (physical condition or mental health), my employer will find out and take negative action against me.

Fact: Your employer has no way of knowing this information unless you tell them. If an employer takes negative action against you because of your VA disability, it could be a violation under the Americans with Disabilities Act (ADA).

Myth #15: If I get a 100% VA rating or P&T status, I can't work anymore.

Fact: Your VA disability rating percentage does not impact your ability to work. Income and VA disability benefits are independent of each other. The only time work status can be affected is if you're rated 100% Total Disability Individual Unemployability (TDIU).

Myth #16: Once I get service connected, I must go to the VA for all my medical care and treatment.

Fact: You do not need to go to the VA for medical care unless you want to. Many veterans have private insurance and choose to see a private doctor in their local area.

Myth #17: I should have a VA rating because the VA medically diagnosed me and is treating me for the condition.

Fact: Just because you receive medical care at the VA for a specific condition does not mean that condition is eligible for VA benefits under the law. All disabilities must be "service connected," meaning they were caused or made worse by your military service or another service-connected disability.

Myth #18: If I go to 90% or 100%, the VA will schedule me for a reexamination of all of my service-connected disabilities.

Fact: Getting a 90% or 100% VA disability does not affect other disability conditions. The VA generally only reviews the specific disability condition(s) you've filed for, and nothing else.

Myth #19: There aren't any additional benefits for my dependents if I get 100% P&T status.

Fact: There are tons of additional benefits available to the dependents of veterans with a 100% permanent and total disability rating. Check out our website at *VAClaimsInsider.com* for a complete list of benefits.

Myth #20: Accredited VSOs and claims agents do what VA Claims Insider does for free.

Fact: Accredited VSOs and claims agents represent veterans with power of attorney (POA) before the VA. They prepare and file your VA claim for you, interact with the VA, and act on your behalf. In contrast, VA Claims Insider is an education company, not a VSO, claims agent, or law firm. We are a dedicated team of fellow veterans and veteran advocates; we are not accredited. Our primary focus is on VA disability education—both live and on-demand—and medical evidence requirements (DBQs, Nexus Letters, and Mental Health Independent Medical Opinions) to help eligible veterans increase their VA rating, win previously denied VA disability benefits, and uncover high-value secondary VA disabilities based on medical evidence of record. VA Claims Insider does not assist veterans with the preparation, presentation, and prosecution of VA disability claims for VA benefits.

FINAL THOUGHTS ON VA DISABILITY CLAIMS

You could be missing out on thousands of dollars' worth of tax-free VA disability compensation benefits you legally deserve every single month! Now you know what to do about it. We've told you exactly what you need to include in your claim and why. At VA Claims Insider, we believe that if you *get your claim strategy right*, the tactics become simpler, and you'll end up winning your claim and getting the rating you deserve in less time.

We talk a lot about accountability as well. Our veteran coaches (VCs) will call a veteran client and say, "Hey, sir/ma'am, you said you were going to do this last week. Well, you didn't. All okay? The only one you're hurting is you and your family. So do it!" I know that you can handle this application process on your own. But if you want the strategy, education, and medical evidence to help you on your VA claim journey, come join the VA Claims Insider community. It's free to start! Via additional coaching, we can help you secure the benefits you deserve. We serve and support each other together, in community. And we will NOT let you fail.

★ ★ ★

Key Takeaway Actions from This Chapter

- Get your butt to the doctor! Tell them everything going on with you and get your condition(s) medically diagnosed and documented in a medical record. It's okay if you've been out of the military for a long time. You simply need to have evidence of your disability documented somewhere in a medical record. VA disability claims are won or lost based on *medical evidence*. Either you have enough, or you don't.

- Consider getting a Medical Nexus Letter from a private provider to help you prove the Nexus requirement for service connection under the law.

- Start preparing for your Compensation and Pension (C&P) exams because being vulnerable doesn't always come easily to veterans. It's important that you prepare to fight a fair fight to secure the benefits you've earned for your honorable service to our country. Would you go to an important job interview without preparing? I think not.

- Log in to *VA.gov right now* and open a new claim, which will automatically start the twelve-month clock for submitting your claim to the VA. Taking this action locks in your effective date for back pay via the opening of a "Notice of Intent to File," so long as you meet the other requirements for that back pay such as being diagnosed.

★ ★ ★

CHAPTER TWO

VA PENSION

The VA pension was actually the first form of benefit provided to American wartime soldiers. Over time, the benefits program transitioned so that either disability compensation or health-care benefits serve most needs. Today, pensions are typically reserved for low-income elderly veterans who don't qualify for disability benefits.

The VA pension program provides monthly payments to wartime veterans who meet certain age or disability requirements and who have income and net worth within certain limits.

One of the most common questions I get, especially from elderly disabled veterans, is, "Brian, can I get both VA disability compensation and pension benefits at the same time?"

The short answer is no. By law, you can't receive pension benefits and disability compensation benefits at the same time. If you do qualify for both, most veterans are better off taking disability compensation, since monthly payment rates for pension benefits tend to be lower.

Okay, now I'll explain the pension eligibility requirements, and then I'll throw in an example.

To receive a VA pension for calendar year 2023, you must meet the following requirements:

- You didn't receive a dishonorable discharge, and

- Your net worth—including your spouse's income and any retirement accounts, among a handful of other assets (but not your home and car)—must be *less* than $150,538. This number gets adjusted each year in the fall based on the new cost-of-living-adjustment (COLA) percentage as determined by the Social Security Administration (SSA).

- At least *one* of these must be true about your service:
  - You started on active duty before September 8, 1980, and you served at least ninety days on active duty with at least one day during wartime.
  - You started on active duty as an enlisted person after September 7, 1980, and served at least twenty-four months or the full period for which you were called or ordered to active duty (with some exceptions) with at least one day during wartime.
  - You were an officer and started on active duty after October 16, 1981, and you hadn't previously served on active duty for at least twenty-four months.

- And at least *one* of these must be true:
  - You are at least sixty-five years old.
  - You have a permanent and total disability.
  - You are a patient in a nursing home for long-term care because of a disability.

- You are getting Social Security Disability Insurance or Supplemental Security Income.

Say, for example, you're seventy-five years old and served in Vietnam. You have a 20% service-connected disability rating for your shoulder, and you were granted a 70% nonservice-connected disability for a heart condition, meaning the heart condition is not due to your active duty military service. You are receiving a small amount of money for your shoulder from disability compensation but nothing for your heart because it's not service connected. However, if your heart condition is making it impossible to work and you have no money, or if it requires you to be in a nursing home with expensive full-time care, then your income and net worth limits may make you eligible for pension benefits, too. Sure, your heart condition is just due to your age and not to your service. Still, you served in the Vietnam War! The VA is going to help you.

★ ★ ★

VA Pension versus VA Disability Compensation

Here's a quick and easy primer on the key differences between these two important benefits.

- **Income and Net Worth:** VA pension benefits are based on income level and net worth limits, whereas VA disability compensation benefits are based on level of disability (aka "severity of symptoms"). Income and net worth are *not* factors in determining VA disability compensation benefits to eligible veterans. You can be 100% permanent and totally disabled (P&T) and still have a great job that pays you well.

- **Service Connection:** Eligibility for VA pension benefits does not require disabilities to be service connected, whereas for VA disability compensation benefits, you must have a service-connected disability, meaning your disability condition was caused or made worse by your active duty military service.

- **Age:** Eligibility for VA pension benefits, assuming you meet the wartime active duty and income and net worth limit requirements, can be based on your age alone. For VA disability compensation benefits, age is *not* a factor unless the VA is deciding P&T disability status. Your age can be a factor in determining P&T status.

- **Monthly Payment Rates:** VA pension benefit monthly payment rates tend to be lower than VA disability compensation rates. Thus, many veterans who qualify for both VA pension benefits and VA disability compensation benefits generally choose to take the latter. Again, you can't get both at the same time in most scenarios.

Bottom line: If you qualify for VA disability compensation benefits, you may not want to mess around with VA pension benefits at all. You will likely be better served by disability compensation. On the other hand, if your disability is not service connected, you meet the income requirements, and your net worth is under the limit, then do apply for a pension.

AID AND ATTENDANCE

If you are a low-income elderly veteran who requires the literal aid and attendance of another person, whether in your home or in a nursing home, the VA may help you pay for that care. It's called a Special Monthly Pension, which just means that it is still a financial benefit but is earmarked for the specific purpose of paying a nurse or other home care provider.

A couple of things to note: First, if you don't require help from another person but are housebound, you might be eligible for Housebound benefits instead of Aid and Attendance benefits. Second, both Aid and Attendance and Housebound benefits are also sometimes available to survivors. You'll want to check the latest eligibility and application requirements online at *VA.gov*.

Eligibility for Aid and Attendance or Housebound Benefits as a Veteran or Survivor

Note: You can't get Aid and Attendance benefits and Housebound benefits at the same time.

Aid and Attendance: You may be eligible for this benefit if you get a VA pension and at least one of these is true:

- You need another person to help you perform daily activities, like bathing, feeding, and dressing.

- You have to stay in bed—or spend a large portion of the day in bed—because of illness.

- You are a patient in a nursing home due to the loss of mental or physical abilities related to a disability.

- Your eyesight is limited (even with glasses or contact lenses you have only 5/200 or less in both eyes, or concentric contraction of the visual field to five degrees or less).

Housebound Benefits: You may be eligible for this benefit if you get a VA pension and you spend most of your time in your home because of a permanent disability (a disability that doesn't go away).

★ ★ ★

How to Apply for Pension Benefits

Applying for a pension is even easier than applying for disability benefits because you don't have to prove ANY kind of service connection. But you will need some supporting documents. Here's a primer to get you ready.

- The pension application is basically a series of questions, such as when and where you served, information about any and all marriages, whether you've been treated at a VA facility, and various questions about your work history.

- There will be a place for you to write about which disabilities prevent you from working. Be as specific as possible about your health and how your conditions limit you.

- Finally, get ready for a lot of financial questions—for both you and your dependents. The VA needs to determine your net worth. That includes not only any kind of salary you might bring in but also all interest-bearing investment accounts, including IRAs, and any real estate property (except your home). You will also need to know how much everything in your home is worth, such as art and furniture. Have all information about your assets with you when you sit down to apply.

- You'll also need your DD 214, Social Security number, or VA file number as well as your bank account direct deposit information.

- Then, if you're also applying for aid and attendance, be prepared to share information about your daily life: how you get around, what your home layout is like, the specific care you require each day, and so forth.

Is it a pain in the butt to pull together all that information before you apply? Yes. That's why I'm telling you *in advance*! This way, you won't quit in the middle of your application and never return to it. We are here to get you through this process, no matter how confusing it all is or how much of a nuisance.

★

Key Takeaway Actions from This Chapter

If your disability is service connected, you probably don't even want to bother with applying for a pension—put your efforts toward acquiring VA disability compensation benefits, which will be more beneficial.

If you don't have a service-connected disability, you're over sixty-five, and your net worth—including everything you and your spouse own, except for your car and house—is less than $150,538, gather the information you'll need and apply for a pension today.

 ★ ★ ★

CHAPTER THREE

VA HEALTHCARE

A few years ago, a gas grill blew up on me, and I suffered second-degree burns all over my legs, torso, arms, and hands, as well as up my neck. I went to the emergency room and racked up thousands of dollars' worth of medical bills. Because my disability rating meets the threshold to receive complete healthcare coverage, the VA paid for *all* of it, including the ambulance. All I had to do was submit a reimbursement request.

One of the VA's primary duties, through the Veterans Health Administration (VHA), is to provide eligible veterans with comprehensive medical care. The VHA is the largest healthcare system in the world. It exists to take care of you, so let it!

Almost all veterans qualify for some type of healthcare benefit, but it won't always be completely free. If you have service-connected disabilities, you will certainly receive free care for those specific injuries or illnesses. The magic number to receive totally free healthcare benefits for everything, without any co-pays, is a disability rating of at least 50%. (Totally free care is also sometimes provided to veterans who couldn't otherwise afford it.)

I am often asked if healthcare benefits extend to your dependents. The answer: Only if you are 100% permanently and totally (P&T) disabled. Your dependents will then qualify for CHAMPVA, which I will cover in this chapter.

Most veterans I talk to generally understand that they can get some amount of healthcare from the VA but don't know how much, how to get it, or how it all works. So let's dive in!

★ ★ ★

Now You Know

Apply for VA healthcare at *VA.gov* as soon as you take off the uniform. In fact, you can submit any disability claims and your healthcare registration at the same time. You don't have to do one before the other.

★ ★ ★

ELIGIBILITY

Congress occasionally changes the laws slightly, but as of the publishing of this book, if you served either twenty-four continuous months or the full period for which you were called to active duty, and you did not receive a dishonorable discharge, you are eligible for some amount of healthcare coverage. (That being said, if you were discharged due to a service-connected disability or for a hardship, or if you served prior to September 7, 1980, you don't have to meet the minimum active duty requirement.)

★ ★ ★

Now You Know

If you're receiving VA healthcare, you meet the Affordable Care Act's minimum essential health coverage requirement. You'll get a letter mailed to you each year for tax purposes.

★ ★ ★

PRIORITY GROUPS

How much will healthcare cost you? Like I said, if you have a disability rating of 50% or higher, it's totally free. You'll be in what's known as Priority Group 1. The VA can't serve all 20 million veterans at the same time, so they created eight priority groupings to prioritize the types of veterans who likely need the most help and when they'll get it.

If you have a disability rating that's less than 50% or no disability rating at all, you will be categorized somewhere between Priority Group 2 and 8. The VA considers a variety of different factors when organizing people into these remaining groups. The higher your priority group, the sooner you'll get your benefits. In addition, your priority group dictates how much, if anything, you'll have to pay toward the cost of your care, also known as co-pays. Generally speaking, the lowest two priority groups, numbers seven and eight, have co-pays associated with benefits.

Disabilities and financial need are not the only factors. If you received honors from the military, you could receive higher priority. This is the military, so there are all sorts of complicated ranking systems in play. I won't detail every factor that goes into priority-group determination. But in a nutshell, the higher the service-connected disability rating and the higher the need, the higher the priority group. The lowest groups are for veterans who have no disabilities and can afford care. So heads up to any able-bodied billionaire readers: you'll have to pay a little more to get your teeth checked!

CHAMPVA

If you are 100% P&T disabled, your dependents will have access to the Civilian Health and Medical Program of the Department of Veterans Affairs (CHAMPVA), which you may have heard of. CHAMPVA has radically improved the lives of many veteran families. It's a *fantastic* healthcare benefits program with literally no drawbacks. The only issue, as of the publishing of this book, is that you must be 100% P&T to qualify. If you do, CHAMPVA has an outpatient deductible ($50 per beneficiary per calendar year or a maximum of $100 per family per calendar year) and a patient cost share of 25% of CHAMPVA's allowable amount, up to the catastrophic cap ($3,000 per calendar year). You can search online for the application, which you'll need to download, fill out, and sign before mailing in for processing. *Note:* It can take eight to twelve weeks for approval.

WHAT ABOUT TRICARE?

You might be wondering about TRICARE, which is what most of us had while we were in the military. Once you're out of the military, though, this program is only available if you retire from a full career of twenty or more years of service. Otherwise, you won't qualify for TRICARE, and neither will your dependents.

★ ★ ★

How to Apply for Healthcare Benefits

First, gather your DD 214, most recent tax return, Social Security numbers for yourself and any qualified dependents, information about your current disability rating if you have one, and the account numbers for any current health insurance you already have.

Log on to *VA.gov* and *let's go!*

★

Key Takeaway Actions from This Chapter

- If you have a disability rating of 50% or higher, go get totally free healthcare for yourself without any co-pays. This benefit does *not* extend to your dependents.

- If you have a disability rating of 100% P&T, go get totally free healthcare, without any monthly premiums, for your dependents with the CHAMPVA program.

- If you have a disability rating that is lower than 50%, get yourself into a priority group so you can find out ASAP what's available for free and what you may need to access elsewhere.

★ ★ ★

★ CHAPTER FOUR ★

VA EDUCATION

You probably already know about the GI Bill.[5] In fact, having the government pay for a college education following your military service may be the reason you enlisted in the first place! I personally know several folks who joined the military specifically because they wanted to go to college but couldn't afford it.

It's true that part of the purpose of the bill—originally called the Servicemen's Readjustment Act of 1944—is to encourage people to commission in our all-volunteer military by sweetening the deal. But that's not the whole story. The GI Bill is one of the grandaddies of all VA benefits. After World War I, returning heroes got only a train ticket and $60. Following World War II, the government was determined to do better by its service members. In addition to helping them pay for education, the GI Bill also instituted unemployment pay as well as loan guarantees for homes, farms, and businesses.

---

5   GI Bill® is a registered trademark with the US Patent and Trademark Office and the VA is the sole owner of the mark.

But the biggest impact was definitely in education. In 1947, a whopping 49% of all college admissions were veterans. That means half of all freshmen in colleges were people like us who had worn the uniform! Imagine the long-term effects that enrollment has had on American culture. I think it's just the coolest.

Today, the GI Bill goes by many names because of updates and improvements made by Congress over the years. I'll briefly explain which affect who and what you need to know in order to apply. For now, here's the bottom line: *Take advantage of this benefit!* Unless you're a millionaire, educational assistance offered through the VA is your best chance to get a four-year college degree. And in the American job market, people with degrees far outearn those without. Further good news: Of all the benefits, this is one of the fastest and easiest to apply for, and you can do it all online at *VA.gov.*

WHAT CAN I GET FROM
THE POST-9/11 GI BILL?

I will spend the bulk of this chapter discussing the Post-9/11 GI Bill, because it's the specific education benefit that the vast majority of readers will qualify for and also the one that offers the most money. (But if your service happened before September 10, 2001, you'll want to pursue a different option; more on this later.)

You may be able to get a maximum of forty-eight months of VA education benefits—not including Veteran Readiness and Employment (VR&E) benefits. But many applicants are eligible for only thirty-six months:

- The VA will pay all your school's tuition and fees up to a capped amount. (For example, in 2022, it was around $26,381.37. The amount typically covers all state-school tuition for in-state residents. The cap allows veterans to apply the money toward a private school or even a foreign school, if they wish.)

- You'll receive a stipend for housing (determined by the cost of living where your school is located).

- You'll get up to $1,000 per school year for books and supplies.

- Depending on where you live and where you're going, the VA might even give you $500 to help you move.

DO I HAVE TO GO TO SCHOOL RIGHT AWAY?

Nope. You should definitely *apply now*, but then you can take some time to figure out exactly how and when you want to use your education benefits. In fact, if you were released or discharged from service on or after January 1, 2013, these benefits will never expire (thanks to the most recent congressional update, dubbed the Forever GI Bill).

If you were released or discharged before January 1, 2013, you can use your benefits anytime within fifteen years after your last separation date from active duty service—which is still pretty fantastic.

BASIC ELIGIBILITY

If you served on active duty and received a Purple Heart on or after September 11, 2001, or you served on active duty for at least 30 continuous days (without a break) and you were discharged with a service-connected disability, you're going to get the full benefit. If you were dishonorably discharged, you won't get anything. Otherwise, how much money you receive will depend on how long you served. You need at least ninety days of active-duty service since September 10, 2001 to receive 50% tuition payment, and from there, the VA prorates the benefit up to the capped amount.

Amount of Active Service = Amount of Benefit Granted

- 90 days to 5 months (90-179 days) = 50% of the maximum benefit

- 6 months to 17 months (180-544 days) = 60% of the maximum benefit

- 18 months to 23 months (545-729 days) = 70% of the maximum benefit

- 24 months to 29 months (703-909 days) = 80% of the maximum benefit

- 30 months to 35 months (910-1,094 days) = 90% of the maximum benefit

- 36 months (1,095 days or more) = 100% of the maximum benefit

★ ★ ★

It's also worth mentioning that if you are a service academy graduate—Air Force Academy, West Point, Annapolis, or Coast Guard—you will not be eligible for the Post-9/11 GI Bill benefits unless you served extra time on top of your five-year active duty service requirement.

★ ★ ★

Now You Know

The VA offers other education benefits besides the Post-9/11 GI Bill, but they are not as robust. If you qualify for the Post-9/11 GI Bill, that's the one you want. However, if you served prior to September 10, 2001, visit *VA.gov* to find more information on the Montgomery GI Bill Active Duty and the Montgomery GI Bill Selected Reserve. *Warning:* The education benefit choice you make is irrevocable. So if you're thinking of going with something other than the Post-9/11 GI Bill (aka the "Forever GI Bill"), be *sure* it's the right choice.

★ ★ ★

GI BILL CALCULATOR

Since the amount of money you'll receive depends on many factors— such as school tuition, zip codes, and changing annual benefit caps—the VA website introduced a brand-new tool called the GI Bill Comparison Tool (colloquially known as the GI Bill Calculator). It's so stinking easy. You just enter your current military status, which benefit you want to use, your amount of cumulative active service, and the school you want to attend. The calculator will then spit out how much money the VA will give you for tuition, housing, and books. How cool is that? Alternatively, you can type in a location, and the calculator will tell you how much the VA will cover for every school in the area! Access the tool for *free* here: *VA.gov/gi-bill-comparison-tool.*

★ ★ ★

Pro Tip: Yellow Ribbon Program

Let's say I go to the University of Texas at Austin to get a four-year undergraduate degree, and I qualify for the full thirty-six months of coverage provided by the Post-9/11 GI Bill. You may have noticed that thirty-six months does not equal forty-eight months or four years of college. I'm going to hit a cap on the amount of benefits I receive. Fortunately, that's where the Yellow Ribbon Program steps in. It's essentially a matching grant that some schools provide to help students cover a portion of any remaining costs, including additional costs associated with being an out-of-state student or attending a private institution. If you're looking to minimize your out-of-pocket costs, choose a school that's part of the Yellow Ribbon Program. You can find out which ones participate at *VA.gov*.

★ ★ ★

BENEFITS FOR DEPENDENTS AND SURVIVORS

Through the Survivors' and Dependents' Educational Assistance (DEA) program, children and spouses of veterans may qualify for education benefits. Specifically, benefits are granted if the military member died or went missing on active duty, died as a result of a service-connected disability, or currently has a rating of 100% P&T for a service-connected disability.

Veterans also sometimes ask me if they can transfer their education benefits to their kids. The answer is yes, but *only* if you have served or will serve for at least ten years. This means you don't have to have completed all ten years before your kid can get the benefits. If you have completed at least six and you sign on for four more, for example, your children can go ahead and apply.

DISABLED VETERAN STUDENT LOAN FORGIVENESS

What I'm about to reveal is a little-known program called the Total and Permanent Disability (TPD) Discharge program for disabled veterans, and it could save you hundreds of thousands of dollars.

The new Disabled Veteran Student Loan Forgiveness Program discharges the federal student loan debt of veterans who are Totally and Permanently Disabled (meaning they have a 100% P&T VA rating) *or* who have received a 100% Total Disability Individual Unemployability (TDIU) status.

The TPD Discharge program has been a huge success to date.

And guess what else, veterans?

Few people know that if you're a veteran with a 100% VA disability rating (even if neither P&T nor TDIU status applies to you), you're also eligible for Disabled Veteran Student Loan Forgiveness!

You can get started right now on this free government website: *DisabilityDischarge.com.*

★ ★ ★

How to Apply for Education Benefits

All you need is your DD 214 and Social Security number. You don't even need to know where you're going to school yet!

You'll hear back in thirty days or less. BOOM!

★

Key Takeaway Actions from This Chapter

- Consider choosing a school based on whether it participates in the Yellow Ribbon Program to take advantage of the most tuition help you can get.

- The Forever GI Bill went into effect in August 2020, and it will get you the *most* money for school. It's fantastic.

- At some point in the next fifteen years, at almost *no* cost to you, go become even smarter than you already are, you dang genius.

- The Total and Permanent Disability (TPD) Discharge program for disabled veterans could literally save you hundreds of thousands of dollars!

★ ★ ★

CHAPTER FIVE

VA HOUSING AND HOME LOAN GUARANTEES

In 2018, when I moved from San Antonio to Austin, I wanted to buy a home instead of continuing to rent. When I was on active duty, my life was always in transit, with no strong connection to any specific location. Now I wanted to put down real roots and settle somewhere. I found a cute spot for my son and me for $385,000. Traditionally, with a mortgage lender, the home buyer has to pay 15%–20% of the total home price as a down payment. For me, that would've been up to $77,000! I didn't have that kind of money sitting around.

Thanks to the VA Home Loan Program, not only did I receive a loan, but I also avoided having to contribute a single dollar toward a down payment. That's right: $0! The actual loan still came from a private lender, but the VA backed the loan and vouched for me. That's how veterans can avoid astronomical down payments: the government guarantees the full loan, which is the main benefit of this program. Some veterans choose to put money down anyway to save on interest over the long term, but they aren't required to.

★ ★ ★

Benefits of a VA-Backed Home Loan versus a Private Lender

- No money down
- No mortgage insurance required
- Competitive interest rates
- Easier to qualify

★ ★ ★

Further, because of my disability rating at 10% or above, the funding fee was waived (more on this later). There was very little stress. Instead, I was just so proud to be able to provide a nice home for my son. And it was a reaffirmation of my military service—I earned this benefit because I served.

If you are an active duty service member or a veteran, you will generally qualify for the VA Home Loan Program, which was created in 1944 to help service members and veterans like you buy homes. Here's what you need to know.

★ ★ ★

Now You Know

If you meet certain demographic requirements, you may be eligible to receive a home loan directly from the VA as part of the Native American Direct Loan program, which can usually provide even better terms than private lenders.

If you are a surviving spouse of a veteran and meet certain requirements, you might also be able to get a Certificate of Eligibility and receive a VA-backed home loan.

If you require your home to be specially adapted to meet the needs of your service-connected disability, you may qualify for additional grants.

Visit *VA.gov* for more information.

★ ★ ★

GET A CERTIFICATE OF ELIGIBILITY (COE)

As you've probably come to expect by now, you'll need to meet a minimum active duty service requirement and not have been dishonorably discharged. If you separated from service after September 7, 1980, you need to have served twenty-four continuous months or the full period for which you were called (at least 181 days, unless you were discharged for a service-connected disability). But then, *that's it!* That's all you'll need to get your COE, which is what a private lender will use to secure VA backing.

Several private lenders out there work exclusively in the VA home loan market. We recommend going through one of these banks instead of a traditional mortgage lender, as a VA purchase lender will be so much more familiar with the process and your specific needs. Did you know we started a VA home loan company for veterans called LendHero? It's stupid simple to complete your application online right now: *LendHeroHomeLoans.com*.

DO I NEED TO MEET A MINIMUM CREDIT SCORE FOR A VA HOME LOAN?

No, the VA does not have a minimum credit score requirement to secure a VA home loan. However, private lenders absolutely do have minimum credit score requirements. Thus, you'll still need to meet your private lender's credit score and income requirements to receive financing, especially if you want more favorable VA home loan terms and conditions. Generally, the higher your credit score, the better the interest rate and loan terms you'll receive from a private lender. Most private VA lenders require a minimum credit score of 620. Note that you may still qualify for a VA home loan with a credit score below 620; however, your options will be limited.

FUNDING FEE WAIVER FOR DISABLED VETERANS

The VA could save you tens of thousands of dollars, but they do charge a fee for this service. It's not to be greedy but to protect taxpayers—the ones ultimately backing your loan. However, there's good news: If you have a service-connected disability of 10% or higher, the VA will waive this fee. That can translate to substantial savings!

The fee is between 1.4% and 3.6% of however much you borrow. Several factors determine the percentage, including whether you made a down payment and whether this is your first mortgage.

★ ★ ★

Pro Tip: Refunded Fee

If you buy your house with a VA-backed home loan, pay a funding fee, and then are later awarded a service-connected disability rating of 10% or higher, you will be eligible for a refund. The VA will actually *pay back* whatever they have charged you in funding fees.

★ ★ ★

CAVEAT

Remember that as with any home purchase, other fees may pop up. There are loan closing costs. There may be a brokerage fee. You may have to pay for an inspection or a termite report, stuff like that. It's always good to be reminded!

★ ★ ★

How to Apply for Home Loan Benefits

Set up a meeting with a private lender that handles VA home loans. You can do some simple internet searches to find the best VA loan deals. You can also apply at LendHero (they'll shop the best rates for you): *LendHeroHomeLoans.com*.

Have a copy of your DD 214—and, if you have a service-connected disability of 10% or higher, a copy of your VA benefits letter—as well as a copy of your VA COE form, which you can download at *VA.gov*.

★

Key Takeaway Actions from This Chapter

- If you want to put down roots and reap all the rewards associated with homeownership in America, the VA will help you substantially.

- You don't have to wait to receive your disability rating before applying for a home loan. You can always get the funding fee refunded later.

CHAPTER SIX

VA JOB TRAINING AND EMPLOYMENT

I f you served in the US military, you are already a darn good candidate for almost any civilian job. First and foremost, remember that. Now, on top of that, the VA offers a variety of programs—from training to hiring preferences—designed to help you get and maintain a good job.

It's scary when you transition out of active duty service and don't know what you're going to do next. When you're in the military, every job and position is assigned to you. Transitioning into a civilian job market can be a significant source of stress and anxiety. It can lead you to question your self-worth. I remember thinking, *Will anybody want to hire me? Do I have the types of skills that make me suitable for civilian employment?*

But then, roughly two weeks after I left active duty service, thanks to a program called Expedited Hiring Authority (EHA), which is part of Veterans Preference for Federal Jobs, the Department of the Air Force hired me on as a civil servant. They literally selected me because I was a veteran, and I already possessed certain skills, training, and experience from my time on active duty.

I knew about this program because other folks at our military installation had previously taken off the uniform and returned as civilian employees. I loved the work I was doing on active duty, and I knew I was good at it, so about three months before I took the uniform off, I reached out to the hiring agency at my military base to say I would be transitioning and was interested in working as a civilian in any available capacity. Because of Veterans Preference, which is one of a few programs you'll learn about in this chapter, they prioritized me over other candidates.

But you certainly don't have to work for the federal government to get a good job. What I want to tell you is that you belong to one of the most employable categories out there. Employers are looking for you. Employers want to hire veterans because we are mission-focused team players. We are leaders. We're able to get the job done at a high level. Do not discount how valuable your military experience, training, and leadership abilities are in the civilian world. There is a direct transfer. You're trained and ready. You matter. You will crush it. Let's go!

VETERAN READINESS AND EMPLOYMENT

If you are disabled, depending on the disability, a lot of jobs may be difficult for you to do. The Veteran Readiness and Employment (VR&E) program—aka "Voc Rehab"—will help you find work appropriate to your abilities and then also help you *get* that work via training services, such as résumé building and job search leads. If your disability is so consuming that you cannot immediately consider work, this program provides services to help you live independently in the meantime.

You'll work with a counselor to determine exactly what your employment handicap is and create an individualized plan based on what kind of help you need. In addition to help with the job search, your program might include on-the-job training, unpaid work experience, compensated work therapy, or other services. Typically, the VA pays for it all, including tuition, fees, books, equipment, and even a subsistence allowance for you, if appropriate.

Eligibility

This service is for service-members or veterans who have both a service-connected disability and an employment handicap. There are two thresholds you could meet: either you have a 20% or higher pre-discharge disability rating (memorandum rating) and an unemployment handicap, or you have a 10% rating and have been determined to have a serious employment handicap. Of course, you must also have been discharged under other-than-dishonorable conditions.

RESERVE AND NATIONAL GUARD REEMPLOYMENT RIGHTS

Hey, all of you who are in the reserves: did you know that if you're called back to duty, you can resume your job when you return? If you're working a full-time job, the employer is required to hold the position for you. They also can't revoke any benefits based on seniority, including pay increases and promotions.

Eligibility

You have to give advance notice of your military service to your employer. With some exceptions, you can't be gone for more than five years total, and you'll have to officially submit an application for reemployment. Keep a record of everything, and if your employer is acting shady, contact the Department of Labor's Veterans' Employment and Training Service.

VETERANS PREFERENCE FOR FEDERAL JOBS

This is the program that helped me get a job right after service. This program recognizes that often, the skills and training veterans receive in the military directly transfer to civil service positions in the federal government. If you're a veteran, you qualify for a five-point preference in your hiring score when applying for federal jobs: all else being equal, if a veteran and nonveteran are equally qualified, the agency is required to pick the veteran. Further, you're also entitled to a retention preference during a reduction in staff.

If you're a disabled veteran, you actually qualify for a ten-point preference, which is huge! In some circumstances, such preferences even extend to spouses of P&T disabled veterans and widow(er)s of veterans who died in service.

★ ★ ★

Now You Know

In this chapter, I have touched on programs that will affect most of you or that offer the most benefit. There are a variety of other job training, education, and career counseling services, for both students and those already in the workforce. Visit *VA.gov* for more information.

★

How to Apply for Veteran Readiness and Employment

- If you already have your disability rating, this is SUPER easy. Just log in to your VA.gov account, look for the "Learn how to apply for VA education benefits" link, scroll down, choose the "Find your education benefits" form, and then answer the questions. If you meet the eligibility requirements (outlined in the section above), you'll be invited to join a program near you.

- If you don't have a disability rating yet, you can still apply! Fill out and submit VA Form 28-0588. Depending on where you are in the disability process, you might not have to wait to start your training.

★

Key Takeaway Actions from This Chapter

- Don't doubt yourself! Civilian employers are looking for leaders like *you*. Because of your military training and experience, you are one of the *strongest* job candidates in the entire market.

- Get an additional leg up by utilizing VA services that will give you additional training and/or help find the perfect job for you.

- If you are in the reserves and get called into service, let your employer know that you will want your job back when you return!

★ CHAPTER SEVEN ★

VA BURIALS AND MEMORIALS

The last thing anyone wants to think about is dying—especially if you just got out of combat. At the same time, whenever you do die, the *last* thing your partner or children will want to deal with is figuring out how to apply for burial reimbursement or get a plot in a national cemetery. Now is a good time to start engaging in these conversations with your family. Make sure you have a will and that your family members know what your wishes are. It's on you, as the veteran, to lead that conversation.

You may want to be buried in private cemeteries with family members who have gone before you. Or you may want to be among other veterans in a federal burial ground, even if your spouse and children will be elsewhere—and I understand that! I don't know a single person who served in the military and didn't come out a different person. The camaraderie, the sense of purpose, the belonging, the fact that you defended freedom in an all-volunteer force—those are probably some of the proudest moments of your life. Whatever your wishes are, you've got to start the process now.

As for reimbursement, a point I really want to hammer home is that there *won't* be that much money. First of all, you're only eligible for any amount if you were already receiving a pension or some kind of compensation (such as disability, for example). Further, the VA will not pay for all the expenses associated with your funeral, which can be incredibly costly. At most, your family will get $2,000 (plus, maybe, the cost of transporting your remains). Still, that will be a welcome amount during a trying time. The fact that the VA helps with funeral costs at all is pretty darn cool in my opinion. Here are the basics you need to know.

NATIONAL CEMETERIES AND MARKERS

Of the 136 currently operating national cemeteries, almost 100 of them are accepting new internments. If you met active duty service requirements and were discharged under conditions other than dishonorable, you are welcome. In some cases, surviving members of your family may *also* be eligible for burial in a national cemetery. Further, the VA will make and deliver a headstone or marker anywhere in the world, along with a burial flag.

The good news is that you can figure all of these logistics out now, instead of leaving the work to your surviving family members. That's what the VA's Pre-Need Burial Eligibility Determination program is for.

BURIAL REIMBURSEMENT

The VA offers more money if your death is service connected. Now, if you are reading this book, you are probably no longer in the service and may assume that you are not eligible for that full amount. However, if your service-connected disability winds up being part of the cause of your death, your family will be eligible for the full $2,000 toward expenses—plus, if you're buried in a national cemetery, some or all the costs associated with transporting your remains.

The VA will pay up to $796 toward burial and funeral expenses for deaths on or after October 1, 2019 (if hospitalized by the VA at time of death), or $300 toward burial and funeral expenses (if not hospitalized by the VA at time of death), and a $796 plot-interment allowance (if not buried in a national cemetery). For deaths on or after December 1, 2001 but before October 1, 2011, the VA will pay up to $300 toward burial and funeral expenses and a $300 plot-interment allowance. For deaths on or after April 1, 1988 but before October 1, 2011, the VA will pay $300 toward burial and funeral expenses (for veterans hospitalized by the VA at the time of death). Like anything having to do with VA benefits, burial reimbursement can be a little confusing. Fortunately, things have recently gotten a bit easier. In 2014, the VA made the payment of burial benefits automatic, meaning your surviving spouse does not have to apply if they're listed with the VBA as the veteran's spouse. However, I recommend familiarizing yourself with the application process anyway in case something changes or you get lost in bureaucracy somehow.

★ ★ ★

How to Apply for Burial Benefits

- Choose where you want to be buried and jump-start the process via the VA's Pre-Need Burial Eligibility Determination Program. Visit *VA.gov/burials-memorials*.

- To get a burial flag, fill out the Application for United States Flag for Burial Purposes (VA Form 27-2008).

- For a headstone, grave marker, or niche cover, fill out the Claim for Standard Government Headstone or Marker (VA Form 40-1330).

- If you're eligible for burial benefits, thanks to the VA's new automated system, your surviving spouse should not have to apply at all. However, in case there is a mix-up, know that your spouse, partner, or family member will have two years to file a claim if it is from a nonservice-related death and will need proof of your death, receipts, and a statement from the funeral home or cemetery. There is no time limit to file for a service-connected burial, plot, or interment allowance.

★

Key Takeaway Actions from This Chapter

- Make plans for where you want to be buried *now* so your family isn't burdened with the process later.

- If you want to save time, you can apply online for burial benefits on the *VA.gov* website.

CHAPTER EIGHT

VA MENTAL HEALTH RESOURCES

D id you know that a veteran is nearly four times more likely to develop post-traumatic stress disorder (PTSD) than a civilian? It's estimated that one in five Iraq and Afghanistan war veterans has either PTSD or major depression.[6] Personally, I think these statistics are way off. Why? Because nearly every veteran I know is suffering from some type of undiagnosed mental health condition, whether they realize it or not. According to my experience with the more than 600,000+ veterans who come to our website properties each month and to the questionnaires we circulate among our member veterans, I believe almost every veteran has issues with mental health to some degree, whether in the form of insomnia, anxiety, panic, or depression. We all experienced trauma while wearing the uniform.

---

6   RAND Center for Military Health Policy Research, "Invisible Wounds: Mental Health and Cognitive Care Needs of America's Returning Veterans," 1.

According to VA statistics, in 2019, 1.7 million veterans received mental health services. This is good and bad: I'm glad millions of veterans receive services, but so many more need help. Mental health is arguably the biggest need right now in the veteran community, especially during the time immediately after you take off the uniform. We try to reintegrate into society and can't figure out why we snap at everybody, why we don't feel like we fit in, or why we abuse alcohol and drugs to try to cope. And then we spiral. Fortunately, the VA has recognized and responded to our needs with a ton of different services and platforms, including telemedicine for those in rural areas.

Need Help Now?

Emergency mental health care is also available 24/7 at VA Medical Centers (if a VAMC doesn't have a twenty-four-hour emergency room, it is required to offer 24/7 mental health care through another local hospital). If you're at your breaking point, put down this book and call 988 and press 1 now, or chat with someone online at *VeteransCrisisLine.net*. America loses twenty-two veterans to suicide every day. I don't want you to be one of them. Your life is important. God created you for a reason, and you matter.

★ ★ ★

The most important thing I can tell you In this chapter is that you're never alone. I encourage you to be open and honest about your struggles and to take advantage of these resources. There is *no* shame in it. The most important thing is your life, which depends on your mental health. When you get help and get better, you can be there for your spouse, your family, and your friends. It's true that you may never be the same again after what you experienced while wearing the uniform, but you can at least develop techniques to help you stabilize and maybe even thrive.

Here's more good news: Mental health care is often a gateway for veterans to achieve a disability rating and then improve their lives even more with financial benefits. Once they get help, they become more aware of their situation and more willing to take action. Plus, the application process is infinitely easier for them because they already have medical evidence and a diagnosis linked to their service. But those steps may be further down the road for you. The most important thing right now is to get help ASAP.

★ ★ ★

Service Risks

The following risks are commonly associated with a veteran's need for mental health care. If any of these applied to your service, please get yourself assessed ASAP.

- Frequent deployments
- Long deployments
- Deployments to hostile environments
- Exposure to extreme stress
- Sexual assault or sexual harassment while in service
- Service-related injuries

★ ★ ★

THE TRANSITION PERIOD

Your readjustment from military life to civilian life will most likely be tough. It's a stressful time. A lot of veterans feel financial stress. There can be worries about getting through school or facing the job market. Many veterans may already know they have mental health issues and, as a result, feel broken and lost. We fill ourselves with self-doubt and limiting beliefs that we are "less than" and will make it on the outside. That couldn't be further from the truth.

★ ★ ★

Now You Know

For a year after your separation, you can get *free* mental health care—no matter your discharge status, service history, or eligibility for VA healthcare.

★ ★ ★

You are *more* capable of succeeding in life than anybody else in America. You're mission focused. You're a team player. You operate with integrity. You're loyal. You're honest. Sure, the transition period will be tough, but that's normal. The VA is here to help you through it and get you out on the other side, ready to succeed at everything you do.

★ ★ ★

Totally Normal Struggles

The following are part of the transition process. Some people will have it tougher than others. If you experience any of these symptoms, don't be alarmed, but do seek care. A whole variety of options are available to you, including professional counseling, buddy guidance, and medical referrals.

• Frequently feeling anxious, tense, or on edge

- Difficulty concentrating
- Anger or irritability
- Trouble sleeping
- Feeling down and depressed for days, weeks, or months

GET YOUR BUTT TO THE DOCTOR!

You probably don't know what you need. I certainly don't know what you need—I am not a medical professional. Find someone who is, and let them decide. Maybe you don't need anything. But when you're struggling, you need help choosing the best course. I'm giving you permission to pick up the phone and make an appointment at the VA mental health facility closest to you, no matter who you are or what you've done. Now get your butt to the doctor!

The fall of 2017, right before my divorce was finalized, was one of the darkest times in my life. My mental health conditions were at their very worst. I struggled at work. I was drinking way too much and abusing drugs. Honestly, I was drunk, high, or both almost every day. I remember thinking that I had failed: as a husband, as a dad, as a worker, as a friend. I shut everybody out because of trust issues. I was angry all the time (and in many ways, still am). The mind has a funny way of piecing together a narrative that you then believe is true.

During that time, I had thoughts like, *Maybe nobody would care if I weren't here. Who would miss me?* I felt estranged from my own kid. I didn't have any friends. Work sucked. And I was abusing substances. What was the point? But then a tiny voice from somewhere urged me to get help. It was most definitely a God moment. And I remembered that every time the VA emailed me its newsletter, it included a number for a suicide hotline, the Veterans Crisis Line.

It was extremely liberating to speak confidentially with somebody who wouldn't judge me. What I said wouldn't go on my official record, be reported to my supervisor, or get back to my family. I knew I'd found a safe space. The person on the other end of the phone put me at ease and helped me understand that even though my brain was telling me a distorted narrative, I do matter. People are counting on me. "Your son needs you, Brian," he said. He helped me remember that tomorrow could be a better day. That phone call helped get me out of a very dark place and onto my path of healing and success, which is why my number one piece of advice to you is to go *see someone* about your mental health, whether you think you have a problem or not. If you're a veteran, you probably do.

★ ★ ★

Now You Know

Sixty-six percent of women in the military report having experienced sexual assault or sexual harassment. And it's not just a women's issue or men's issue—it's an all-of-us issue. Sexual harassment and sexual assault have *no* place in the military or our society. These statistics are shameful and unacceptable, and I'm on a mission to change them. The VA provides free, *confidential* counseling and treatment to female and male veterans for both mental and physical health problems linked to military sexual trauma.

★ ★ ★

Even if you don't qualify for VA healthcare, you may still be able to get certain mental health services for free. You can seek help in person or through the VA's TeleMental Health program. Care is also available via phone apps. You can do individual counseling or group counseling, either for yourself or your family. If you want to talk to other veterans facing similar challenges, check out the peer assistance program BeThere and the peer coaching program Military OneSource. There are so many ways to receive help—choose one and get yourself seen.

God created you for a purpose. You are here for a reason. You are not alone. You are enough. Your life matters. I lived to tell you that.

★ ★ ★

VA Vet Centers

VA Vet Centers are community-based centers located off-base, across the country, that provide a broad range of free counseling, outreach, and referral services to veterans, active duty service members, and their families. They offer individual, group, marriage, and family counseling in a safe and confidential environment. You can access Vet Center services regardless of your character of discharge, and you do not need a disability rating or service connection for injuries from either VA or DoD. All Vet Center services are available without time limitation and at no cost. They offer nontraditional hours to accommodate busy schedules. Some communities have Mobile Vet Centers that travel to places where there is no permanent local Vet Center. And more than 70% of staff are veterans, the majority of whom served in combat theaters.

★ ★ ★

THANKS, VA

It's worth taking a minute to thank the VA, along with our elected officials and the general public who support them, for shining so much light on the mental health needs of veterans. At the time of writing this second edition in January 2023, I had been out of the service for ten years. Mental health care options now are light-years ahead of where they were even just a decade ago. Care is exponentially more accessible and available. According to a Pew Research study, 75% of Americans support increasing spending for veteran benefits and services. If you ever think for a second that you don't matter, remember that the majority of America thinks you *do*.

TESTIMONIAL: PTSD RELIEF

"*Eighteen years after serving in the US Marine Corps, I finally got the VA to establish that my PTSD was combat related. After a three-year battle and constantly being sent by the VA for more anger management and psych evaluations, I received a 70% rating—but only, I think, because I had reached out to a senator I served closely with. Unfortunately, my lifestyle did not change much, as the PTSD was still not properly addressed. I came to VA Claims Insider in 2017 but didn't feel ready for another three-year fight. Brian encouraged me. The team and I had a fully developed claim built in two weeks, including an independent medical opinion, a personal impact statement, and buddy letters. Sixty days later, I saw $6,000 in my bank account and assumed the VA had overpaid. I checked eBenefits and saw that I was now 100% P&T. This was a life-changing event. Instead of struggling to provide for my family through severe PTSD, my new rating gave me protections that allowed me to retire and focus on my family and my mental health. My life has completely turned around. Thank you, VA Claims Insider.*"

★ ★ ★

How to Access Mental Health Resources

- Call or walk into any VA medical center 24/7, 365 days a year. Check *VA.gov/find-locations*.

- For readjustment counseling, call or walk into one of 232 different Vet Centers across America during clinic hours. Check *VetCenter.VA.gov* for locations.

- Call 1-877-222-8387 Monday through Friday, 8:00 a.m. to 8:00 p.m. ET, for help finding the right resources suited to your needs.

- At any time, you can call the Veterans Crisis Line at 1-800-273-8255 (and then press 1) or text 838255.

★

Key Takeaway Actions from This Chapter

- You matter—to those around you and because you were put on this earth for a purpose. The VA wants to help you. I want to help you.

- Get your butt to the doctor! This is me urging you right now to pick up the phone and call the nearest VA mental health facility.

★ ★ ★

PART 2

STATE BENEFITS

Now that you are aware of the support, services, and programs available to you through the federal Department of Veterans Affairs (VA), let's talk about what your state of residence offers. Get psyched: many more financial benefits are coming your way in this section! For example, Texas has an entire comprehensive platform for state benefits called the Texas Veterans Commission. They help with disability, education, and employment. Texas offers grants, help for small businesses, healthcare advocacy, mental health support, and so much more.

Other states also offer great support, such as property tax waivers or free hunting and fishing licenses. I mention Texas first because I am very familiar with its programs and systems—I live there. My last duty assignment was at JBSA-Randolph in San Antonio. Although I wasn't thrilled when I was assigned there, I soon fell in love with Texas. Once I was a veteran, I stayed in part because I started learning about the benefits available, such as help with buying my first home. While I was on the house-buying journey, I did more research. I kept a small notebook where I jotted down any information I gathered. And I always kept my discharge paperwork and certifications with me so I could use them whenever needed.

Soon, I had a notebook full of information. I started reaching out to other veterans, especially disabled veterans, to share my knowledge. Many discovered they had been paying full price for services and programs they were eligible to receive for free or at a reduced price.

Now my team and I have collected this information for every state in America. If you're already settled, you can skip straight to your state (organized alphabetically by region of the country). If you're just out of the service or about to take off the uniform, we strongly suggest taking state benefits into consideration when choosing where to live. Like Texas, many states have entire programs funded through the state's budget and staffed by state-funded workers. Others don't.

Overall, we feel there is a "Top Ten" list of states based on how they support veterans. These are Texas, Florida, North Carolina, Pennsylvania, New York, California, Ohio, Virginia, Georgia, and Illinois. It's not a coincidence that almost half of all veterans in the United States live in one of those states. To whittle down the list even more, based on our research and reports from veterans, the three most vet-friendly are Texas, Florida, and North Carolina.

For each state, we have listed the number of veteran residents as a percentage of total state population based on data available at the time of publishing.

When deciding where to live, state benefits obviously won't be your only decision. You'll need to come up with a detailed budget, consider opportunities for work and hobbies, and so forth. But if one state can make that budget lighter or enhance your job or hobbies, those are factors you shouldn't ignore. Also, just as the VA offers veterans preference points when hiring for federal jobs, every state also offers some kind of veteran preference for state, county, and/or city jobs. (Since some offer more than others, I recommend that veterans check each state's website for updated information on hiring regulations.)

When I hear from veterans about how our information has helped them, the hair on my arms and neck stands up because I know we are truly making a difference in their lives. Helping veterans get the benefits they deserve is our mission, which extends far beyond federal benefits offered by the VA.

This section provides information on all fifty states but with a concentrated focus on the benefits available to disabled veterans. These lists are by no means comprehensive. (For example, every state offers some kind of special license plate and/or designation for veterans, and this information is relatively easy to find. Therefore, we didn't include it.) There's so much information out there, and we don't want to overwhelm you. This is just a starting point. This list was also accurate as of the time of publication, but you'll want to check the resources directly from the most up-to-date details.

Once you've mastered the information in these pages that is relevant to your specific state, we encourage you to dig deeper on your own to find any other benefits or resources pertinent to your needs.

How to Approach Part 2

- If you're already settled, turn straight to the pages associated with your state. You'll find them organized by US region and then alphabetized by state within each section.

- If you are still considering where to live (or move), review any states of interest to you.

- In each listing, there is information about the programs and benefits available to you. Please note that eligibility requirements apply. For example, you will always need to have been honorably discharged, and you will almost always need to be a resident of the state offering the benefit. Further, many benefits are available only to veterans with service-connected disabilities. For full eligibility information, visit *VAClaimsInsider.com/blog* and search by state.

★ ★ ★

CHAPTER NINE

THE MIDWEST REGION

ILLINOIS

Veteran population: 4.6% (591,267)[7]

Financial Benefits

Income Tax. Active duty, National Guard, reserve, retired pay, and Survivor Benefit Plan (SBP) payments are tax-free.

General Financial Bonuses. The state of Illinois offers a one-time bonus for veterans who served honorably during a time of war. Certain medals are needed to qualify. Veterans or their survivors may apply at their nearest service office.

---

7   For each state, veteran population statistics were calculated using veteran-population numbers from *VA.gov* and state population numbers from the US census.

Bonuses for Veterans of Certain Wars (and Survivors). Monthly or one-time bonuses are also available to qualifying veterans (and sometimes to their survivors) of the following engagements: World War II, the Korean War, the Vietnam War, the Persian Gulf War, and the Global War on Terrorism.

POW Compensation. Qualifying veterans who were taken and held prisoner by hostile forces in Southeast Asia are entitled to a bonus for each month or portion thereof while being held captive.

Specially Adapted Housing Tax Exemption. Up to a $100,000 reduction in the property's value for taxation purposes is available for homes that were purchased or modified with the Specially Adapted Housing Grant for as long as the veteran, spouse, or unmarried surviving spouse lives there. Mobile homes purchased with the Specially Adapted Housing Grant are also exempt from county mobile home tax.

Returning Veterans' Homestead Exemption. Qualifying veterans receive a $5,000 reduction to their home's assessed value for two consecutive years.

Disabled Veterans' Standard Homestead Exemption. A reduction in the assessed value of the home is available to a veteran with a service-connected disability. Depending on the disability rating, exemptions range from $2,500 to 100%. The unmarried surviving spouse of a service member killed in the line of duty is exempt from paying property taxes on the primary residence. You must file an annual application with the county to receive this exemption.

Housing and Healthcare Benefits

Veterans' Homes. The state of Illinois operates several veterans' homes.

- **The Veterans' Home at Quincy.** The Veterans' Home at Quincy, the largest in the state, is located in Adams County. The home provides a broad range of facilities and services, including domiciliary, intermediate, and skilled care. Anderson and Somerville Barracks offer a home to up to 132 domiciliary residents. Sunset State Veterans' Cemetery, located on the campus, provides internment and perpetual care for eligible veterans and spouses. Over 7,000 veterans and spouses dating back to the Civil War rest there.

- **The Veterans' Home at LaSalle.** The Veterans' Home at LaSalle is located in LaSalle County. The home provides skilled nursing care for 184 residents and an additional forty people in a special needs unit for veterans suffering from Alzheimer's disease or related dementia.

- **The Veterans' Home at Anna.** The Veterans' Home at Anna is located in Union County. The home provides skilled nursing care services to eligible veterans and can accommodate fifty skilled nursing care residents and twelve people in six adjoining apartment-style domiciliary units.

- **The Veterans' Home at Manteno.** The Veterans' Home at Manteno is located in Kankakee County. The home can accommodate 249 skilled care residents and forty in the

Alzheimer's/dementia unit. Manteno offers a diverse range of programs and services to eligible veterans.

- **The Prince Homeless/Disabled Veterans' Home.** Located at the Veterans' Home at Manteno, this fifteen-bed program is staffed with social service professionals and provides permanent supportive housing to veterans, helping them obtain medical and education benefits to which they are entitled, and assisting them with learning and reinforcing the life skills necessary to live independently.

- **The Veterans' Home at Chicago.** The Veterans' Home at Chicago will be located in Cook County on the northwest side of the city onsite at the Chicago-Read Mental Health Center. It is scheduled to have a 200-bed capacity with a wing for Alzheimer's/dementia patients. (As of this book's publication, construction on the almost completed project had been paused due to COVID-19.)

Employment Benefits

Education Requirements for Police and Firefighters. The educational requirements needed to join the Illinois State Police will be waived for veterans who have been honorably discharged with a campaign service medal for Afghanistan or Iraq. The Illinois Conservation Police will waive their educational requirements for honorably discharged veterans who have certain campaign medals. The educational requirement for a firefighter or municipal police officer is waived for veterans discharged honorably after twenty-four months of active duty or 180 days in combat.

State Licenses and Credentials. Licenses and credentials testing and fees for EMT,IA, EMR, and CDL may be waived if you have military experience in that job.

Education Benefits

Deceased, Disabled, and MIA/POW Veterans' Dependents Scholarship. The state of Illinois provides an education scholarship for the dependents of veterans who are either Missing in Action or a Prisoner of War, died while on active duty, are 100% disabled due to service-connected disabilities, or died as a result of a service-connected disability. 105 ILCS 5/30-14.2 (Deceased, Disabled, and MIA/POW Scholarship) establishes the benefit and 95 Ill. Admin Code 116 (Deceased, Disabled, and MIA/ POW Scholarship) provides the rules governing the administration and eligibility of dependents.

Illinois Veterans' Grant (**IVG**). The IVG Program pays tuition and mandatory fees at all Illinois state-supported colleges, universities, and community colleges for eligible Illinois veterans. An individual must meet the following criteria:

- Be an honorably discharged veteran
- Reside in Illinois six months before entering the service or be a resident of Illinois for at least fifteen consecutive years after having active duty as of the date of application
- Have at least one full year of active duty in the US Armed Forces (this includes veterans who were assigned to active duty in a foreign country in a time of hostilities in that country, regardless of length of service)
- Return to Illinois within six months of discharge from the service

Applications and additional information are available from the VSO Offices of the Illinois Department of Veterans' Affairs, college financial aid offices, or the Illinois Student Assistance Commission (ISAC), located at 1755 Lake Cook Road, Deerfield, IL 60015; telephone 847-948-8550 or 1-800-899-ISAC.

Illinois National Guard (ING) Grant Program. The ING Grant Program will pay tuition and certain fees (registration, graduation, general activity, matriculation, and term fees) for undergraduate or graduate study for eligible Illinois National Guard service members. Benefits can only be used at an Illinois two- or four-year public college. The value of benefits a service member can receive is based on years of service:

- For less than ten years of National Guard service, the grant can be used up to the equivalent of four academic years of full-time enrollment.
- For ten years or more of National Guard service, the grant can be used for a maximum of the equivalent of six academic years of full-time enrollment.

Who is eligible for ING? To be eligible, service members must meet the following requirements:

- Currently serving Illinois National Guard service member
- Completed one full year of service in the Illinois National Guard
- Enrolled at an Illinois public two- or four-year college
- Not be in default on any student loan or owe a refund on any state or federal grant
- Maintain satisfactory academic progress as determined by the educational institution

Service members who served in the Illinois National Guard for at least five consecutive years and whose education was interrupted due to being called to federal active duty for at least six months can receive an exemption from the currently serving requirement. For more information, service members should contact their chain of command or the Education/Incentives Branch of the Military Personnel Office at 217-761-3782.

University of Illinois Children of Veterans Scholarship. Each county in the state is entitled, annually, to one honorary scholarship at the University of Illinois, for the benefit of children of veterans of World War I, World War II, Korean War, the Vietnam conflict, at any time on or after August 2, 1990, and until those persons in service are no longer eligible for the Southwest Asia Service Medal. Preference is given to the children of deceased and disabled veterans. Such children are entitled to receive, without charge for tuition, instruction in any or all departments of the university for a term of at least four consecutive years. Details may be obtained from the University of Illinois's Financial Aid Office.

Veteran Coordinators at Public Universities and Colleges in Illinois. Veteran coordinators are tasked with being the central point of contact for all veterans, service members, and dependents at universities and colleges. Veteran applicants and student veterans are encouraged to contact these staff members to learn about eligibility for veteran education benefits, benefit application processes, academic counseling, financial aid counseling, and student support services.

VA Work Study Locations. The Illinois Department of Veterans' Affairs provides VA work-study opportunities at its numerous offices throughout Illinois. The federal VA work-study program provides part-time employment to students receiving VA education benefits who attend school three-quarter time or more. Work-study students are paid either the state or federal minimum wage, whichever is greater. Other available opportunities may exist at the school veteran's office, VA medical facilities, the VA Regional Office, and approved VSOs.

Academic Credit for Military Training. The Office of the Governor and the Illinois Department of Veterans' Affairs—in cooperation with the Illinois Community College Board, several community colleges, the Illinois Board of Higher Education, and MyCreditsTransfer—completed a collaborative project to grant student veterans appropriate academic credit for the education and training they've gained in military service.

INDIANA

Veteran population: 5.9% (402,386)

Financial Benefits

Income Tax. Indiana resident service members in an active or reserve component of the US Armed Forces are eligible for an income tax deduction of $5,000 for their military pay. Service members on duty outside of the United States and Puerto Rico, filing Indiana income tax, are authorized for an automatic sixty-day extension to file taxes. Military pay earned while in a combat zone is exempt from Indiana state income tax.

Property Tax Deductions. There are several property tax deductions that range from $12,480 to $24,960. The amount of the deduction depends on a number of criteria, including disability status, wartime service, and property value.

- *Deduction for Totally Disabled Veteran or Veteran age 62 and Partially Disabled:* There is a $14,000 deduction available to veterans who have served at least ninety days in the US Armed Forces and received an honorable discharge (can be peacetime service) and have a total disability rating from the VA (does not have to be service connected), *or* who are sixty-two years old or older and have a 10% or more service-connected disability rating. The surviving spouse of an eligible veteran can claim this deduction. *Note:* This deduction is not available if the assessed value of the property is greater than $200,000.

- *Deduction for Veteran with Partial Disability:* A $24,960 tax deduction is available for veterans who received an honorable discharge for service in the US Armed Forces during World War II (December 7, 1941 through December 31, 1946), Korea (June 27, 1950 through January 31, 1955), Vietnam (August 5, 1964 through May 7, 1975), or the Gulf War (August 2, 1990 through a future date to be set by law or presidential proclamation) *and* are least 10% service-connected disabled. The surviving spouse of an eligible veteran can claim this deduction.

- *Deduction for Property Received from a Tax-Exempt Organization:* Indiana offers a property tax deduction on the assessed value of property given to disabled veterans by charitable organizations. The property tax deduction is equal to the percentage of service-connected disability the VA has awarded the veteran. Veterans must have served during a wartime period for at least ninety days, received an honorable discharge, and been given a service-connected disability rating greater than 50%.

- *Vehicle Excise Tax Deduction for Disabled Veterans:* For veterans or their spouses who are eligible for any of the deductions above but for whom the assessed value of their property is less than the deduction can apply the overage toward the excise tax on up to two vehicles. Veterans and their spouses can receive a $2 credit to be applied toward the excise tax for every $100 of remaining property tax deduction. An individual cannot claim a vehicle credit and a property tax credit at the same time.

Military Family Relief Fund (MFRF). The MFRF emergency grant may be used by families for needs such as food, housing, utilities, medical services, transportation, and other essential family support expenses that have become difficult to afford. A grant up to $2,500 may be awarded.

Housing Benefits. The Indiana Veterans' Home, located in West Lafayette, was originally created to care for veterans of the Civil War and is now a full-service care facility offering a complete array of services for all eligible Indiana veterans.

Employment Benefits

Military CDL Skills Waiver Program. The BMV may waive the required driving skills test for veterans who have received specific training and who were truck drivers during their military service when they apply for an Indiana Commercial Driver's License.

Next Level Veterans Program. The state will help you apply for a job with dozens of corporations and, if hired, will pay you $5,000 to relocate to Indiana.

Education Benefits

Indiana Wartime Veterans High School Diploma Program. Indiana offers high school diplomas to veterans who left high school to serve in the US Armed Forces during the following wartime periods:

- December 7, 1941 through December 31, 1946 (World War II)
- June 27, 1950 through January 31, 1955 (Korea)
- August 5, 1964 through May 7, 1975 (Vietnam)

Veterans must meet these requirements:

- Were students in good standing at an Indiana high school prior to entering the military
- Did not graduate or receive a diploma due to entering the US Armed Forces
- Received an honorable discharge

Free Tuition for Children of Disabled Veterans. Indiana offers free or discounted tuition at state schools to children of eligible disabled veterans, Purple Heart recipients and their children, and children of former POW/MIA.

Indiana National Guard Supplemental Grant (NGSG). Indiana offers 100% tuition and regularly assessed fees for service members in the Indiana National Guard at Indiana public colleges and universities. Service members can attend either full time or part time during only the spring and fall semesters.

Indiana Resident Tuition for Veterans. Nonresident veterans and former Indiana National Guard service members who enroll in an Indiana public college or university within twelve months after receiving an honorable discharge are eligible for resident tuition rates.

Veteran or former Indiana National Guard Service member who received an honorable discharge within twelve months of enrolling in an Indiana public college or university.

Within one year of enrollment, the veteran or former service member must take steps to establish Indiana residency, such as by:

- registering to vote in Indiana
- obtaining an Indiana driver's license or state ID card
- registering a motor vehicle

Recreational Discounts, Licenses, and Passes

State Parks. A Hoosier Golden Passport provides unlimited admission to all Indiana state-owned parks, recreation areas, reservoirs, forests, historic sites, museums, memorials, and other Department of Natural Resource facilities. The pass is good for one calendar year and is available to all persons eligible for a Disabled American Veteran license plate.

Hunting and Fishing Licenses for Disabled Veterans. Any Indiana resident who is service-connected disabled by the US Department of Veterans Affairs may purchase a license to hunt and fish in the state of Indiana for a reduced fee.

IOWA

Veteran population: 6.1% (194,953)

Financial Benefits

Injured Veterans Grant. This grant provides up to $10,000 to service members or discharged veterans who sustained serious or very serious combat-related injuries in a combat theater of operations after September 11, 2001.

Homeownership Assistance. A $5,000 grant is available to eligible service members who buy a home in the state of Iowa.

Property Tax Exemption. This benefit reduces an eligible veteran's assessed home value for property tax purposes by $1,852.

Disabled Veteran's Homestead Tax Credit. This legislation, from the year 2014, provides 100% exemption of property taxes for 100% service-connected disabled veterans and Dependency and Indemnity Compensation recipients.

Military Retirement Tax Exemption. This legislation, from the year 2014, exempts federal retirement pay received for military service and survivor benefits from state individual income tax.

Military Spouse Residency Relief Act (MSRRA). Under the MSRRA and Iowa law, a nonresident service member's spouse's income from wages, salaries, tips, and so forth, may be excluded from Iowa income tax if they meet the following requirements:

- The service member is serving in the US Armed Forces and is in Iowa in compliance with their orders.
- The spouse is in Iowa only to be with the service member.
- The spouse has the same state of residence as the service member.

Iowa Veterans Trust Fund. The state of Iowa has established a multi-million-dollar fund to provide relief for Iowa veterans and their families. Currently, funds are used for unemployment or underemployment assistance due to service-related causes, counseling and substance abuse services, vehicle repairs, housing repairs, transitional housing in an emergency, and assistance with vision, hearing, dental care, durable medical equipment, and prescription drugs. Trust fund expenditures are approved through the Iowa Veterans Commission.

Housing and Healthcare Benefits

Iowa Veterans Home. The Iowa Veterans Home provides a continuum of care to Iowa's veterans and their spouses in an environment focusing on individualized services to enhance their quality of life. One of the largest state veterans homes in the nation, it provides services to more than 550 Iowa veterans at a time, with multiple levels of care.

Employment Benefits

Workforce Development: Home Base Iowa. Iowa is committed to providing quality employment services to all veterans at its IowaWORKS Centers through Home Base Iowa, a one-of-a-kind program that connects businesses with qualified veterans and transitioning service members to career opportunities. The program also provides resources to help connect veterans and their families with education and transitioning to a new community. Claimants who have questions about their claim status or benefit payments should visit *IowaWorkForce Development.gov*.

Education Benefits

National Guard Tuition Benefits. Present Iowa National Guard members in good standing are eligible for up to $2,700 per semester for full-time enrollment. Part-time students are eligible for $196 per semester hour. Additionally, guard members who are mobilized will receive a tuition refund.

Operation Recognition High School. This program furnishes an honorary high school diploma to qualifying veterans who did not complete high school (in Iowa) due to armed service enlistment.

War Orphan Tuition Assistance. Children of Iowa veterans killed in action following September 11, 2001, are eligible for up to $11,844 per year in tuition assistance at an Iowa postsecondary institution. Dependents of those killed in action prior to September 11, 2001 are eligible for $600 per year, with a maximum of $3,000. Residency is required.

Branstad-Reynolds, Children of Fallen Iowa Service Members Scholarship Fund. The Branstad-Reynolds Scholarship Fund provides postsecondary educational scholarships for children of service members who died while serving on active duty in the US Armed Forces after September 11, 2001.

Scholarships may be used to pay for the costs of tuition, books, fees, housing, special tools, and equipment required for coursework, school-approved tutoring, and any other required educational expenses. Once all educational expenses are met, any remaining funds will be released to the student to cover other expenses as needed. This is a state-funded program and may be used in conjunction with any federal benefits.

Recreational Discounts, Licenses, and Passes

Lifetime Hunting and Fishing License. Eligible veterans can receive a lifetime hunting or fishing license for a $7 fee.

KANSAS

Veteran population: 6.6% (192,963)

Financial Benefits

Income Tax. Military retirement pay and SBP payments are tax-free.

Homestead Act. Eligible disabled veterans can claim a homestead refund.

Kansas National Guard and US Armed Forces Reserve Service Members Emergency Relief. Kansas National Guard Service members or Kansas resident US Armed Forces Reserve service members and their families can request financial assistance to help them make ends meet in emergency situations when all other options have been exhausted. For more information and to apply, service members should speak to their chain of command.

Housing and Healthcare Benefits

Kansas Veterans' Homes. Kansas runs two veterans' homes, in Fort Dodge and Winfield. Veterans seeking admission must have active federal service. Veterans who have no adequate means of support receive first priority for admission. Kansas residents also receive priority for acceptance. On a space-available basis, spouses and surviving spouses may qualify for admission.

Education Benefits

Kansas Military Service Scholarship. This scholarship covers tuition and fees at a public Kansas institution for eligible veteran students who are residents of Kansas. Financial need is a priority in awarding this scholarship.

Kansas National Guard Educational Assistance Program. This program pays tuition at state colleges and will pay up to fifteen hours per term for eligible students.

Kansas Tuition Assistance for Dependents of Deceased Resident Service Members, Disabled Veterans, and Former Prisoners of War (POWs). Kansas public educational institutions will waive tuition and fees for the spouse, unremarried surviving spouse, and dependent children of the following resident service members or veterans:

- Service members who died in the line of duty while serving on state or federal active duty in the US Armed Forces on or after September 11, 2001
- Veterans with an 80% or greater service-connected disability rating
- Former POWs

Those eligible can receive a waiver for the equivalent of ten semesters of undergraduate instruction at Kansas state universities, community colleges, or vocational technical colleges.

Kansas Educational Benefits for Dependents of Veterans of the Vietnam War. The child of a veteran who dies as a result of service in Vietnam is eligible to attend a Kansas public institution of higher learning without paying tuition and fees. This benefit is for up to the equivalent of twelve semesters of instruction. Once a person is eligible for this benefit, they may not be disqualified.

Recreational Discounts, Licenses, and Passes

Free Hunting and Fishing Licenses. National Guard members and Kansas resident veterans with a 30% disability rating or greater can get free hunting and fishing licenses.

Hunting Licenses for Active Duty Members. Active duty military personnel stationed in Kansas can purchase all annual state licenses, permits, and stamps at the resident rate. Military permits for elk draw are available for active duty military personnel stationed at Fort Riley.

Discounted State Park Admission. Kansas Army and Air National Guard service members and veterans with a disability rating of 30% or greater receive discounted admission to state parks.

MICHIGAN

Veteran population: 5.5% (554,281)

Financial Benefits

Property Tax Exemption. Eligible resident veterans may be exempt from paying taxes on their home. Surviving spouses who have not remarried are also eligible.

Income Tax. Active duty, retired pay, and SBP payments are tax-free.

Income Tax Credit for Property Tax Paid. The state's income-tax code provides a credit for property tax paid by a disabled veteran or surviving spouse. This benefit varies depending on disability rating and the family's income.

Emergency Assistance. Emergency assistance is available to those experiencing temporary financial issues and who require assistance with utility bills, vehicle or home repairs, medical bills, or other debts. There are many resources available, including county Soldiers & Sailors Relief Fund, the Michigan Veteran Trust Fund, and the National Guard Family Program.

Michigan Military Family Relief Fund. The Michigan Military Family Relief Fund Act authorizes financial assistance grants to qualifying families of service members in either the Michigan National Guard or Army Reserve who are called to active duty as a result of the national response to the September 11, 2001 terrorist attacks. These grants can be used for clothing, food, housing, utilities, medical services or prescriptions, insurance payments, vehicle payments, or other related necessities of daily living.

Michigan National Guard State Retirement Pay. Michigan provides a state retirement benefit for all former members of the Michigan National Guard who have served a minimum of nineteen years, six months, and one day of active service. Retired Service members will be paid $600 annually ($50 per month) beginning at age fifty-five or the effective date of application, whichever is later. Active members of the Michigan National Guard may not receive the benefit until they retire.

Housing and Healthcare Benefits

There are three Michigan Veteran Homes; they are located in Marquette, Grand Rapids, and Chesterfield Township. Veterans eligible for VA healthcare or financial assistance for long-term care may be admitted. Michigan residency is not required, and spouses or surviving spouses may be admitted if space is available. Fees are income-based.

D. J. Jacobetti Home for Veterans. Located in Marquette near the shores of Lake Superior, the Jacobetti Home offers physician coverage as well as the following services: pharmacy, respiratory therapy, physical therapy, rehabilitation (in-patient), mental health, social work, routine dental examination, speech therapy, occupational therapy, laboratory services, recreation therapy, EKG, and specialty clinics.

Additional services such as podiatry, dental services, and vision services are available on a fee-for-service basis. The amount of the monthly payment is based on income, expenses, marital status, and assets. Staff will assist members in applying for pensions, social security, VA, and long-term care insurance payments.

Grand Rapids Home for Veterans (GRHV). The GRHV is a long-term care state veterans home located on ninety acres of land near the mighty Grand River. Initially founded in response to the needs of veterans in the aftermath of the Civil War, GRHV has capacity for 450 nursing care beds and more than 100 domiciliary beds. The nursing care beds include 115 special needs beds, with two thirty-five-bed nursing units for the care of Alzheimer's and dementia patients and one forty-five-bed nursing unit for dual diagnosis patients.

Chesterfield Township Home for Veterans. There is a brand-new home in Chesterfield Township available to Michigan veterans residing in metro Detroit (Wayne, Oakland, and Macomb Counties), with four homelike neighborhood buildings catering to 128 members. The 33,000-square-foot community center houses administrative offices, occupational and physical therapy spaces, and amenities like a multi-faith prayer room, a café and bistro, a barbershop, a beauty parlor, multipurpose rooms, and a large space for full membership and community gatherings. The surrounding grounds are designed for additional recreation and exercise opportunities, with walking paths and gardens.

Education Benefits

The Children of Veterans Tuition Grant. This grant provides undergraduate tuition assistance to the child of an eligible veteran who is between sixteen and twenty-six years old. Undergraduate students may receive scholarship assistance for up to four academic years and a total of $11,200.

Michigan National Guard State Tuition Assistance Program (MINGSTAP). MINGSTAP provides tuition assistance to members of the Michigan National Guard who are attending any public or private college, university, vocational school, technical school, or trade school located in Michigan.

Employment Benefits

Michigan State Employment Veterans' Hiring Preference. Michigan offers eligible veterans and their spouses preference when hiring for state civil service positions. Applicants must meet the minimum qualifications for the job and any position-specific selection criteria, and preference can only be used for an initial (first) appointment to a Michigan civil service position.

Michigan Department of Licensing and Regulatory Affairs (LARA) Service Members, Veterans, and Spouses Benefits. LARA offers the following benefits for active duty service members, veterans, and their spouses:

- Temporary exemption from renewal fees, continuing education requirements, and any other related requirements until ninety days after release from active duty but not more than thirty-six months after the expiration of the license
- Temporary licenses for an active duty service member's spouse
- Waiver of initial license or initial registration fee and initial application processing fee for veterans

Recreational Discounts, Licenses, and Passes

Disabled Veteran Hunting and Fishing Licenses. Permanently and totally disabled veterans can get any resident hunting or fishing license for which a lottery is not required, free of charge.

State Parks. One hundred percent permanently and totally disabled veterans receive free entry into Michigan state parks.

MINNESOTA

Veteran population: 5.3% (304,276)

Financial Benefits

Short-Term Financial Assistance (Subsistence). The Subsistence program provides temporary assistance with shelter payments (rent or mortgage), current utility bills, and health insurance premiums to eligible veterans and their dependents. This benefit is income- and asset-based and is designed to assist veterans for up to six months.

Minnesota Special Needs Grant. The Minnesota Special Needs Grant provides a once-per-lifetime financial grant to help veterans and their dependents during a financial crisis and to promote stability and prevent homelessness. Requests are reviewed and approved on a case-by-case basis, and applicants must demonstrate future sustainability beyond the requested amount of assistance. Approved amounts of assistance are paid directly to the vendors chosen by the applicant as part of their application.

Income Taxes. Military pay, retirement pay, and SBP payments are tax-free.

Minnesota Tax Credit for Past Military Service. Veterans of the US Armed Forces who have a federal adjusted gross income less than $37,500 may qualify for a nonrefundable tax credit of up to $750. Part-year residents or nonresident veterans may qualify for the credit, based on the percentage of their income that is taxable in Minnesota.

Minnesota Tax Credit for Military Service in a Combat Zone. Service members who served in a combat zone or qualified hazardous duty area can receive a refundable tax credit of $120 per month for each month they served in a qualifying area. Partial months will count as whole months. Service members may qualify to receive this credit even if they have no income or owe no tax.

Disabled Veterans Market Value Exclusion on Homestead Property. Disabled veterans may qualify for a reduction in the assessed value of their home. The reduction varies depending on the amount of disability. Surviving spouses may also qualify.

Housing and Healthcare Benefits

Minnesota Veterans Homes. Minnesota Veterans Homes are located in Fergus Falls, Hastings, Luverne, Minneapolis, and Silver Bay. Each facility offers a variety of services to meet veterans' physical, social, and spiritual needs.

Minnesota SOAR, Homeless Veterans Assistance Program. The MDVA has partnered with the Minnesota Department of Human Services and the US Social Security Administration to provide homeless and at-risk veterans with expanded access to Social Security Income and Social Security Disability Insurance benefits.

Minnesota Homeless Veteran Registry. The Minnesota Homeless Veteran Registry connects veterans experiencing homelessness with housing and services in their community. It also helps programs and partners serving veterans to coordinate their efforts. Anyone who served in an active or reserve component of the US Armed Forces can join the registry, regardless of the type of discharge or length of time in the service. Veterans who join can receive assistance from a team of housing and service professionals to help them access housing and services that meet their needs.

Employment Benefits

Resources for Veterans Looking for Employment. MDVA partners with the Minnesota Department of Employment and Economic Development to support veterans as they put their military skills to work in a new career.

Minnesota CareerForce Veteran Resources. Minnesota CareerForce assists veterans to meet their career development needs. Local Veterans Employment Representatives can help with career planning, job searches, and finding education and training opportunities, in addition to connecting veterans with other resources. Veterans will receive priority services in all CareerForce locations across the state.

Education Benefits

Minnesota GI Bill. The Minnesota GI Bill program provides eligible Minnesota veterans up to the age of sixty-two with assistance of up to $10,000. Eligible participants can use the benefit in higher education, on-the-job training, apprenticeship, or license and certification.

Minnesota Veteran Education Assistance. Minnesota Veteran Education Assistance is a one-time $750 grant for tuition for veterans who have exhausted their GI Bill benefits to assist them in completing a bachelor's degree. This grant is paid directly to the institution or may be reimbursed to veterans upon verification that their tuition has been paid.

Surviving Spouse and Dependent Education Benefit. If found eligible, resident survivors are allowed admission to most Minnesota post-secondary education institutions, can attend free of tuition until they obtain a bachelor's degree, and will receive an annual stipend for fees, books, supplies, and/or room and board.

Minnesota Higher Education Veterans Programs. MDVA's Higher Education Veterans Programs help connect veterans with education benefits and resources to help them succeed in college. The programs support veterans, current service members, and their families who are attending Minnesota's colleges and universities by providing on-site comprehensive information about benefits and resources as well as supporting the unique needs of these students.

Minnesota National Guard State Tuition Reimbursement (STR) Program. STR reimburses Minnesota National Guard service members up to 100% of the tuition cost at an accredited educational institution. The lifetime maximum STR benefit is 208 quarter or 144 semester credits.

The undergraduate reimbursement rate is up to 100% of the undergraduate rate of the University of Minnesota, Twin Cities, with a maximum yearly benefit of $18,000 per fiscal year (July 1 through June 30). The graduate reimbursement rate is up to 75% of the graduate rate of the University of Minnesota, Twin Cities, with a maximum yearly benefit of $28,000 per fiscal year.

Recreational Discounts, Licenses, and Passes

Minnesota State Parks. All active duty personnel and disabled veterans get free admission to Minnesota state parks. You do not have to be a Minnesota resident to qualify.

Resident Disabled Veterans Hunting and Fishing License. Minnesota 100% disabled veterans get a free lifetime fishing license and a free annual hunting license.

MISSOURI
Veteran population: 6.7% (413,742)

Financial Benefits

Income Tax. Military retirement and disability are tax-free.

Property Tax Credits. The Missouri Property Tax Credit gives credit to eligible senior citizens and residents who are 100% disabled as a result of military service for a portion of the real estate taxes or rent paid for the year. The credit is for up to a maximum of $750 for renters and $1,100 for homeowners.

Housing and Healthcare Benefits

Missouri Veterans Homes. The Missouri Veterans Homes manage a total of 1,238 beds that provide long-term skilled nursing care. The homes are located in Cameron, Cape Girardeau, Mexico, Mount Vernon, St. James, St. Louis, and Warrensburg.

Missouri Homeless Veterans Assistance. VA Medical Centers in Missouri have a Homeless Veterans Coordinator who can provide information about the services available for homeless veterans through the VA. Services include outreach, case management, referrals to benefits counselors, linkage to healthcare, and housing assistance. Homeless veterans who need assistance after hours should contact any VA medical center emergency room.

Education Benefits

Missouri Returning Heroes Act. The act limits undergraduate tuition at any state college to no more than $50 per credit hour.

War Veteran's Survivor Grant Program. Children and spouses of eligible veterans may receive up to the state average for tuition per semester plus up to $2,500 for room, board, and textbooks.

Missouri National Guard State Tuition Assistance (STA) Program. STA provides tuition assistance to eligible National Guard service members pursuing an undergraduate degree or below. STA can be used for up to thirty-nine semester hours per state fiscal year (July 1 through June 30), up to the tuition rate charged at the University of Missouri, Columbia. Service members must use federal tuition assistance before STA. Service members are authorized to take fifteen credits in the spring and fall semesters and up to nine credit hours during a summer session with a lifetime limit of 150 undergraduate credit hours.

Recreational Discounts, Licenses, and Passes

Free Fishing and Hunting Licenses for Disabled Veterans. Eligible veterans can fish or hunt without a permit (except for deer and turkey). You must have proof of eligibility on your person; some trout or turkey tags may be required.

Missouri Camping Discounts for Veterans, Active Duty Service Members, and Their Family Members. Service members, veterans, and family members of active duty service members are eligible for a $2 per night discount on camping fees year-round at Missouri state parks. Those eligible must show a Military Common Access Card, Uniformed Services ID card, VA ID card, or Missouri driver's license or ID card with a "Veteran" designation at check-in to receive their discount.

NEBRASKA

Veteran population: 6.3% (124,300)

Financial Benefits

Income Taxes. Retirement pay, Military Disability Retirement Pay, and SBP payments are tax-free.

Nebraska Veterans Aid (NVA) Fund. The NVA Fund was established in 1921 to temporarily assist eligible veterans, their spouses, and dependents when an unforeseen emergency disrupts their normal method of living and when other resources are not immediately available.

Aid can only be used for food, fuel, shelter, apparel, funerals, medical care, and surgical items.

Homestead Exemption. Totally disabled veterans with an honorable discharge or general discharge under honorable conditionse and their unmarried surviving spouses may qualify for a reduction in the amount of property taxes owed. Some surviving spouses of members killed in action may also qualify; however, there are income limits and home value limits.

Housing and Healthcare Benefits

Nebraska Veterans Homes. Veterans who served on active duty in the US Armed Forces may be eligible for admission to one of the Nebraska veterans homes; eligibility may extend to the spouse, surviving spouse, and Gold Star parent. Homes are located in Bellevue, Norfolk, Kearney, and Scottsbluff.

Employment Benefits

Occupational Licensure Benefits. Licensure by endorsement, expedited licensing, and temporary licensing are available for certain occupations.

Education Benefits

Waiver of Tuition. This state program is available to resident dependents of an eligible veteran and may be used to waive 100% of a student's tuition charges and tuition-related fees to the University of Nebraska campuses, Nebraska state colleges, and Nebraska community colleges. Waiver of tuition can be used to receive one degree, diploma, or certificate from a community college and one baccalaureate degree from the university or a state college.

Operation Recognition. Operation Recognition is a joint effort between the Nebraska Department of Veterans' Affairs and the Nebraska Department of Education to award honorary high school diplomas to veterans who left school to serve their country during World War II, the Korean War, or the Vietnam War and did not complete their education after their release from service. Since the implementation of the program in 1999, more than 1,700 honorary diplomas have been awarded to eligible veterans.

Nebraska Residency for Tuition Purposes for Service Members, Veterans, and Their Dependents. Nebraska offers residency for tuition purposes to eligible service members serving in the US Armed Forces, veterans, and their dependents.

Nebraska Reservist Tuition Credit Program. Nebraska residents serving in a Nebraska-based unit of a reserve component of the US Armed Forces may be eligible for a 75% tuition credit (50% for graduate or professional degree) at University of Nebraska campuses, Nebraska state colleges, and Nebraska community colleges. This program allows 200 new applicants each calendar year. There is no lifetime limit on tuition credit for any qualifying service member.

Recreational Discounts, Licenses, and Passes

Hunting and Fishing Licenses. Nebraska resident veterans who are at least 50% disabled can get free lifetime hunting and fishing licenses.

Any veteran aged sixty-four or older can get a hunting and fishing license for $5.

Active duty members stationed in Nebraska for thirty days or more can buy hunting and fishing licenses at the resident rate.

Nebraska residents who have been deployed out of the state within the last twelve months can get an Annual Small Game Hunt/Fish Permit on a one-time basis for $5. This permit includes all state stamps.

Nebraska Free Disabled Veterans Lifetime Park Entry Permit. Nebraska disabled veterans may be eligible for a free Disabled Veterans Lifetime Park Entry Permit. This permit authorizes free entry to Nebraska state parks.

NORTH DAKOTA
Veteran population: 6.8% (52,603)

Financial Benefits

Income Tax Exemption. One hundred percent of military retirement pay is exempt from North Dakota state income tax.

North Dakota Renter's Refund Program for Senior Citizens and Disabled Persons. The North Dakota Renter's Refund program provides a partial refund on rent paid for living quarters or for a mobile home lot. Refunds can be up to, but not exceeding, $400.

Disabled Veterans (VA Rating 50% or Higher) Exemption. Eligible disabled veterans may reduce the taxable value of a homestead. A homestead can include a house, the land the house is on, and/or other buildings on the same land. If a qualified veteran moves to a different homestead, the credit can be applied to the new property. If two disabled veterans are married and living together, the combined credits may not exceed 100% of $8,100 of taxable value of the homestead. In the event of the applicant's death, the surviving spouse is eligible for the credit. The spouse whoeceiveeiving US Department of Veterans Affairs dependency and indemnity compensation receives 100% of the credit, until remarrying.

Loan Program. The Veterans Aid Fund is a permanent fund to be used solely for the purpose of making loans to veterans or their widow(er)s.

The maximum loan amount is $5,000. One half of the interest paid will be refunded, provided the loan is repaid under the agreed-upon terms.

Military Operations Adjusted Compensation. In order to ease the financial hardships and personal and family sacrifice sustained by members of the North Dakota National Guard, North Dakota residents of the Army Reserve, and active duty components who were mobilized after December 5, 1992 in support of military operations around the world, additional compensation will be provided to those resident veterans. It is the further intent of the legislative assembly to encourage those North Dakota resident veterans to continue their voluntary membership in the National Guard, reserve component, and active military force.

Disabled American Veteran License Plates. Qualified veterans with DAV licensed vehicles can park in marked handicap spots in North Dakota. Eligibility for the DAV license plates includes eligibility for exemption on the sales tax on up to two purchased or leased vehicles.

Post War Trust Fund (PWTF) Hardship Assistance Grant. The purpose of this assistance is to provide money to give aid and comfort to veterans and their spouses, or unremarried widow(er)s of eligible veterans. The individual must have an unmet need of dental and/or denture work (routine and maintenance procedures are not covered), optical or hearing care, transportation (for medical treatment), other special medical care, or housing deposit, or other emergency needs approved by the Commissioner of Veterans Affairs.

Grant available for ND Veterans with PTSD. North Dakota veterans suffering from PTSD may apply for a grant that may provide them with a specially trained service dog. The dogs address the special needs of the veteran they serve, whether it is calming anxiety attacks, providing comfort and assurance in public settings, or waking a veteran from a nightmare. PTSD service dogs have been proven to greatly assist veterans in returning to a more normal life and reintegrating back into their community.

Housing and Healthcare Benefits

The North Dakota Veterans Home, located in Lisbon, North Dakota, consists of ninety-eight basic care and fifty-two skilled nursing beds. Staff members strive to provide residential healthcare excellence to the veterans and/or spouses in their care and offer a variety of enjoyable social activities and relaxing environments to meet the varied interests of the residents.

Employment Benefits

Priority of Service for Veterans and Eligible Spouses at Job Service North Dakota Locations. Job Service North Dakota helps service members who are leaving the US Armed Forces, veterans, and their spouses to transition to a rewarding career by offering employment, training, and placement services.

Job Service North Dakota, Veterans' Employment Team. Job Service North Dakota has a Veterans' Employment Team that is trained to provide one-on-one assistance to help veterans and their eligible spouses to work through employment barriers.

North Dakota Professional and Occupational License Benefits for Service Members and Military Spouses. North Dakota offers professional and occupational license benefits to active or reserve component service members and military spouses.

Education Benefits

Veterans Educational Training (VET). Available to honorably discharged North Dakota veterans, VET is a free program of study funded by the state of North Dakota to prepare veterans for a certification program or two-year or four-year college degree. The program provides refresher training as well as training in English, computers, math, and study skills.

Dependent Tuition Waiver. Tuition waivers are available to dependents of resident veterans who were killed in action, died from wounds or other service-connected causes, or were totally disabled as a result of service-connected causes. Dependents can attend any North Dakota state school and not pay any tuition or fees.

North Dakota National Guard (NDNG) Tuition Assistance and 25% Tuition Waiver. NDNG service members can receive a 25% waiver of tuition charges at participating North Dakota state-supported schools.

The NDNG will provide financial assistance for the remaining 75% of tuition charges.

The waiver and tuition assistance may be used for certificate courses, undergraduate and graduate degrees for a lifetime total of 144 semester or 208 quarter credit hours. The sum of all tuition assistance—including federal tuition assistance, VA tuition assistance, State Tuition Assistance (STA), and so forth—cannot exceed 100% of tuition.

Recreational Discounts, Licenses, and Passes

Hunting Licenses. A resident disabled veteran can get a combined general game, habitat stamp, small game, and fur-bearer license for $3, with an additional $1 fee to purchase the resident certificate.

Eligible veterans pay only $5 for a resident fishing license, with an additional $1 fee to purchase the resident certificate.

State Parks. North Dakota veterans with a 50% or greater service-related disability and former POWs are eligible for one free annual permit for state parks.

OHIO
Veteran population: 6.2% (725,991)

Financial Benefits

Military Injury Relief Fund. The fund grants a one-time, tax-exempt monetary payment to military service members injured in active service as a member of the US Armed Forces while serving after October 7, 2001, as well as to individuals diagnosed with post-traumatic stress disorder while serving after October 7, 2001.

Veterans Bonus for Service in Afghanistan and Other Locations. This program provides $100 per month to Ohio residents who served in Afghanistan and $50 per month to those who served elsewhere, up to a maximum of $1,500.

Education Benefits

Fast Track to College Credit for Veterans. Military Transfer Assurance Guides provide a statewide guarantee that certain types of military training, experience, and/or coursework align to existing college and university courses and will be awarded appropriate college credit. Ohio's public colleges and universities are required to provide priority course registration and academic and career counseling for veterans as well as other veteran support services on campus. Each public college and university has an on-campus contact to provide more information about the program and help determine eligibility.

Ohio GI Promise. Ohio GI Promise authorizes the chancellor of the Ohio Department of Higher Education to deem qualified veterans as Ohio residents for the purpose of qualifying for in-state tuition rates. The residency officer at each public institution has sole authority to request any documentation in order to make the final determination of residency status.

Ohio War Orphans Scholarship. The Ohio War Orphans Scholarship program provides tuition assistance to children of deceased or at least 60% VA-rated service-connected disabled Ohio veterans who served in the US Armed Forces during a period of declared war or conflict.

Ohio Safety Officers College Memorial Fund. Tuition waivers are also available (for up to four years of undergraduate education) for the spouse or qualified former spouse of a member of the US Armed Forces killed in the line of duty during Operation Enduring Freedom, during Operation Iraqi Freedom, or in an officially designated combat zone.

Military Interstate Children's Compact Commission. As a member of this national organization, Ohio ensures the fair and equal treatment of military children and the children of recent military retirees and service members who died on active duty. The compact provides support for children transferring between school districts and states, ensuring that their records, course placement, extracurricular participation, and graduation needs are accommodated.

Ohio National Guard Scholarship Program. This scholarship program provides—subject to available funding—100% tuition to army and air guard members attending a two- or four-year public college or university. It is available for up to twelve full-time quarters or eight full-time semesters.

Employment Benefits

OhioMeansJobs Centers. Veterans and military spouses can access free one-on-one personal coaching for their job search at any of the eighty-eight county OhioMeansJobs Centers. Eligible veterans receive additional intensive services under the Jobs for Veterans State Grant program. Priority is given to serving those who are economically or educationally disadvantaged, including homeless veterans and veterans with barriers to employment. Veterans who register on the site will have their résumés seen first by employers who have jobs matching their skills.

Ohio Troops to Teachers Program. The Ohio Troops to Teachers Program was established to help transitioning service members and veterans start new careers as public school teachers. The goal of the Ohio

Troops to Teachers Program is to identify potential teachers and help facilitate the process for them to earn a teaching certificate and find employment as an Ohio teacher.

Tax Relief

Mobilized Military Member Tax Exemption. Service members are allowed to deduct military pay from federal adjusted gross income received for active duty while stationed outside of the state of Ohio for more than thirty days.

Military Retirement Pay—State Tax Exemptions. Military retirement pay and SBP benefits are exempt from Ohio income tax and local school district income taxes. Surviving spouse benefit plans are also exempt from Ohio income tax and local school district income taxes.

Homestead Exemption. Veterans who are rated by the VA as 100% disabled due to a service-connected disability can exempt $50,000 of the assessed value of their primary residential home from property taxes. These veterans are also exempt from the $30,000 limit on annual income applied to other applicants; eligible veterans have no limit on their annual income.

Financial Assistance

County Assistance. Each County Veterans Service Office provides short-term financial assistance to veterans and their families. The amount and type of assistance varies according to the individual abilities of each county.

Healthcare Benefits

Ohio Cares for the National Guard. Ohio Cares is a collaboration of state and local agencies supporting the behavioral health of current active Ohio National Guard personnel and their families. For emergencies: VA Telenurse is available twenty-four hours a day at 1-888-838-6446.

Transportation to VA Medical Appointments. The County Veterans Service Office in each county provides transportation to VA medical appointments. Contact your local office for specific information.

Veterans Homes

The Ohio Veterans Homes have three facilities in two locations.

- Located near Lake Erie in Sandusky, Ohio (approximately sixty miles west of Cleveland), the **Sandusky Home** offers standard and memory care in its licensed nursing home. The Sandusky Home also offers Veterans Hall, a domiciliary (DOM) for those who are able to function in an independent living situation and DOM+ for those who require very limited assistance (supervised care) but do not require the level of care provided to nursing home residents.

- Located in scenic, rural Georgetown, Ohio (approximately forty-five miles east of Cincinnati), the **Georgetown Home** offers skilled nursing services providing two levels of nursing care: standard care and memory care.

Home Loans and Assistance

Ohio Heroes Program. The Ohio Housing Finance Agency offers all benefits of their first-time home buyer program to Ohio's heroes at an interest rate that is lower than the going interest rate.

Short-Term Assistance. Each County Veterans Service Office provides short-term financial assistance to veterans and their families. The amount and type of assistance varies according to the individual abilities of each county.

Legal Assistance

Ohio Legal Help. Ohio Legal Help is a nonprofit organization founded in 2018 to help Ohioans access the civil justice system. The organization provides plain language legal help information, interactive self-help tools, and connections to local legal and community resources that can assist people with resolving legal issues.

Patriot Program. The Ohio attorney general provides services for the Ohio military.

- **Legal Assistance:** This pro bono program provides volunteer lawyers to assist military personnel and their families. Legal assistance is available for wills, powers of attorney, living wills, and durable powers of attorney for healthcare.

- **Consumer Protection:** This section provides information to enable active duty personnel and veterans to protect themselves from scams and assists those who have fallen victim.

- **Civil Rights:** Ohio law prohibits discrimination against disabled active duty persons or veterans for military status in employment, housing, and public accommodations, including service animals for those who need them.

- **Identity Theft:** This section helps identity theft victims by working with the credit report agencies, creditors, collectors, and so forth.

134 ★ YOU DESERVE IT

Ohio's Veterans' Courts. Courts throughout Ohio are implementing special Veterans' Courts, where the emphasis is on treatment and diversion rather than punishment. The Ohio Department of Veterans Services has established effective working relationships with these courts in order to provide guidance and assistance on issues like sustainable funding and obtaining certification from the Ohio Supreme Court.

Recreational Discounts, Licenses, and Passes

Free Licenses. Ohio Revised Code provides for eligible resident disabled veterans and former prisoners of war to receive a fishing license, hunting license, fur taker permit, deer permit, wild turkey permit, wetlands habitat stamp, or any combination of these licenses free of charge. Contact 1-800-WILDLIFE (945-3543) to learn more.

Free Registration of Watercraft. Free watercraft registration is available to 100% service-related disabled veterans (as rated permanently and totally disabled by the VA) or former POWs, Medal of Honor recipients, or Veterans Car Assistance Program participants. Contact Veteran's Boat Registration, Ohio DNR Division of Watercraft, at 1-877-4BOATER (426-2837).

Discounts at Ohio State Parks. Free camping is available to 100% disabled veterans (as rated permanently and totally disabled by the VA) or former POWs. A 10% discount on camping, getaway rentals, cottages, and lodge rooms is available to active duty military and veterans.

SOUTH DAKOTA

Veteran population: 7.1% (63,950)

Financial Benefits

Veterans Bonus. South Dakota pays a bonus to eligible members of the US Armed Forces who were legal residents of the state for no less than six months before their period of active duty.

Veterans with qualifying service from August 2, 1990 to December 31, 1992 (Desert Storm) may receive one bonus of up to $500. Veterans with qualifying service after January 1, 1993 may receive another bonus of up to $500.

Property Tax. Dwellings or parts of multiple-family dwellings that are specifically designed for use by paraplegics as wheelchair homes and are owned and occupied by veterans with the loss, or loss of use, of both lower extremities, or by the unremarried widow(er)s of such veterans, are exempt from taxation.

A partial property tax exemption of up to $150,000 of the full and true value of a dwelling owned and occupied by a veteran who is rated permanently and totally disabled from a service-connected disability is exempt from taxation. The surviving spouse of a veteran who was rated as permanently and totally disabled from a service-connected disability qualifies for the same property tax exemption.

Veterans Home

A local physician regularly comes to the Michael J. Fitzmaurice State Veterans Home, located in Hot Springs, and is on call for other medical services. The nursing staff of the Nursing Care Unit provides whirlpool baths, assistance with activities of daily living, supervised medications, and other personal services. Prescribed medications are available to members without extra charge. Physical therapy and occupational therapy departments work toward the rehabilitation of residents.

Education Benefits

Free Tuition for Veterans. Certain veterans are eligible to take undergraduate courses at a state-supported university without the payment of tuition, provided they are not eligible for educational payments under the GI Bill or any other federal educational program.

Eligible veterans may receive one month of free tuition for each month of qualifying service, with a minimum of one and up to a maximum of four academic years.

Free Tuition to Child or Spouse of South Dakota National Guard Member Disabled or Deceased in the Line of Duty. Any resident of South Dakota who is less than twenty-five years of age and whose parent (or any resident whose spouse) has died or has sustained a total disability, permanent in nature, resulting from duty as a member of the South Dakota National Guard, while on state or federal active duty or any authorized training duty, is entitled to tuition without cost and is entitled to attend any course or courses of study in any state educational institution under the control and management of the board of regents.

Reduced Tuition for South Dakota National Guard Members. South Dakota National Guard service members are eligible for a 50% reduction in undergraduate tuition at any state-supported school for up to 128 credits for undergraduate programs and thirty-two credits for graduate programs. Service members also have the option to use this benefit at state-supported vocational schools for a 50% tuition reduction.

South Dakota Veterans Upward Bound (VUB) Program. VUB helps veterans improve their educational skills and prepare for college, university, or technical school.

VUB provides the following programs and assistance:

- Academic refresher classes
- Tutoring (individual and group)
- Study skills
- College curriculum information
- Preparation for college, university, or technical school entrance
- GED preparation assistance

In addition, VUB offers career services such as:

- Career interest inventories
- Follow-up information on specific job outlooks
- Help finding training opportunities
- Career exploration
- Help defining choices and planning
- Education funding information
- Financial aid application assistance
- Employment Benefits

Credited Military Service for South Dakota Retirement System (SDRS). Members of SDRS who are reserve component service members in the US Armed Forces and are called to federal active duty service do not lose credit for retirement. Employees will continue to earn credited service if they are employed before going on military leave, return to public service within one year of discharge, and remain employed for at least one year after their return.

South Dakota State Employment Wage Compensation Adjustment during Active Duty Service. State employees who are members of a reserve component of the US Armed Forces and are ordered to state or federal active duty (not active duty for training) will receive the difference between their state salary and their military salary for the duration of their active duty service. The difference will be paid on a quarterly basis.

Recreational Discounts, Licenses, and Passes

State Parks. Certain resident veterans may obtain free admission to any South Dakota state park and are eligible for a 50% discount on any camping fee or associated electrical fee.

Hunting and Fishing. Eligible resident veterans will receive a Total Disability Reduced Fee Hunting and Fishing License. This license card will be a replacement for the resident small game license and resident fishing license.

Individuals who are missing an upper limb or are physically incapable of using an upper limb or who are confined to a wheelchair may use a crossbow to take game birds and animals once they have obtained a disabled hunter permit. A legally blind or quadriplegic, legally licensed individual who possesses a disabled hunter permit and who is physically present and participating in the hunt may claim game birds and animals taken by a designated hunter in accordance with the license or licenses possessed by the disabled hunter.

WISCONSIN
Veteran population: 5.8% (342,822)

Financial Benefits

Wisconsin Veterans Assistance Grants. The WDVA Wisconsin Veterans Assistance Grant program provides limited financial assistance to those who are in need and have exhausted all other sources of aid. The grants may be used for specified healthcare and subsistence needs up to maximum grant limits.

Military Retirement Benefits Exemption. Military retirement benefits are exempt from Wisconsin state taxation.

Disabled Veterans Property Tax Credit. The Wisconsin Veterans and Surviving Spouses Property Tax Credit gives eligible veterans and unremarried surviving spouses a refundable property tax credit for their primary, in-state residence and up to one acre of land. Veterans rated 100% disabled or unemployable by the VA are eligible. Surviving spouses may also be eligible if they receive DIC.

Housing and Healthcare Benefits

Veterans Homes. Wisconsin has three veterans homes in Chippewa Falls, King, and Union Grove, serving nearly 1,000 veterans and their spouses, providing twenty-four-hour skilled nursing care to our nation's heroes.

Wisconsin Veteran Housing and Recovery Program (VHRP). VHRP helps veterans who are homeless or at risk of becoming homeless receive the job training, education, counseling, and rehabilitative services that they need to find steady employment, affordable housing, and the skills to sustain a productive lifestyle.

Wisconsin Department of Veterans Affairs, Veterans Outreach and Recovery Program (VORP). VORP is designed to connect veterans to community services and provide case management and support, with a special focus on treatment and recovery.

Employment Benefits

Veterans Retraining Grants. Recently unemployed or underemployed veterans may receive up to $3,000 per year, for a maximum of two years, if they have a financial need while being retrained for employment. Other education or retraining grants will be considered when determining the veteran's financial need for this program and should be included in the application.

Job Center of Wisconsin (JCW), Veterans Employment Assistance. JCW helps veterans who are looking for a job or want to start a new career. Conveniently located across the state, JCWs offer priority of service for veterans.

Wisconsin Hire Heroes Transitional Jobs Program for Veterans. The Hire Heroes Transitional Jobs Program for Veterans offers local businesses access to subsidized veteran employees to help veterans with high barriers to employment gain job skills needed for long-term sustainable employment.

Veterans can enter subsidized employment for up to 1,040 hours to gain new or updated skills through on-the-job training. Employers will be reimbursed federal minimum wage while they train eligible veterans.

Education Benefits

VetEd Reimbursement Grant. The Veterans Education (VetEd) grant program provides a reimbursement grant to eligible veterans who have not yet been awarded a bachelor's degree, based on a credit-bank system that is based on length of active duty military service. The grant reimburses tuition and fees following successful course completion at an eligible University of Wisconsin, technical college, or approved private institution of higher learning.

Veterans may currently receive federal VA Chapter 30 Montgomery GI Bill benefits and VetEd for the same semester. Individuals eligible for Wisconsin GI Bill benefits must apply for and use those benefits in order to be eligible for VetEd reimbursement. VetEd reimbursement will be reduced to the extent that tuition and fees have already been paid by other grants, scholarships, and remissions provided for the payment of tuition and fees, including federal VA Chapter 33 Post-9/11 GI Bill tuition benefits.

Wisconsin GI Bill. The Wisconsin GI Bill remits (forgives) full tuition and segregated fees for eligible veterans and their dependents for up to eight semesters or 128 credits, whichever is greater, at any University of Wisconsin System or Wisconsin Technical College System school. The Wisconsin GI Bill is a state program that is entirely separate from the federal GI Bill.

For additional information, eligibility criteria, and instructions on applying for the Wisconsin GI Bill program, see the Wisconsin GI Bill information and application booklet.

Wisconsin Veteran Student Assistance Grant. The Wisconsin Veteran Student Assistance Grant provides financial assistance for eligible veterans, their spouses, and their children to attend private nonprofit educational institutions that are members of the Wisconsin Association of Independent Colleges and Universities. The amount of the grant is the lesser of $2,000 or 50% of the tuition charged per semester. For each grant, the private institution will match the amount of the grant to offset the tuition charged to the student.

Grants may be made for up to 128 credits or eight semesters, less the number of credits or semesters the student received tuition assistance under the Wisconsin GI Bill. Veteran Student Assistance Grants will be paid only after all grants and scholarships, including VA educational benefits, are paid.

Wisconsin Veterans Upward Bound (VUB) Program. VUB is a free program offered at the University of Wisconsin-Milwaukee and the Zablocki VA Domiciliary Veterans Center that helps eligible veterans become college-ready and enroll in a postsecondary school (university, community college, or vocational/technical programs).

Recreational Discounts, Licenses, and Passes

Hunting Licenses. Wisconsin disabled veterans with a VA disability of at least 70% are eligible for a reduced-fee fishing license.

Recently returning Wisconsin resident veterans can get a one-time free small game, archery, gun, deer, or annual fishing license.

State Parks. Disabled veterans with at least 70% disability may receive waivers of vehicle admission and trail pass fees to Wisconsin state parks.

CHAPTER TEN

THE NORTHEAST REGION

CONNECTICUT

Veteran population: 4.4% (157,947)

Financial Benefits

Property Tax Exemptions. Eligible veterans may receive a $1,500 exemption for property tax purposes (e.g., real property or automobiles). Veterans below a certain income level and service-connected disabled veterans are eligible for additional property tax exemptions (up to $10,000 for paraplegics). Surviving spouses of veterans may also be eligible for this benefit.

Income Tax. Active duty pay is tax-free for veterans stationed out of state, provided they don't own a home in Connecticut or live there for more than thirty days per year. Military retirement pay and SBP payments are tax-free.

Wartime Bonus. Connecticut National Guard members are eligible for a bonus of $50 for every month of mobilized service after September 11, 2001, with a maximum payment of $500 for non-combat or $1,200 for combat service.

Connecticut Military Family Relief Fund. The Military Relief Fund provides monetary grants to service members and their families experiencing financial hardship as a result of military service. The amount of the grant award is dependent on the unique circumstances of each case but may not exceed $5,000.

The Soldiers', Sailors', and Marines' Fund (SSMF). The SSMF provides funding for temporary financial assistance for clothing, food, medical and surgical aid, and general care and relief. For further information, please call 860-953-4345.

Housing and Healthcare Benefits

Veterans Home at Rocky Hill. The department has a healthcare center with a capacity of 125 beds, a 50-bed substance abuse recovery program, and a 400-bed residential program. Professional services are provided by staff physicians, advanced practice registered nurses, OT, PT, RT, dietitians, and social workers, and they are augmented by community specialists, as well as networking to local VA and major area hospitals when appropriate.

The Veterans' Home at Rocky Hill features a 125-bed long-term care facility. The healthcare facility has five units and offers specialty programs for dementia care, respite care, assisted living, and hospice care.

The residential program provides eligible veterans with a continuum of rehabilitation designed to ultimately return them to independent living in the community. Components include room and board, substance abuse treatment if appropriate, temporary employment, training and education, job placement, and transitional living.

Connecticut Department of Veterans Affairs, Patriots' Landing. Connecticut's Patriots' Landing, located in Rocky Hill, has five separate single-family, three-bedroom homes for homeless veterans, their spouses, and their children. All homes are completely furnished and equipped with kitchen supplies, bedding, furniture, washers and dryers, and full kitchens.

Connecticut Military Support Program (MSP). The MSP is a partnership between the Connecticut Department of Mental Health and Addiction Services and the Connecticut National Guard to provide confidential behavioral health services to veterans, Connecticut National Guard service members, and their families.

Sgt. John L. Levitow Veterans Healthcare Center. The Sgt. John L. Levitow Veterans Healthcare Center at the Connecticut State Veterans' Home provides long-term care to veterans with chronic and disabling medical conditions.

Education Benefits

Tuition Waiver. State law provides that tuition at state educational institutions be waived for certain veterans and certain dependents.

High School Diplomas and Veterans of World War II. Local boards of education may award diplomas to those World War II veterans who did not receive them when they left high school before graduation for military service (Public Act 00-124).

Recreational Discounts, Licenses, and Passes

State Parks. Connecticut offers a free lifetime pass to all state parks and forests for Connecticut residents with a service-connected disability.

Hunting Licenses. Any active duty military member, no matter where they are stationed, can buy hunting, trapping, and fishing licenses for the resident rate.

DELAWARE
Veteran population: 6.9% (68,850)

Financial Benefits

Veterans Trust Fund. The Delaware Veterans Trust Fund provides assistance to Delaware's veterans in financial crisis. Established in 2013, it has brought relief to veterans in need of help with reintegration, housing, utilities, and incidental expenses for health and welfare.

Delaware Taxes on Military Disability Retirement Pay. Military Disability Retirement Pay received as a pension, annuity, or similar allowance for personal injury or sickness resulting from active service in the US Armed Forces should not be included in taxable income.

Modifications to Taxable Income. People under the age of sixty receiving pensions from employers, the United States, the state, or any subdivision thereof, may deduct up to $2,000 from their federal adjusted gross income. Amounts received as pensions by persons aged sixty or older may deduct up to $12,500 off their federal adjusted gross income.

Delaware Disabled Veterans School Tax Credit. Delaware resident disabled veterans may be eligible for a tax credit of 100% of their nonvocational school district property tax. This credit may only be used toward property taxes assessed on a primary residence.

Pension Benefits for Paraplegic Veterans. Paraplegic veterans eligible for benefits may receive a pension from the state of $3,000 per year, payable in equal monthly installments.

Delaware Joining Forces (DJF) Network. The DJF network provides solutions that improve the quality of life and welfare of the Delaware military community. This community-level effort directly supports service members, veterans, and their families by addressing critical issues and needs, including financial and legal assistance, job training and employment, homelessness and housing, behavioral health and wellness, and education.

Housing and Healthcare Benefits

Delaware Veterans Home (DVH). The DVH has 150 beds with both private and semiprivate rooms. The facility includes physical therapy, a main dining room, a multipurpose room, and a town square with amenities such as a canteen, barber/beauty shop, library, and chapel. The home is located on Airport Road in Milford on twenty-four acres, adjacent to a sixteen-bed hospice, a Boys & Girls Club, and nearby facilities for dialysis, professional medical offices, and Milford Memorial Hospital.

Delaware Supportive Services for Veteran Families (SSVF). SSVF provides assistance to veterans and their families who have housing stability issues or are homeless. SSVF will provide case management, benefit application assistance, financial assistance (including rental, security deposit, and utility assistance), and access to benefit enrollment.

Delaware People's Place Veterans Outreach Program. The Delaware People's Place Veterans Outreach program offers a wide range of services for Delaware veterans who live in areas from lower New Castle County to the Delaware-Maryland state line.

Education Benefits

Delaware Veterans Education Benefits. The state of Delaware provides educational benefits for eligible children of certain deceased veterans of the military services of the United States, military service personnel held prisoner of war, and military service personnel officially declared to be missing in action.

Delaware National Guard Tuition Assistance. Delaware National Guard service members can receive waivers of up to 100% tuition at state-supported colleges and universities or the average of in-state tuition at a private college or university in Delaware.

Employment Benefits

Veterans Employment Opportunity Credit. Employers are eligible for a tax credit of 10% of a qualified veteran's wages, up to a maximum of $1,500, and may take the credit the year a veteran is hired and the two subsequent tax years.

Licenses and Permits for Military Spouses. Professional regulations will issue a six-month temporary occupational license, when required, to a military spouse relocating in Delaware. The temporary license will allow for the spouse to obtain employment in their discipline, pending application for endorsement or reciprocity.

Recreational Discounts, Licenses, and Passes

State Park Admission. Any veteran who honorably served or is honorably serving, including members of the Delaware National Guard, who resides in the state of Delaware, and who owns a motor vehicle registered in Delaware can receive a 50% discount on the annual fee for vehicle entrance to state parks and recreational areas.

Hunting, Trapping, and Fishing Licenses. Any member of the US Armed Forces, while stationed within the state, is deemed a resident of the state for the purpose of obtaining a license. Veterans with a disability rating of 60% or more by the US Department of Veterans Affairs may obtain a no-fee license.

Registration and Inspection of Motor Vehicles of Disabled Veterans. A motor vehicle owned by a disabled veteran who is eligible for adaptive equipment benefits is exempt from the payment of registration fees (limited to one automobile per eligible veteran at any one time).

MAINE
Veteran population: 7.8% (106,832)

Financial Benefits

Veterans' Emergency Financial Assistance (VEFA). VEFA was created to provide assistance for Maine veterans who suffer an emergency and do not have sufficient savings or access to other financial assistance to resolve the emergency. Examples of emergencies may include:

- Damage to the veteran's home due to fire, flood, or hurricane that is not covered by insurance

- Illness of the veteran or family member that results in hardship
- Prevention or resolution of homelessness
- Any other condition that puts the veteran at risk of not having the basic necessities of food, shelter, or safety

The bureau may approve up to $2,000 to a veteran who is currently a resident of Maine.

Pension Taxation. Military pensions, military income earned out of state, and military retired pay are tax-free.

Property Tax Exemption. A veteran who served during a recognized war period and is sixty-two years of age or older—or is receiving 100% disability as a veteran or became 100% disabled while serving—is eligible for a $6,000 property tax exemption. A disabled veteran or the surviving spouse of an eligible deceased veteran who received a federal grant for a specially adapted housing unit may receive a $50,000 exemption.

Vehicle Registration Fee. Veterans who are 100% permanent and total, service-connected disabled are exempt from one registration fee, title fee, and driver's license renewal fee.

Maine National Guard Foundation Fund. The Maine National Guard can award loans and grants for emergencies and other special needs to resident service members in the Maine National Guard or the US Armed Forces Reserves and their families. For more information, please contact the Maine National Guard Family Program Office at 1-888-365-9287 or *ng.me.mearng.list.me-mil-fac@army.mil.*

Housing and Healthcare Benefits

Maine Veterans' Homes (MVH). MVH opened its first home in Augusta in 1983 and has since established homes in Caribou, Scarborough, South Paris, Bangor, and Machias. MVH is a nonprofit organization and receives no state funding. It's independent from the VA but works closely with them to access federal funding for veterans' benefits and care.

Salute ME and Salute Home Again. The Maine State Housing Authority offers active duty service members, veterans, and retired military personnel a 0.50% discount on mortgages through the SaluteME or Salute Home Again programs. Limits can vary depending on how many people live in your household and where the home you plan to buy is located. Mortgage loans are available with little or no down payment.

Education Benefits

Dependents Education Benefit Program. Maine offers a 100% waiver of tuition and fees at state schools for resident dependents of Maine veterans who are permanently and totally disabled, died of a service-connected disability, or were killed in action. Spouses have ten years from the date of first entrance to complete the program; children have six academic years from the date of first entrance to complete eight semesters.

Maine Guard Tuition Assistance. Maine offers a 100% tuition waiver for Maine's National Guard members to attend any of the schools in the University of Maine and Maine Community College Systems, as well as Maine Maritime Academy.

Maine Veterans Upward Bound (VUB) Program. VUB is a federally funded precollege program that provides free assistance to eligible veterans interested in pursuing a college degree. VUB is designed to develop the academic and personal skills necessary for admission to and success in a postsecondary education program.

Recreational Discounts, Licenses, and Passes

Hunting Licenses. A disabled veteran who has a service-connected disability of at least 50% can get a free license to fish, trap, and hunt. This includes archery, muzzle load, bear, migratory bird, pheasant, spring/fall wild turkey, coyote night hunt, crossbow, one expanded archery antlerless deer permit, and upon meeting the qualifications, a license to guide. This license remains valid for the life of the license holder as long as they meet residency requirements.

State Parks. The following people are eligible for free admission to Maine state parks, museums, and sites:

- All Maine veterans with an other-than-dishonorable discharge
- 100% disabled Maine veterans and their dependents
- Maine residents who are enlisted active duty members and their dependents

MARYLAND

Veteran population: 6.1% (377,772)

Financial Benefits

Property Tax Exemption. A property tax exemption is available to the following individuals for their primary residence located in the state of Maryland: veterans who are 100% disabled for service-connected causes (exemption passes to the veteran's spouse upon their death) and surviving spouses of active duty military personnel who died in the line of duty.

Military Retired Pay Income Tax Exemption. Eligible military retirees are exempt from Maryland income tax on the first $5,000 of their retirement income. At age fifty-five, this exemption increases to $20,000.

Maryland Pension Exclusion. Veterans who are age sixty-five or older, totally disabled, or married to someone who is totally disabled may qualify for Maryland's maximum pension exclusion of $34,300.

Maryland Military Spouses Residency Relief Act. Spouses of nonresident service members remain nonresidents for state tax purposes when they are in Maryland due to military orders and do not have to pay taxes on wages earned in Maryland.

Maryland Tax Forgiveness for Deceased Service Members. Maryland will abate the taxes owed by a service member serving on active duty in the US Armed Forces who dies in a combat zone or hazardous duty area (qualifying area) or from wounds, disease, or injury they incurred while there. The abatement will apply to the tax year in which death occurred, as well as any earlier tax year ending on or after the first day the service member started serving in a qualifying area.

Vessel Excise Tax. A member of the active duty US Armed Forces residing in Maryland is exempt from the 5% vessel excise tax for one year. This exemption applies only to vessels currently registered elsewhere and brought into Maryland because of a permanent duty station change. New purchases are not exempt.

Motor Vehicle Excise Tax Credit. Returning military members may claim an exemption as new residents of Maryland if they title their vehicle within sixty days of moving to Maryland. Active duty military personnel who are residents of Maryland seeking to register an out-of-state vehicle may not be required to pay the full Maryland excise tax if they apply for a transfer of title and tags to Maryland within one year of becoming Maryland residents or within a year of returning from deployment.

Veterans Trust Fund. State legislation authorizes the Maryland Department of Veterans Affairs to receive donations and then make grants and loans to veterans and their family members who are in dire financial situations—or to private organizations that help veterans (homeless programs, substance abuse programs, etc.).

Death Benefit for Survivors or Estate of Maryland Resident Service Members Killed in Action. Maryland offers a death benefit of up to $125,000 to the beneficiaries of any resident service member who is killed in action or as a direct result of a wound suffered in action in Iraq or Afghanistan.

Housing and Healthcare Benefits

Charlotte Hall Veterans Home. Charlotte Hall Veterans Home meets the needs of those veterans who are looking for assisted living, skilled care, long-term care, or a rehabilitation program. Located on 125 acres of beautifully maintained plush green landscaping, Maryland's Veterans Home provides a continuum of care from its 168-bed assisted living unit to a higher level of care in its 286-bed nursing home. In 2012, a sixteen-bed women's nursing care unit was opened to accommodate the growing female veteran population. An electronic medical records system was implemented in 2014 and an on-site pharmacy in 2015. Both of these services ensure patient care, safety, and accountability.

Housing Services. In Maryland, a number of agencies, organizations, and nonprofits provide services for homeless veterans and veterans who are at risk of homelessness. For a list of resources, visit the Maryland Department of Veterans Affairs website at *Veterans.Maryland.gov/housing-services*.

Behavioral Health. Maryland's Commitment to Veterans assists veterans and their families with coordinating behavioral health services, including mental health and substance abuse treatment, with either the VA or Maryland's public health system.

Employment Benefits

The US Department of Labor (USDOL) provides grant funds to the state of Maryland, providing employment and training services to eligible residents and workers. As a condition of receiving those funds, Priority of Service is given to qualified veterans when referring individuals to job openings, USDOL-funded training programs, and related services. Veterans' services representatives, specifically Disabled Veterans' Outreach Program Specialists, commonly referred to as DVOPs, provide specialized employment services to veterans. The Maryland Department of Veterans Affairs sends biweekly Jobs for Maryland Veterans emails, which consist of position announcements shared by employers seeking veteran candidates. If you would like to become a subscriber, email *mdveteransinfo@maryland.gov*.

CDL License. The Maryland Motor Vehicle Administration will waive the CDL skills test requirements for eligible veterans within twelve months of their discharge if they have received training for those qualifications in the service.

Small Business No-Interest Loan Program. The state of Maryland supports veterans who have served our country, as well as the small businesses that employ them. The Maryland Department of Business and Economic Development, in consultation with the Maryland Department of Veterans Affairs, provides no-interest financial assistance to small businesses that fall within one of the listed categories of businesses: a small business owned by a military reservist or a National Guard member called to active duty, a small business that employs a military reservist or National Guard member called to active duty, a small business owned by a veteran or in plans to be started by a veteran, or a small business that employs a service-disabled veteran. No-interest loans range from $1,000 to $50,000.

Education Benefits

Two state scholarships are available to veterans, military personnel, and dependents in Maryland. The requirements and availability of funds vary. To get the most up-to-date information and eligibility requirements, visit Maryland Higher Education Commission's website at *mhec. maryland.gov.*

Veterans of the Afghanistan and Iraq Conflicts (VAIC) Scholarship. The VAIC Scholarship program provides financial assistance to US Armed Forces personnel who served in the Afghanistan or Iraq campaigns. The sons, daughters, or spouses of veterans enrolled in an eligible accredited Maryland postsecondary institution may also be eligible.

Edward T. and Mary A. Conroy Memorial Scholarship & Jean B. Cryor Memorial Scholarship Program. This program provides veterans and their family members with tuition assistance and financial aid for other educational expenses if they are attending a Maryland postsecondary institution.

Recreational Discounts, Licenses, and Passes

State Parks. Active duty military may enter state parks free of charge by showing a military ID. Visitors with a disability may apply for a free lifetime universal disability pass. Visitors over the age of sixty-two may apply for a Golden Age Pass, which has a one-time $10 administrative fee.

Hunting Licenses. Maryland residents serving in the US Armed Forces and stationed in Maryland must purchase a Resident Hunting License before hunting, unless they are on official leave and possess a copy of their official leave orders. Maryland residents serving in the US Armed Forces, while hunting during official leave in Maryland, do not need to purchase a hunting license, deer stamps, or DNR Managed Hunt Permit; however, they must purchase a Maryland migratory game bird stamp, a federal migratory bird hunting and conservation stamp, and a furbearer permit.

Any nonresident serving in the US Armed Forces who is on leave in Maryland but not stationed in Maryland must purchase a Nonresident Hunting License before hunting.

A complimentary lifetime hunting license is available to Maryland residents certified as former prisoners of war or 100% service-con-nected disabled American veterans (VA documentation required). The lifetime license is available only at DNR Licensing and Registration Service Centers and includes the bow stamp, muzzle-loader stamp, and furbearer permit.

Maryland Park Service Wounded Warrior and Veteran Outreach Program. The Maryland Park Service offers recreational opportunities for wounded warriors, veterans, and their families to enjoy. The Wounded Warrior and Veteran Outreach Program is designed to provide Maryland's servicemen and -women with unique opportunities to work, learn, volunteer, and relax in the rich natural habitats of Maryland. To learn more, visit *dnr.maryland.gov/publiclands/pages/armed_forces.aspx* or call 1-800-830-3974.

MASSACHUSETTS

Veteran population: 4.4% (305,707)

Financial Benefits

Retired Military Pay Income Tax Benefit. Retired military pay is not taxed in Massachusetts.

Military Disability Retired Pay. In Massachusetts, US Department of Veterans Affairs disability benefits are excluded from state gross income.

Property Tax Exemptions. Veterans and surviving spouses may qualify for a range of tax exemptions ranging from $400 to $1,500, depending on different criteria. Contact the Department of Revenue at 617-626-2300 to see if you qualify.

Massachusetts Vehicle Sales Tax Exemption for Disabled Veterans. Disabled veterans who suffered the loss of, or permanent loss of the use of, two limbs or who have a Massachusetts disabled veteran license plate are eligible for a motor vehicle sales tax exemption for one motor vehicle for personal, noncommercial use.

Public Assistance. Under Massachusetts General Laws, Chapter 115, the commonwealth provides a needs-based, means-tested program of financial and medical assistance for indigent veterans and their dependents. Qualifying veterans and their dependents receive necessary financial assistance for food, shelter, clothing, fuel, and medical care in accordance with a formula that takes into account the number of dependents and income from all sources. Eligible dependents of deceased veterans are provided with the same benefits as if the veteran were still living. Contact your local VSO to apply.

Veterans' Bonuses and Annuities

Bonuses. The Commonwealth of Massachusetts provides a bonus to veterans of certain designated campaigns who were domiciled in Massachusetts immediately prior to entry into the armed forces. In case of the death of a veteran, a bonus may be provided to the eligible spouse and children, parents, siblings, or other dependents of the deceased veteran, in that order. Persian Gulf veterans should contact the Veteran's Bonus Division at 617-210-5927 or email *mdvs@vet.state.ma.us* to see if they qualify. All other veterans should contact the Office of the Treasurer at 617-367-933 x859 or email *veteransbonus@tre.state.ma.us.*

Annuities. The Commonwealth of Massachusetts and the Department of Veterans' Services provide an annuity in the amount of $2,000 to 100% service-connected disabled veterans. This annuity is payable biannually on August 1 and February 1 in two installments of $1,000 each. It is granted to 100% service-connected disabled veterans as well as surviving Gold Star parents and unremarried Gold Star spouses of certain deceased veterans who gave their lives in the service of their country during wartime. Each has a separate application form. Contact the Department of Veterans' Services at 617-210-5480 or email *mdvs@vet. state.ma.us* to apply.

Education Benefits

National Guard Tuition and Fee Waiver. Members of the National Guard are eligible for a waiver of both fees and tuition at all state colleges and universities. Please contact the college or university veterans' representative for details about this program.

Public Service Grant Programs. Scholarships will be awarded to the following groups:

- Children of prisoners of war or military or service persons missing in action in Southeast Asia whose service was between February 1, 1955, and the termination of the Vietnam campaign
- Children of veterans (as defined by MGL Chapter 4, Section 7) whose service was credited to the commonwealth and who were killed in action or otherwise died as a result of such service

Scholarships will be for undergraduate studies at an institution of higher education in the commonwealth. Visit *osfa.mass.edu* for more information.

Veterans Upward Bound (VUB) Program. The VUB program has two locations in Massachusetts: UMass Boston and Suffolk University. VUB is a free precollege program to help veterans develop the academic and personal skills necessary for success in a program of postsecondary education. Visit *Veterans-UB.UMB.edu* to see if you qualify.

Massachusetts Soldiers Legacy Fund. The Massachusetts Soldiers Legacy Fund provides funds for current and future college/university students whose parents were killed on deployment during Operation Enduring Freedom or Operation Iraqi Freedom. Visit *MSLfund.org* for more information.

Housing and Healthcare Benefits

State-Aided Public Housing. Veterans who are applying for state-aided public housing through a local housing authority and are to be displaced by any low-rent housing project or by a public slum clearance or urban renewal project or were displaced within three years prior to applying for low-rent housing, when equally in need and eligible for occupancy as other applicants, are given preference in tenant selection in the following order:

- Families of disabled veterans whose disability has been determined by the US Department of Veterans Affairs to be service connected
- Families of deceased veterans whose death has been determined by the US Department of Veterans Affairs to be service connected
- Families of all other veterans, including the spouse, surviving spouse, dependent parent or child of a veteran, as well as the divorced spouse of a veteran who is a legal guardian of a child of a veteran

Continued Occupancy. State-aided low-rent housing projects cannot deny continued occupancy to veterans, widow(er)s of veterans, or a Gold Star mother who has lived there for the last eight consecutive years, provided that the unit is two bedrooms or less and the rent is not more than three months in arrears.

Homeless Shelters, Transitional Housing, and Supportive Housing with Services. The Department of Veterans' Services provides some funding to select nonprofit organizations that provide housing services to eligible veterans. Housing services range from emergency homeless shelters and group residences to single occupancy (SRO) quarters. All require that residents maintain a sober and drug-free environment. Services are available to both male and female veterans.

Soldiers' Homes. Massachusetts Soldiers' Homes provide a variety of services to veterans, such as acute hospital care, domiciliary care, long-term care, physical and occupational therapy, laboratory and radiology services, an outpatient department, and a social services department. There are two state Soldiers' Homes, one in Chelsea and the other in Holyoke. More information on eligibility and admission is available directly from the respective homes:

- **Chelsea Soldiers' Home**: 91 Crest Avenue, Chelsea, MA 02150, 617-884-5660
- **Holyoke Soldiers' Home**: Admissions Office, 110 Cherry Street, Holyoke, MA 01040, 413-532-9475

Tenancy Preservation Program (TPP). Through the TPP, MassHousing works to prevent homelessness among people with disabilities, acts as a neutral party between landlord and tenant, and provides clinical consultation services to the Housing Court.

For more information, call 617-854-1089 or *MassHousing.com.*

VA-Supported Housing (VASH) Program. The VASH program is a joint project of the Department of Veterans Affairs and the Department of Housing and Urban Development. VASH provides Section 8 vouchers to chronically homeless veterans with substance abuse or mental health issues. The voucher provides a rent subsidy that generally covers rental costs in excess of 30% of the veterans' income. The goal of the program is to transition veterans from homelessness to independent subsidized housing by providing supportive, community-based case management services.

To be eligible, veterans must:

- Not be a lifetime sexual offender
- Be homeless or at-risk for homelessness
- Have a substance abuse or mental illness history
- Clinically stabilized applicants
- Those with a need and willingness to accept case management services over a period of time to be determined by the case manager
- Applicants within income guidelines
- People who have a savings account

For more information, contact the VASH Program Assistant at a VA Medical Center near you.

- Bedford: 781-687-2000
- Boston: 617-232-9500
- Northampton: 413-584-4040

Employment Benefits

Veterans' Employment and Training Service (VETS). The VETS program receives grant funding from the US Department of Labor. The grant allows the Division of Career Services to provide Disabled Veteran's Outreach Program (DVOP) specialists and Local Veteran Employment Representatives (LVERs) at One-Stop Career Centers throughout the commonwealth.

One-Stop Career Centers. One-Stop Career Centers are located across the state in every major city, with branch offices in additional communities. Although centers design services to meet local needs, there are core services that are similar across the statewide network. There is no charge for these services for veterans. DVOPs and LVERs at the centers give priority service to veterans. For a complete listing of the One-Stop Career Centers, visit *ServiceLocator.org/nearest_onestop.asp* or call toll-free: 1-877-US2-JOBS (872-5627).

Transition Assistance Program (TAP). TAP is an intensive five-day course designed to ease the transition of military personnel into civilian life. TAP workshops are facilitated regularly by DVOP and LVER staff at Hanscom Air Force Base in Bedford, Fort Devens in Acton, and the US Coast Guard Base in Boston. TAP is available to transitioning military personnel and their family members who are within twelve months of separating or twenty-four months of separating if retiring from the military. Visit *Mass.gov/orgs/department-of-career-services* for more information.

Green Jobs and Training Grants. The Veterans' Workforce Investment Program (VWIP) grant, called the Green TEAM (Training and Employment Access for MA) veterans' initiative, assists eligible Massachusetts veterans residing in the I-495/Boston Metropolitan area—especially those who have been recently discharged, are disabled, and are most in need—in accessing information leading to green training, certification and licensure, and employment opportunities. Green training and green jobs are a priority; however, traditional training and career paths are also included within the VWIP program opportunities. This program is administered through Veterans Northeast Outreach Center, with staff in Haverhill, Wellesley, South Shore, and Boston. Visit *GreenJobs4vets.org* for more information.

Additional VWIP services. Another program received DOL/VWIP funding and serves the geographic area beyond I-495 by providing training and employment services for green jobs. Contact *VeteransInc.org* for more information.

Job Training for Homeless Veterans. Homeless Veterans' Reintegration Program grants are available to veterans who are homeless or currently residing in a shelter and provide training, job assistance, and housing services.

Work Opportunity Tax Credit (WOTC) for Hiring Veterans. For-profit employers in Massachusetts may be eligible for a federal tax credit through the WOTC program if they hire a qualifying unemployed veteran, defined as a person discharged or released from the military during the five years preceding the hiring date who received unemployment benefits for at least four weeks during the one-year period ending on the hiring date. Individuals must be identified as members the targeted groups before a job offer is made. The WOTC program has two purposes: to help individuals who qualify as members of a target group to get a job, and to help employers who hire qualified individuals by giving them a credit on their federal taxes. The person hired must be employed for at least 120 hours. For more information on this federal program, ask a DVOP/LVER at a Career Center or call 1-877-872-5657 (toll-free) for the Career Center locations near you.

Recreational Discounts, Licenses, and Passes

Free Fishing or Hunting License for Disabled Veterans. Blind or paraplegic Massachusetts residents may qualify for a free freshwater fishing license, and paraplegic Massachusetts residents may qualify for a free hunting license.

Resident Hunting/Fishing Licenses for Nonresident Military Personnel. Nonresident military personnel stationed in Massachusetts may apply for and receive hunting and fishing licenses at the resident rate.

Free State Park Parking for Disabled Veterans and Purple Heart Recipients. Day-use parking fees are waived for vehicles bearing a disabled veteran license plate or placard, or a Purple Heart recipient license plate. This waiver does not apply to camping fees and is subject to available parking.

NEW HAMPSHIRE

Veteran population: 7.0% (97,270)

Financial Benefits

Financial Bonuses. Eligible veterans who actively served as members of the US Armed Forces during the Vietnam War, Persian Gulf War, or Global War on Terrorism are entitled to a $100 bonus.

Tax Credits. Certain wartime veterans or their surviving spouses may be eligible for a property tax credit between $51 and $750. The widow(er) of a veteran killed while on active duty in the military may be eligible for a tax credit of between $700 and $2,000 on real estate or personal property. There is a $700 tax credit on real estate occupied as a principal residence by a permanently and totally disabled service-connected veteran. Permanently and totally disabled veterans who meet certain requirements are exempt from all taxation on the homestead, as are their surviving spouses.

New Hampshire Veterans and Dependent Families Relief. Honorably discharged veterans who served during wartime and their families who have become unable to support themselves are eligible to receive assistance from the town or city where they live.

Housing Benefits

New Hampshire Veterans Home. Located at Tilton, the New Hampshire Veterans Home is a 250-bed facility for honorably discharged veterans who have served in the US Armed Forces in time of war and who have been New Hampshire residents for one year preceding application or who were residents of New Hampshire when they entered the military.

Education Benefits

Tuition and Scholarship. The child of a missing person who was domiciled in New Hampshire serving in or with the US Armed Forces after February 28, 1961 is entitled to free tuition at vocational-technical college so long as said that missing person is reported or listed as missing, captured, and so forth. Children of military members who died in service during wartime, and children of certain wartime veterans who died from a service-connected disability, may qualify for free tuition at New Hampshire public institutions of higher learning. A scholarship for board, room, rent, books, and supplies up to $2,500 per year for a period of no more than four years at such educational institutions may be furnished to these children if they are in need of financial assistance.

Training. Qualified veterans receive priority in obtaining training funded in whole or part by the federal government or the state of New Hampshire.

Employment Benefits

Peddler's License. Service-connected disabled veterans and their unremarried widow(er)s may be exempt from fees for a peddler's license.

Recreational Discounts, Licenses, and Passes

Fish and Game License Fee Exemption. Honorably discharged veterans who are residents of New Hampshire and who are permanently and totally disabled from service-connected disability may be issued a free perpetual fish and game license.

A veteran with a discharge other than dishonorable who is at least 80% service-connected disabled may apply for a lifetime license at 50% of the cost.

Patients at the VA Medical Center in Manchester, New Hampshire, and residents of the New Hampshire Veterans Home may be issued free fishing permits under certain conditions.

The New Hampshire Fish and Game Department offers free or reduced-fee perpetual fish and game license depending on veterans' disability percentage.

State Parks. New Hampshire veterans with any VA service-connected disability rating, as well as members of the New Hampshire National Guard who are legal residents of the state and are serving or who retired in pay grades E-1 through E-6, are not charged a fee for day-use admission to New Hampshire state parks. Disabled veteran license plates issued by the state of New Hampshire or a letter issued by the VA certifying the veteran suffers from a service-connected disability are considered proof of entitlement. Any fees for the use of enterprise activities (including ski lifts, food service, campgrounds, etc.) will still be charged.

NEW JERSEY
Veteran population: 3.5% (328,958)

Financial Benefits

Income Tax Exemption for Veterans. Military veterans honorably discharged or released under honorable circumstances from active duty in the US Armed Forces on or any time before the last day of the tax year are eligible for a $6,000 exemption ($3,000 for tax years 2017 and 2018) on their New Jersey income tax return. This exemption is in addition to any other exemptions they are entitled to claim and is available on both the resident and nonresident returns. The exemption does not apply to domestic partners or dependents unless the legal partner is also an eligible veteran, and it does not pass through to a surviving spouse.

Property Tax Deduction. Veterans certified by the VA as 100% permanent and total disabled based on active duty service may qualify for an annual property tax exemption. Veterans with active wartime service may qualify for an annual $250 property tax deduction. Veterans who served in peacekeeping missions and operations, as well as surviving spouses or domestic partners, may also qualify.

Catastrophic Entitlement. Eligible veterans or surviving spouses receive a monthly entitlement of $62.50 if they are New Jersey residents in receipt of a permanent service-connected disability rating from the VA that resulted from wartime service resulting in one of a handful of catastrophic disabilities.

Veterans Status for Pensions. Veterans employed by the state can qualify for special retirement benefits from the New Jersey Public Employees' Retirement System or New Jersey Teachers' Pension and Annuity Fund.

Housing and Healthcare Benefits

New Jersey Veterans Memorial Homes. The state of New Jersey runs veterans' homes in Menlo Park, Paramus, and Vineland. The homes are open to honorably discharged wartime veterans, their spouses, and Gold Star parents. Preference is given to New Jersey residents. Applicants must meet certain asset limitation criteria, and residents pay according to ability based on income. Homes include the Paramus Veterans Memorial Home (able to accommodate 336 residents and located across the street from the Bergen Regional Medical Center), the Menlo Park Veterans Memorial Home (with capacity for 312 beds and adjacent to Roosevelt Hospital), and Vineland Veterans Memorial Home (serving 300 residents).

Transitional Housing. Veterans Haven is a transitional housing program for homeless veterans, divided into three phases: treatment, self-reclamation, and community reintegration. Each phase lasts three to six months and is tailored to individual treatment needs and vocational interests.

Employment Benefits

New Jersey Department of Labor One-Stop Career Centers. New Jersey Local Veterans' Employment Representatives (LVERs) and Disabled Veterans' Outreach Program (DVOP) specialists provide services to veterans at One-Stop Career Centers throughout the state.

New Jersey Helmets to Hardhats (NJ H2H) Program. NJ H2H helps transitioning service members and veterans from active or reserve components of the US Armed Forces find careers in the building and construction industry.

Transportation Program. Free transportation is offered to VA medical centers, clinics, pharmacies, private physicians, regional VSOs or job service offices, and other community services in most counties. For more information, contact the Veterans Service Officer in the county.

Military Commercial Driver License (CDL) Skills Waiver Program. By waiving the CDL Skills Test (behind-the-wheel exam), this program ensures qualified military applicants will no longer need access to a commercial vehicle in order to obtain a New Jersey CDL.

Education Benefits

War Orphans Tuition Assistance. Resident children of military members who died while in the military, who died due to service-connected disabilities, or who are officially listed as MIA can get $500 per year for four years of college or equivalent training. To qualify, the child must be between the ages of sixteen and twenty-one, and the veteran must have been a state resident.

New Jersey State Approving Agency (SAA). The SAA operates under contract with the VA, maintaining the state's authority to supervise programs at traditional colleges. The agency also approves and supervises programs at nontraditional "for profit" schools, including nondegree programs, apprenticeships, on the-job training, and flight and correspondence schools. The SAA has its foundation in federal law, under USC, Title 38. To find out if your program of study is approved, call 609-530-6849 or visit *nj.gov/military/veterans/services/saa*.

Recreational Discounts, Licenses, and Passes

Hunting Licenses. Honorably discharged New Jersey disabled veterans can get free hunting and fishing licenses as well as pheasant, quail, and trout stamps. Active duty members, no matter where they are stationed, can get New Jersey hunting, fishing, and trapping licenses at the resident rate. Eligible active New Jersey National Guard personnel are entitled to free licenses, permits, and stamps.

NEW YORK
Veteran population: 3.6% (714,107)

Financial Benefits

Blind Annuity Program. The Blind Annuity Program benefit is for legally blind wartime veterans or their surviving unremarried spouses who live and are domiciled in New York State. Blindness need not be a service-connected disability. If veterans met all the criteria for the Blind Annuity benefit but never actually received the benefit during their lifetime, their unremarried surviving spouses may still be eligible to receive the benefit.

New York Gold Star Parent Annuity. The New York Gold Star Parent Annuity is a semiannual annuity payment to each Gold Star parent of a US Armed Forces service member who died in armed conflict.

Income Tax Exemptions. Military pay received for active service as a member of the US Armed Services in an area designated as a combat zone is exempt from New York State, New York City, and Yonkers income taxes.

Property Tax Exemptions. There are three different property tax exemptions available to veterans who have served in the US Armed Forces. The exemption applies to county, city, town, and village taxes and may apply to school district taxes. Veterans can receive one of the three following exemptions: Alternative Veterans' Exemption, Cold War Veterans' Exemption, or Eligible Funds Exemption.

Military Service Credit for State and Local Retirement System Members. Veterans may be entitled to receive additional credit toward retirement for their military service through the New York State and Local Retirement System. In most cases, purchasing additional service credit will increase the pension. However, there are certain situations in which additional service credit may not increase the pension at retirement. More information regarding complete eligibility requirements, buy-back cost, and instructions to apply can be found on the Office of the State Comptroller website.

FreshConnect Checks. New York State employees who are veterans, their immediate family members, and their unremarried surviving spouses are eligible to receive FreshConnect checks, which recipients can use to purchase fresh produce and other food items at participating farmers markets throughout the state. Each recipient receives a booklet of FreshConnect checks worth a total of $20 at participating markets and farm stands. Only one booklet of checks is available per household.

Employment Benefits and Volunteerism

Experience Counts. In the first step of the "Experience Counts" campaign, the governor announced a series of reforms to state licensing and higher education that will ensure military experience is appropriately credited when service members return to civilian life.

Volunteering with the Division of Veterans' Services. Wait, volunteering is a benefit? You bet. Many veterans feel lost after they take off the uniform and are no longer technically of service. Volunteering is a great way to find a sense of purpose while connecting with fellow veterans. NYS Division of Veterans' Services (DVS) is seeking volunteers ages eighteen and older who are committed to DVS's mission of advocating on behalf of New York's veterans, service members, and their families.

State Employment Services. The New York State Department of Labor (DOL) gives veterans priority service in all New York State employment and training programs. Services include career assessment, job referrals, résumé preparation, job-search planning, 55-c civil service positions, and more.

Hire-a-Vet Credit. The Hire-a-Vet Credit encourages hiring qualified veterans. Businesses that employ a qualified veteran for no less than thirty-five hours per week for one full year may earn up to $5,000 for hiring a qualified veteran and up to $15,000 for hiring one who is disabled.

Veterans with Disabilities Employment Program (55-c). New York State wants to employ veterans. Section 55-c of the New York State Civil Service Law authorizes 500 positions to be filled with qualified wartime veterans with disabilities. Applicants must meet the minimum qualifications for the position but are not required to take an examination. Eligible veterans are not guaranteed state employment and are not placed on a hiring list.

New York State Peddler's License. New York State veterans with other-than-dishonorable discharges from the US Armed Forces are eligible to apply for a free lifetime Veterans Peddler's License, provided the veteran served overseas in peace or war. This license provides veterans and surviving spouses with the right to peddle, vend, and sell goods, wares, or merchandise, or solicit trade on the highways within a specific jurisdiction.

Veteran-Owned Business. Through the Center for Veterans Enterprise, the VA established specific programs to help veterans start a business and become qualified as a Veteran-Owned or a Service-Disabled Veteran-Owned Business, which will enable qualified business owners to be eligible for federal set-asides.

Education Programs

Operation Recognition. Veterans who left high school in New York State without graduating are eligible to earn New York State high school diplomas. Operation Recognition, created by Section 305 of New York's Education Law, recognizes the devotion and sacrifice of all veterans who left school early by presenting them with a high school diploma. Deceased veterans can also receive a diploma: the child or spouse of a deceased veteran who met the criterion listed above may apply and accept a posthumous diploma on the veteran's behalf.

Military Enhanced Recognition Incentive and Tribute (MERIT) Scholarship. The MERIT Scholarship provides financial aid to children, spouses, and financial dependents of members of the US Armed Forces or state-organized militia who, at any time on or after August 2, 1990, while New York State residents, died or became severely and permanently disabled while performing their military duties, whether in combat or not.

Regents Awards for Children of Deceased and Disabled Veterans. Through the New York State Higher Education Services Corporation, the Regents Awards are for children of deceased and disabled veterans and provides up to $450 per year to students whose parent(s) served in the US Armed Forces during specified times of war or national emergency, and as a result of such service, the veteran either died, suffered a 40% or greater VA service-connected disability rating percentage, was classified as missing in action, or was a prisoner of war. The veteran must currently be a New York State resident or have been a New York State resident at the time of death.

Military Service Loan Deferment. Student loan borrowers who are called to active duty (or are performing National Guard duty) during a war, military operation, or national emergency may be eligible to defer federal student loan payments from the time of mobilization for up to 180 days following qualifying service.

Post-Active Duty Service Deferment. Members of the National Guard or other reserve components of the US Armed Forces (including retired members) called to active duty while enrolled at a postsecondary institution may defer federal student loan repayment.

Veterans Tuition Awards. The Veterans Tuition Awards, managed by the New York State Higher Education Services Corporation, are for full-time or part-time study for eligible veterans matriculated at an undergraduate or graduate degree-granting institution or in an approved vocational training program in New York State.

Housing Benefits

Homes for Veterans. The Homes for Veterans program, administered through the State of New York Mortgage Agency (SONYMA), offers fixed-rate mortgages with interest rates 0.375% below the already low interest rates charged on SONYMA mortgages with down payment assistance. Veterans and their spouses or co-borrowers need not be first-time home buyers.

Down payment assistance is provided for up to the greater of $3,000 or 3% of the home purchase price (not to exceed $15,000). There are no points or origination fees. The minimum borrower cash contribution is only 1% (the remaining 2% can come from a gift or other acceptable source).

Real Property Tax Deadline Extension. New York State localities are permitted, at their discretion, to extend the payment period for any tax owed on real property.

Recreational Discounts, Licenses, and Passes

Lifetime Liberty Pass for Veterans with Disabilities. The Lifetime Liberty Pass benefits provide eligible, disabled, resident veterans with free vehicle entry to state parks and day-use areas operated by the Department of Environmental Conservation (DEC), as well as numerous state boat launch sites, historic sites, arboretums, and park preserves; free golf at twenty-eight state park golf courses; free swimming pool entrance at thirty-six state park pools; and discounted camping and cabin rentals at all 119 state park and DEC campgrounds.

Reduced-Fee Hunting and Fishing Licenses for Disabled Veterans. Veterans with a service-related disability of 40% or more can get reduced-fee hunting and fishing licenses and preference for deer management permits from the New York State Department of Environmental Conservation.

PENNSYLVANIA
Veteran population: 5.9% (770,806)

Financial Benefits

Real Estate Tax Exemption. Any eligible 100% P&T veteran who is a resident of Pennsylvania is exempt from the payment of all real estate taxes levied on any building, including up to five acres of land on which it stands, provided that all eligibility criteria are met. Upon the death of a qualified veteran, tax exemption may pass on to the unmarried surviving spouse if financial need can be shown.

Veterans Temporary Assistance (VTA). The VTA program provides temporary financial aid to eligible disabled veterans and their beneficiaries who reside in Pennsylvania for the necessities of life (food, shelter, fuel, clothing, and medical expenses). If eligible, a veteran or their beneficiary can qualify for an amount not to exceed $1,600 in a twelve-month period.

Pension. Residents who suffered a service-related injury or incurred a disease that resulted in loss of vision, or the loss or loss of use of two or more extremities may be eligible for a pension of $150 per month.

Military Family Relief Assistance Program (MFRAP). MFRAP provides emergency financial assistance to eligible Pennsylvania service members and their eligible family members to address a direct and immediate financial need resulting from circumstances beyond their control.

The Veterans' Trust Fund (VTF). The VTF assists Pennsylvania veterans and their families in need of shelter and necessities of living by issuing grants to statewide charitable organizations that serve veterans, Veterans Service Organizations, and County Directors of Veterans Affairs. Learn more at *vtf.pa.gov.*

Educational Benefits

Educational Gratuity. The Commonwealth of Pennsylvania provides financial assistance of up to $500 per term or semester for up to eight semesters to children of honorably discharged veterans who have service-connected disabilities and served during a period of war or armed conflict.

Pennsylvania Higher Education Assistance Agency. To learn more about state educational grants and financial aid for veterans, call 1-800-692-7392.

Employment Assistance

CareerLink. Contact a veterans employment representative at a Pennsylvania CareerLink office for free job counseling, training referrals, and placement services for veterans.

Veterans' Homes

Pennsylvania offers its eligible veterans or surviving spouses six extended care facilities across the state that provide personal care, skilled nursing care, and dementia care:

- Hollidaysburg Veterans' Home (Hollidaysburg)
- Pennsylvania Soldiers' and Sailors' Home (Erie)
- Southeastern Veterans' Center (Spring City)
- Gino J. Merli Veterans' Center (Scranton)
- Southwestern Veterans' Center (Pittsburgh)
- Delaware Valley Veterans' Home (Philadelphia)

Recreational Discounts, Licenses, and Passes

Free Hunting Licenses. Certain disabled veterans are eligible for free hunting, fishing, and fur trapper licenses and can apply via the county treasurer.

Deer License. Antlerless deer license applications can be made at a county treasurer of the veteran's choice, regardless of the county allocation.

RHODE ISLAND

Veteran population: 5.5% (60,506)

Financial Benefits

Property Tax Exemption. Eligible veterans residing in Rhode Island may receive an exemption on either their real estate tax bill or their motor vehicle tax bill. The seven exemption categories have their own regulations, forms, and exemption amount, which include:

- Veterans' regular exemption
- Unmarried widow(er) of qualified veteran
- Veterans' exemption for totally disabled through service-connected disability
- Veterans' exemption for partially disabled through service-connected disability
- Gold Star parents' exemption
- Prisoner of war exemption
- Specially adapted housing exemption

Free Vehicle Registration for Disabled Veterans. Any honorably discharged veteran who lost a limb or the use of a limb in combat gets a lifetime exemption for the annual vehicle registration and license. Totally disabled veterans also get this benefit.

Rhode Island Bus Pass Program for Disabled Veterans. The Rhode Island Public Transit Authority Bus Pass Program offers free and half-fare bus passes for eligible veterans.

Operation Stand Down Rhode Island (OSDRI) Assistance. OSDRI helps active and reserve component service members, veterans, and their families secure stable housing and employment. It also provides need-based assistance, including case management, basic human need support, referrals, education, and training services.

Rhode Island Veterans Home

A 110-acre complex located on Mount Hope Bay, the **Rhode Island Veterans Home** offers 208 nursing care beds in six long-term care units, including an Alzheimer's care unit. Additional services include dental, X-ray, pharmacy services, and transportation to and from the Veterans Administration Hospital clinics in Providence, as well as rehabilitation services, social services, transitional services, and activities.

Education Benefits

Free Tuition for Disabled Veterans. Veterans who are permanent residents of the state and have 10%–100% service-connected disability get free tuition at Rhode Island's public colleges and universities.

Free Tuition for Surviving Spouses and Children of Deceased Rhode Island National Guard Service Members. Rhode Island will pay the tuition at a state-supported college or university for a surviving spouse or child of a Rhode Island National Guard service member who died in the line of duty. This financial assistance only applies to tuition and may be used for up to four years.

Employment Benefits

Rhode Island Department of Labor and Training (DLT) Career Centers Veteran Services. DLT Career Centers offer specialized assistance and "priority of service" to eligible veterans and their spouses. Priority of service gives eligible individuals preference over others for Workforce Investment Act employment, training, and placement services. This priority includes providing first access to services when offered for a limited time and giving preferred registration in limited enrollment situations.

Recreation Discounts, Licenses, and Passes

Hunting Licenses. Every 100% disabled veteran can get a hunting and fishing license for free. Nonresident military members stationed in Rhode Island can get hunting and fishing licenses for the resident rate.

Free Golf. Any veteran who is a resident of the state and determined by the VA to be totally disabled through service-connected disability is exempt from paying any fee to play golf at the Goddard State Park Golf Course.

State Recreational Fees. No fee is charged to any 100% service-connected disabled veteran or an automobile transporting the disabled veteran at any recreational facility owned by the state. Fee waivers include parking, admittance, or other user fees for playing golf but not licensing, camping, picnic table, or specialized facility-use fees (including but not limited to fees for the use of equestrian areas, performing art centers, game fields, and the mule shed).

Other Benefits

Providence VAMC. Providence VA Medical Center, Rhode Island, offers a variety of health services to meet the needs of veterans.

Homeless Veterans. Contact VA's National Call Center for Homeless Veterans at 1-877-4AID-VET (424-3838) to speak to a trained VA responder. The hotline and online chat are free, and neither VA registration nor enrollment in VA healthcare is required to use either service. Available resources include shelters, food banks, legal services, emergency rent and utility assistance, housing counselors, educational resources, help hotlines, and other forms of support.

Veterans Benefits Counseling. The Rhode Island Veterans Affairs Office offers benefit counseling including a variety of social services to Rhode Island Armed Forces personnel, veterans, and their dependents who are seeking assistance.

LGBT Veteran Training. The Lesbian Gay Bisexual and Transgender (LGBT) Program oversees educational programs on LGBT health in VHA and provides ongoing educational programs for VHA staff about best practices in LGBT healthcare, which are designed to shape the environment of care for enhanced health, well-being, and quality of life for LGBT veterans.

VERMONT
Veteran population: 6.4% (41,221)

Financial Benefits

Tax Exemptions. Some veterans are eligible to receive discounts on their property taxes and fees at the Department of Motor Vehicles. Property tax exemption levels vary from town to town. State law mandates a minimum $10,000 exemption, although towns are given the option of increasing the exemption to $40,000.

Emergency Financial Assistance. Low-income Vermont veterans without the funds to take care of their critical life needs can receive temporary financial assistance from various state and local programs. These programs won't cure long-term financial difficulties, but they can help prevent a financial problem from becoming a crisis.

Mortuary and Burial Benefits. Programs provided by the VA and the state honor deceased veterans and military members through financial assistance and burial benefits. These include the Vermont Veterans Memorial Cemetery, grave markers, and financial assistance for burials.

Purchasing a Home. Learn more about the VA Guaranteed Home Loan Program that helps veterans buy a home.

Disability Benefits

State Division of Disability and Aging Services. In addition to seeking assistance from the VA, disabled veterans should also visit the state's Division of Disability and Aging Services to learn more about the resources available to help them and their families.

Other Veteran Benefits

Recognition. Vermont understands the need to show those who have defended our nation appreciation for their service and sacrifice, including through medals, license plates, and high school diplomas.

Home and Vehicle Modification. Various programs provide help to disabled veterans who need to have their home or vehicle modified to accommodate their disability.

Other Benefits. Sometimes the benefits that can best help veterans and their families are those not specifically created for veterans. To talk with a benefits specialist to find out what is available in your area, regardless of who provides the benefit, just dial 211 for a free call that is available twenty-four hours a day.

Healthcare Options

The VA operates a hospital and four clinics in or adjacent to Vermont. They provide a full range of services for veterans, including prescription benefits. Veterans returning from a combat theater have expanded eligibility for VA healthcare for a temporary period after their discharge.

PTSD and other mental health conditions, such as anxiety and depression, are normal reactions to abnormal situations, such as life in a combat theater. Veterans and family members who would like to talk to counselors have many options in Vermont, from VA healthcare and vet centers to community mental health.

Many people call traumatic brain injury (TBI) the signature injury of the War on Terror, as military members exposed to explosive forces can have a TBI, even if there are no outward signs of injury. But TBI also affects people who have had falls, been in car accidents, or had a blow to the head. You might be eligible for screening and care via VA healthcare in Vermont.

Veterans and their families have additional options when it comes to long-term care, both in nursing homes and in their own home.

Transition Assistance

Veterans and Family Outreach Program. The outreach program gives veterans and their families a point of contact in their area to learn more about the assistance available to help them.

Education Benefits. Since the end of World War II, education benefits have helped veterans obtain the training and education needed to improve both their lives and the lives of their families. Visit the state's website on Veterans Affairs to learn more.

Vocational Rehabilitation. Learn more about the two programs in Vermont that help veterans with disabilities train for new careers.

Business Development. There are many different business-focused government and nonprofit organizations that help people start businesses. Many of them also have programs specifically for veterans.

Employment and Other Protections. Military members have protections to limit the impact of military service on their civilian lives.

Special Groups

A variety of resources about special groups and support for veterans in Vermont can be found at *Veterans.Vermont.gov/benefits-and-services/special-groups.*

CHAPTER ELEVEN

THE SOUTHERN REGION

ALABAMA

Veteran population: 7.1% (357,520)

Claims Representation and Counseling

The primary function of the Alabama Department of Veterans Affairs (ADVA) service offices is to assist veterans, their dependents, and survivors in the application and processing of claims for benefits and entitlements available from the VA and the benefits provided for veterans by law from the state of Alabama earned by honorable service in the US Armed Forces.

Services include the processing of compensation and pension applications, appealing VA decisions, filing for survivors' death benefits, applying for aid and attendance and housebound benefits, certifying claim documents, requesting military service records, upgrading military discharges, and applying for special veteran license plates.

ADVA veterans service officers are accredited to perform claims actions by nationally chartered VSOs to include the American Legion,

American Ex-Prisoners of War, Fleet Reserve Association, and Blinded Veterans Association.

Veteran Education Benefits

Tuition Waiver for Purple Heart Medal Recipients. Purple Heart recipients may be eligible for free education at Alabama public institutions of higher learning, including two-year and four-year technical colleges, community colleges, and junior colleges. Check with your school to see if they participate in the program.

Alabama National Guard Education Assistance Program (ANGEAP). ANGEAP provides financial educational assistance to Alabama National Guard service members enrolled in an Alabama state-supported school. The current award amount per semester is $5,080 for up to 120 academic hours. ANGEAP will cover tuition and fees that are not covered by any VA education benefits. You must be over seventeen, active in the AL Guard, an Alabama resident, show financial need, and maintain a cumulative 2.0 GPA in undergraduate studies or 3.0 GPA in graduate studies at the end of each semester.

GI Dependent Scholarship Program. Eligible children and stepchildren of qualified veterans may receive five standard academic years (ten semesters) at any Alabama state-supported institution of higher learning or a prescribed course of study at any state-supported technical college to be used for undergraduate courses of study at the in-state tuition rate. Spouses or unremarried widow(er)s of a qualified veteran may also receive scholarships.

Tuition will be limited to the Department of Defense Tuition Assistance Cap (currently $250 per semester hour), and required textbooks and applicable fees will be limited to a combined $1,000 total per student for each semester. Schools may waive any overages of these charges at their discretion. All scholarships and grants must be applied to education expenses first (unless otherwise prescribed by state law), and the Alabama GI Dependent Scholarship Program will be applied for any applicable remaining charges pursuant to current state law.

Housing and Healthcare Benefits

State Veteran Home Program. The hospitals maintained by the VA have filled the needs of acutely ill or injured veterans, but a different type of facility is needed for aging or chronically disabled veterans. The state of Alabama extends this special kind of care to veterans through a partnership with the federal government and private industry by proudly operating four state-of-the-art veterans homes located within the state.

The Bill Nichols State Veterans Home in Alexander City has been home to thousands of veterans since its opening in November 1989. In July 1995, Alabama opened two more homes to veterans, the Floyd E. "Tut" Fann State Veterans Home in Huntsville and the William F. Green State Veterans Home in Bay Minette. In November 2012, the Colonel Robert L. Howard State Veterans Home opened in Pell City.

Tax Benefits

Property Tax for Homes of Totally Disabled Persons over Age Sixty-Five. Any Alabama resident is exempt from ad valorem taxes on their home and adjacent 160 acres of land if they are permanently and totally disabled or sixty-five years of age or older and have a net annual income of $12,000 or less.

Property Tax for VA Specially Adapted Houses. Any home acquired under the VA's specially adapted housing grant is tax exempt as long as it is owned and occupied by the veteran or their unremarried surviving spouse.

Income Tax. All military retirement pay and SBP payments are exempt from any Alabama state, county, or municipal income tax.

Employment Benefits

Membership in Employees'/Teachers' Retirement System of Alabama (RSA) Benefits for Service Members. State employees and teachers who enter the US Armed Forces and return to state employment can keep their RSA benefits and may receive credit for up to four years of military service.

Alabama Reduced Cost Business and Occupational Licenses for Disabled Veterans. Eligible disabled veterans are charged a reduced fee of $25 for state, county, and municipal business or occupational license taxes.

Recreation Discounts, Licenses, and Passes

State Parks. Active duty and honorably discharged veterans who are residents of Alabama are granted free admission to state parks.

Fishing and Hunting Licenses. Alabama resident veterans who are at least 20% disabled can get a discounted freshwater fishing license. A special hunting license is available to 100% service-connected veterans at a cost of $3.15 and to 50% service-connected veterans at a cost of $14.75.

Pistol Permit. A pistol permit is available for free to individuals who are otherwise eligible for a pistol permit and who retired from active duty, the reserves, or the National Guard.

ARKANSAS

Veteran population: 6.5% (195,685)

Financial Benefits

Military Retirement Pay Exemption. State law exempts military retired pay from Arkansas state income taxes.

Homestead and Personal Property Tax Exemption. Disabled veterans living in Arkansas who have been awarded special monthly compensation by the VA for the loss of or the loss of use of one or more limbs, for total blindness in one or both eyes, or for service-connected 100% total and permanent disability are exempt from payment of all state taxes on the homestead and personal property owned by the disabled veteran. Surviving unremarried spouses and dependent children under the age of eighteen continue this entitlement. Entitlement is also available if the veteran was killed or died within the scope of military duties, is missing in action, or died from service-connected causes.

Housing and Healthcare Benefits

Veterans Homes. Arkansas State Veterans Home at Fayetteville offers registered nurse, licensed practical nurse, and certified nursing assistant skilled care around the clock; an on-site medical director; physical, occupational, and speech therapy; a licensed clinical social worker; transportation; and daily activities.

Arkansas State Veterans Home at North Little Rock is the first veterans home in Arkansas developed from the ground up for the sole purpose of long-term care for veterans. The facility consists of eight individual homes that serve twelve residents each. The small home concept seeks to deinstitutionalize care and provide a warm, homelike environment in a setting that encourages social activity. As a result of the design, the operating model differs substantially from that of a traditional skilled nursing facility.

Education Benefits

State Educational Benefits. The Arkansas Department of Higher Education has the authority to provide free tuition and fees at any state-supported college, university, technical school, or vocational school to the spouse or surviving spouse and children of any Arkansas resident who has been declared to be a prisoner of war, placed in a missing-in-action status, or killed in action since January 1, 1960.

In-State Tuition. Regardless of residence, state-supported institutions of higher education, trade schools, and vocational schools classify a student as in-state, in-county, in-district, or resident for the purpose of tuition and fees applicable for all programs of study, including distance learning programs, if the student is

- an eligible veteran
- a dependent of a veteran
- a member of the US Armed Forces
- a spouse of a member of the US Armed Forces

Diplomas for Veterans. High school diplomas can be obtained for veterans of World War II, the Korean War, and the Vietnam War who were called up for active duty service before finishing high school. Qualifying veterans should contact their school superintendent or the Arkansas Department of Education.

Employment Benefits

The Arkansas Department of Workforce Services provides employment counseling and referral services tailored to the special needs of veterans, in addition to maintaining an ongoing program of job development designed to create jobs and preferences for all veterans, through Local Veterans Employment Representatives (LVERs) and the Disabled Veterans Outreach Program (DVOP).

Recreational Discounts, Licenses, and Passes

State Parks. The Arkansas Department of Parks and Tourism provides Arkansas resident veterans who have a permanent service-connected 100% disability rating the ability to camp for half price in Arkansas state parks.

Fishing and Hunting Licenses. The Arkansas Game and Fish Commission provides discounted hunting and fishing licenses to Arkansas veterans who are 100% totally and permanently disabled or military retirees over the age of sixty:

- The Resident Disabled Military Veteran Lifetime Fishing License ($1.50) entitles totally and permanently disabled veterans to the privileges of the Resident Fisheries Conservation License.

- The Resident Disabled Military Veteran and Military Retiree Lifetime Hunting License ($25) entitles totally and permanently disabled veterans to the privileges of the Resident Sportsman's License.

- The Resident Disabled Military Veteran and Military Retiree Lifetime Combination License ($35.50) entitles totally and permanently disabled veterans to the privileges of the Resident Sportsman's License (hunting) and the Resident Fisheries Conservation License (fishing).

- The Resident Military Retiree Lifetime Fishing License ($10.50) entitles military retirees to the privileges of the Resident Fisheries Conservation License.

FLORIDA
Veteran population: 6.9% (1,492,176)

Home Loans and Property Taxes

Basic Property Tax Exemptions. Eligible resident veterans with a VA-certified service-connected disability of 10% or greater are entitled to a $5,000 deduction on the assessment of their home for tax exemption purposes. The veteran must establish this exemption with the county tax official in their county of residence by providing documentation of this disability. The unremarried surviving spouse of a disabled ex-service member is also entitled to this exemption.

Property Tax Exemption for Permanent and Total Disability. Any real estate owned and used as a homestead by a veteran who was honorably discharged and has been certified as having a service-connected permanent and total disability is exempt from taxation if the veteran is a permanent resident of Florida and has legal title to the property on January 1 of the tax year for which exemption is being claimed.

Property Tax Exemption for Partial Disability. Any service-connected partially disabled, honorably discharged veteran who is age sixty-five or older may be eligible for a discount from the amount of ad valorem tax on the homestead commensurate with the percentage of the veteran's permanent service-connected disability. Eligible veterans should apply for this benefit at the county property appraiser's office.

Property Tax Exemption for Quadriplegia, Wheelchair Use, or Legal Blindness. Any real estate used and owned as a homestead by any quadriplegic is exempt from taxation. Veterans may be exempt from real estate taxation if they are paraplegic, hemiplegic, or permanently and totally disabled; must use a wheelchair for mobility; or are legally blind.

Education Benefits

Congressman C. W. Bill Young Tuition Waiver Program. Florida waives out-of-state tuition fees for all honorably discharged veterans who reside in the state and who are enrolled in Florida public postsecondary institutions through the Congressman C. W. Bill Young Tuition Waiver Program. The out-of-state tuition and fee waiver are extended to spouses and dependent children who reside in Florida and who are using GI Bill benefits for enrollment in Florida public postsecondary institutions.

Purple Heart Undergraduate Tuition Waiver. Florida waives undergraduate-level tuition at state universities and community colleges for Florida recipients of the Purple Heart and other combat-related decorations superior in precedence to the Purple Heart. The waiver program also includes the state's career and technical training facilities.

Priority Course Registration. Each Florida College System institution and state university offering priority course registration for segments of the student population must provide priority course registration to veterans of the US Armed Forces who are receiving GI Bill educational benefits. The benefit also applies to spouses and dependent children receiving GI Bill benefits.

Credit for Service. Florida state colleges and universities allow current members of the US Armed Forces and honorably discharged veterans to earn academic college credit for college-level training and education acquired in the military.

High School Diploma. Honorably discharged veterans who were inducted into the US Armed Forces prior to completing their high school education can be awarded a state of Florida high school diploma.

Veterans' Homes

The Florida Department of Veterans' Affairs operates seven skilled nursing facilities and one assisted living facility. Two additional skilled nursing facilities are under development. The homes are supervised around the clock by registered and licensed nurses.

- The **Robert H. Jenkins Jr. Veterans' Domiciliary Home** in Lake City (150 beds) is an assisted living facility providing a combination of housing, personalized supportive services, and incidental medical care to eligible veterans. Veterans must be able to feed and dress themselves and be in need of assisted living care.

- The **Emory L. Bennett State Veterans' Nursing Home** in Daytona Beach (120 beds) provides skilled nursing care to its veteran residents.

- The **Baldomero Lopez State Veterans' Nursing Home** in Land O' Lakes (120 beds) provides skilled nursing care and can accommodate sixty residents with dementia or Alzheimer's disease.

- The **Alexander "Sandy" Nininger State Veterans' Nursing Home** in Pembroke Pines (120 beds) offers skilled nursing care and can accommodate sixty residents with dementia or Alzheimer's disease.

- The **Clifford C. Sims State Veterans' Nursing Home** in Panama City (120 beds) offers skilled nursing care and can accommodate sixty residents with dementia or Alzheimer's disease.

- The **Douglas T. Jacobson State Veterans' Nursing Home** in Port Charlotte (120 beds) offers skilled nursing care and can accommodate sixty residents with dementia or Alzheimer's disease.

- The **Clyde E. Lassen State Veterans' Nursing Home** in St. Augustine (120 beds) offers skilled nursing care and can accommodate sixty residents with dementia or Alzheimer's disease.

- The **Ardie R. Copas State Veterans' Nursing Home** in Port St. Lucie (120 beds) will offer skilled nursing care and accommodate sixty residents with dementia/Alzheimer's disease.

- **Alwyn C. Cashe State Veterans' Nursing Home** is a new state veterans' home in Orlando which will be a 112-bed skilled nursing facility.

Motor Vehicle, Licensing, and Fee Exemptions

Driver License and State ID Fee Exemptions. Any honorably discharged veteran who has a valid FDVA 100% disabled veteran ID card or who has been determined to have a 100% total and permanent service-connected disability and is qualified to obtain a driver's license is generally exempt from all fees.

Handicapped Toll Permit. Licensed drivers can pass free through all toll gates if they operate a vehicle specially equipped for the handicapped and are certified by a licensed physician or the VA as having permanent upper limb impairments or disabilities substantially affecting their ability to deposit coins in toll baskets. A window sticker from the Florida Department of Transportation must be obtained and displayed.

Commission as a Notary Public. The state's $10 commission fee is not required for a commission as a notary public to a veteran with wartime service who has been rated 50% or more for a service-connected disability. Other fees will apply.

Disabled Veterans' Exemption from Fees. Totally and permanently disabled Florida veterans are exempt from county and municipality building license or permit fees when making certain improvements to their residence in order to make the dwelling habitable or safe. Restrictions apply.

Employment Services

CareerSource. Employment services for veterans, military members, and their families are offered through the CareerSource Florida network, which includes the Department of Economic Opportunity, Florida's twenty-four local workforce development boards, and more than 100 career centers. Available services include interview preparation, résumé writing assistance, job and training-related referrals, career planning, vocational guidance, job search and placement assistance, and internet access.

LVER and DVOP. Local Veterans' Employment Representatives conduct outreach to employers and business associations and engage in advocacy efforts with hiring executives to increase employment opportunities for veterans and encourage the hiring of disabled veterans. The Disabled Veterans Outreach Program provides individualized career services to veterans with significant barriers to employment, with the maximum emphasis directed toward serving veterans who are economically or educationally disadvantaged.

Employ Florida Vets. The Florida Veterans Program Portal is an online resource from Employ Florida for veterans' employment and employer recruitment information. The portal provides information and resource links to assist veterans, their families, and employers in accomplishing their employment goals and is available 24/7.

Troops to Teachers. Troops to Teachers is a program designed to help transitioning service members and veterans begin new careers as K–12 teachers. Some program participants are eligible for financial assistance.

Uniformed Services Employment and Reemployment Rights Act (USERRA). USERRA protects the employment rights and ensures the reemployment of veterans, reservists, and National Guard members after a period of active service and prohibits employment discrimination because of past, current, or future military obligations. It covers all employers, regardless of size, in the public and private sectors.

License and Consumer Services Fee Waivers. The Department of Business and Professional Regulation may waive the initial licensing fee, application fee, and unlicensed activity fee for military veterans and their spouses at the time of discharge who apply for a state professional license.

The Florida Department of Health has programs in place to aid veterans in finding employment in health-related fields. The department offers expedited healthcare practitioner licensure through the Veterans Application for Licensure Online Response system. They also offer expanded licensure fee waivers for military veterans and their spouses applying for healthcare licensure in Florida.

The Florida Department of Agriculture and Consumer Services now waives first-time licensing application fees for specific veterans of the US Armed Forces, their spouses, or a business entity in which the veteran or spouse has a majority ownership stake. For more information, visit *fdacs.gov*.

The Florida Department of Agriculture and Consumer Services is now expediting all Florida concealed weapon or firearm license applications submitted by active military members and veterans. For more information, visit *fdacs.gov*.

Florida Veteran Certified Business Enterprises. The Department of Management Services' Office of Supplier Diversity (OSD) certifies eligible Florida-based veteran-, woman-, and minority-owned small businesses. The OSD also provides technical assistance, certification support, and pertinent information about state contract opportunities, special events, and networking activities. Learn more by visiting *DMS. MyFlorida.com/osd*.

Career Opportunities. Veteran-friendly businesses in high-growth fields such as aerospace, manufacturing, logistics, research and development, and technology seek to hire veterans and provide them with the training they need to build a long and fruitful career. Veterans Florida has career specialists to help veterans, transitioning service members, and members of the National Guard and Army Reserve translate their military skills for employers, assist with résumé and interview preparation, and get placed into skills-based jobs. Visit *VeteransFlorida.org/careers* to submit your résumé.

Entrepreneurship. The skills you learned in the military like discipline, attention to detail, and leadership directly correlate to being a successful entrepreneur. Veterans Florida offers a world-class and proven entrepreneurship program just for veterans. They've joined forces with top Florida universities, colleges, and startup incubators to deliver the Veterans Florida Entrepreneurship Program, a training initiative for veterans seeking to start their own business. As part of the program, veterans gain access to small business development resources. Visit *VeteransFlorida.org* to sign up.

Legal Help

Legal Advice and Counsel. The Governor's Initiative on Lawyers Assisting Warriors (GI LAW) draws from the talent of Florida's leading law firms to provide pro bono services for military members. There are discussions to expand this service to veterans in the future.

The Florida Bar, in conjunction with the American Bar Association, administers a free virtual legal advice clinic for Floridians. Learn more at *Florida.FreeLegalAnswers.org*.

Veterans Courts. Veterans returning from combat may suffer from PTSD or have difficulty reintegrating into society. Due to alienation and lack of support, some veterans fall into drug and alcohol abuse or develop mental health issues. Thirty veterans courts in Florida have been established as of July 2018 to address the substance abuse and mental health needs of veterans within the criminal justice system. Successful completion of veterans court has helped decrease the recidivism rates of its participants through the proper diagnosis and treatment of mental health issues and as a result of the supportive roles mentors play in the process. Recent legislation has expanded the pool of eligible veterans. There is a helpful Veterans Resource Guide for the Florida State Court System you can download online.

Recreational Discounts, Licenses, and Passes

State Parks. The Florida Department of Environmental Protection provides a 25% discount on annual passes to Florida's state parks for all active duty and honorably discharged veterans of the US Armed Forces, National Guard, or reserve units of the US Armed Forces or National Guard. Veterans with service-related disabilities, surviving spouses, and parents of members of the US military who have fallen in combat, and law enforcement officers and firefighters who have died in the line of duty will receive a free lifetime family annual entrance pass.

Local Parks. County and municipal departments of parks and recreation provide a full or partial discount on park entrance fees to current military service members, honorably discharged veterans, service-connected disabled veterans, and the surviving spouse or parents of a military service member who died in combat.

Hunting Licenses. The Military Gold Sportsman's License is available for a reduced fee of $20 to any resident who is an active or retired member of the US Armed Forces, US Armed Forces Reserve, or National Guard upon submission of a current military ID card.

State hunting and fishing licenses and permits are issued without fees for five years to any veteran who is a Florida resident and is certified or determined to be 100% totally and permanently disabled by the VA or the US Armed Forces, or who has been issued a valid disabled veteran ID card by FDVA.

Operation Outdoor Freedom. The Operation Outdoor Freedom program provides wounded veterans with outdoor activities to enjoy at no cost. Designated state and agricultural lands throughout Florida provide qualified veterans with unique opportunities for recreation and rehabilitation.

Other Services

County Veteran Service Offices. Information on current federal, state, and local veterans' programs, entitlements, and referral services is available in Florida through a network of County Veteran Service Offices. Counselors are trained and accredited annually by the Florida Department of Veterans' Affairs. All services are provided free of charge. A list of offices can be found online at *FloridaVets.org/benefits-services*.

Women Veterans. The Sunshine State is home to approximately 144,000 women veterans. Many women veterans don't know they are eligible for the full range of federal and state benefits. To help connect women veterans with earned benefits and services, FDVA hosts an annual state women veterans conference. A Woman Veteran license plate is also available for purchase. For more information on women veterans' issues, visit *FloridaVets.org/our-veterans/women-veterans*.

Veterans Florida. Veterans Florida is a nonprofit corporation created by the state of Florida to help veterans find a new career, start a business, or connect to other helpful resources in the Sunshine State. Visit *VeteransFlorida.org* to learn more.

GEORGIA
Veteran population: 6.4% (689,274)

Financial Benefits

Abatement of Income Taxes for Combat Deaths. Georgia law provides that service personnel who die as a result of wounds, disease, or injury incurred while serving in a combat zone as a member of the US Armed Forces are exempt from all Georgia income taxes for the taxable year of death. Additionally, such taxes do not apply for any prior taxable year ending on or after the first day served in the combat zone.

Ad Valorem Tax on Vehicles. This exemption is for veterans who are verified by the VA to be 100% totally and permanently service-connected disabled and veterans rated unemployable who are receiving or are entitled to receive statutory awards from the VA for loss or permanent loss of use of one or both feet or hands, loss of sight in one or both eyes, or permanent impairment of vision of both eyes to a prescribed degree.

Business Certificate of Exemption. Georgia veterans are eligible for a certificate granting exemption from any occupation tax, administrative fee, or regulatory fee imposed by local governments for peddling, conducting business, or practicing a profession or semiprofession for a period of ten years if they were discharged under honorable conditions and have a service-connected disability rating of 10% or more.

Sales Tax Exemption for Vehicle Purchase and Adaptation. A disabled veteran who receives a VA grant for the purchase and special adaptation of a vehicle is exempt from paying the state sales tax on the vehicle (only on the original grant).

Homestead Tax Exemption. Veterans with 100% disability, those receiving VA disability for loss of vision or limbs, and their surviving unremarried spouses may be exempt from property tax on their homes. The maximum exemption, which changes every year, is currently $93,356, but several factors determine the amount.

Housing and Healthcare Benefits

War Veterans Homes. There are two skilled nursing care homes for eligible war veterans located in Georgia. One is in Augusta, and the other is in Milledgeville. The primary mission of these homes is to provide high-quality skilled nursing care to eligible veterans while seeking to improve their quality of life and overall health.

Education Benefits

Georgia HERO Scholarship. The Georgia HERO Scholarship program provides educational scholarships to members of the Georgia National Guard and US Armed Forces Reserve who served in combat zones, as well as the children and spouses of eligible service members.

University System of Georgia Resident Waiver of Mandatory Fees for US Armed Forces Reserve and Georgia National Guard Combat Veterans. Combat veterans attending a University System of Georgia institution can receive a waiver of all mandatory fees. This waiver does not apply to housing, elective food service, any other elective fees, special fees, or other user fees and charges (e.g., application fees). Veterans must meet the admissions requirements of the applicable institution and be accepted for admission.

Employment Benefits

Business Licenses. Some honorably discharged veterans with at least a 10% disability are exempt from payment of occupational taxes and other fees for peddling, conducting a business, or practicing a profession or semiprofession.

Recreational Discounts, Licenses, and Passes

Hunting and Fishing Licenses. Returning veterans are entitled to a free honorary hunting and fishing license for a period of one year following issuance. Veterans rated permanently and totally disabled by the VA or DOD are eligible for a discounted sportsman's license.

State Parks. Any Georgia resident veteran with a service-connected disability and an honorable discharge can get a discount card good for 25% reduced entrance fees to Georgia state parks, historical sites, and recreational areas.

KENTUCKY
Veteran population: 6.3% (284,803)

Financial Benefits

Veterans Program Trust Fund (**VPTF**). The VPTF directs funding to projects and programs that help Kentucky's veterans but that do not have other funds available. It supports many veterans' programs and projects throughout the commonwealth, like the University of Louisville's free behavioral health treatment for traumatized children of military families.

Income Tax. Military income is tax-free. The portion of a member's benefits earned after January 1, 1998 is subject to Kentucky income tax; however, this income may be excluded up to a certain amount. See Schedule P in the Kentucky income tax forms for the exclusion amount and calculation. Retirement credit for unused sick leave is treated as being earned at the time of retirement.

Property Tax for Disabled Veterans. Totally disabled veterans are eligible for a deduction on the assessed value of their home for property tax purposes. The adjustment for the 2021 and 2022 assessment years was $40,500.

Housing and Healthcare Benefits

Kentucky Veterans Centers. The Office of Kentucky Veteran Centers administers four long-term care facilities:

- Eastern Kentucky Veterans Center (Hazard)
- Carl M. Brashear Veterans Center (Radcliff)
- Thomson-Hood Veterans Center (Wilmore)
- Western Kentucky Veterans Center (Hanson)

Kentucky Homeless Veterans Trust Fund. The Kentucky Department of Veterans Affairs has a Homeless Veterans Trust Fund that can provide financial assistance, in the form of a grant, to veterans who served in the US Armed Forces and were discharged under conditions other than dishonorable. Qualifying applicants must meet the income restrictions and show immediate need, such as via an eviction notice or utility disconnect. For more information or to start the application process, call 502-782-5730.

Employment Benefits

KyVETS. The Kentucky Veterans Employment, Training, and Support (KyVETS) program provides resources and support to assist veterans across the commonwealth in gainful employment and training services. The KyVETS program director maintains a database of Kentucky veterans seeking employment, which includes only those Kentucky veterans who have volunteered their information to KDVA. The strictly confidential information in this database is used to match employment-seeking veterans with veteran-seeking employers. Complete the online form at *Veterans.KY.gov/employment_info*.

Education Benefits

State Educational Benefits. Kentucky's High School Diploma Program allows veterans to receive an official high school diploma if they left school to enroll in the military and then served during World War II, the Korean War, or the Vietnam War. Since the beginning in 2002, the program has proven highly popular and deeply moving for veterans and their families.

Kentucky Tuition Waiver Program. Eligible children, stepchildren, spouses, and unremarried widow(er)s of veterans may receive a tuition waiver to attend any two-year, four-year, or vocational technical schools that are operated and funded by the Kentucky Department of Education. Private or out-of-state schools do not qualify for the waiver.

Recreational Discounts, Licenses, and Passes

Fishing Licenses. Kentucky veterans with 50% or more service-connected disability are authorized a discounted license. Kentucky residents home on leave can fish for free without a license.

State Parks. Kentucky resident veterans who are permanently and totally disabled pay no overnight accommodation fees at any state park. Those eligible can stay for a maximum of three overnight stays per calendar year, three nights maximum for each visit.

LOUISIANA

Veteran population: 6.1% (282,998)

Financial Benefits

National Guard Death and Disability Benefit. Louisiana National Guard service members suffering a permanent and total disability while on federal or state active duty on or after September 11, 2001, or the beneficiary of record of those killed in action, may qualify for a $100,000 disability or $250,000 death benefit from the state of Louisiana.

Homestead Exemption. Qualifying veterans can receive additional tax benefits on their homestead exemption. Additional special property tax exemptions are also assessed for some disabled veterans or active duty service members killed in action.

Combat Pay Exception. Military pay that is exempt from federal taxation, such as combat pay or hazardous duty pay, is also exempt from Louisiana state taxation.

Military Retiree Pay Tax Exemption. Military retirement benefits are exempt from Louisiana state taxation.

Military Family Assistance (MFA) Fund. The MFA Fund can provide financial support to Louisiana veterans and their families when they experience financial hardships. It can pay up to $10,000 for one claim per active duty order in a twelve-month period and is funded by private donations from individuals and corporations.

Housing and Healthcare Benefits

Veterans Homes. LDVA proudly operates five state-of-the-art veterans homes across the state. Homes are located conveniently across the state in Jackson, Bossier City, Monroe, Reserve, and Jennings. Each facility offers a variety of services, including but not limited to long- and short-term care, rehabilitative therapies, Alzheimer's and intermediate care, skilled nursing, mental health services, and centralized pharmacy services.

Employment Benefits

Veterans First Business Initiative. The Louisiana Veterans First Business Initiative allows for veterans, active duty or reserve military, or Gold Star spouses who have a 51% ownership in a business to apply for and gain certification to recognize and promote their businesses. In addition, a searchable database is provided for anyone seeking to patronize a veteran, active duty, reserve military, or Gold Star spouse business. For more information, visit *LaVeteransFirst.org/search.*

Louisiana's Veterans Initiative (LAVETBIZ). LAVETBIZ is a certification program designed to help eligible Louisiana veteran-owned and service-connected disabled-veteran-owned small businesses gain greater access to purchasing and contracting opportunities at the state government level.

Licensing and Certification. Open new doors to employment by getting licensed or certified as a mechanic, medical technician, attorney, or other professional position. Often required for work in certain fields, these tests may be eligible for GI Bill reimbursement. Eligibility requirements apply.

Military Training toward Education or Certification Credits. Louisiana recognizes that the skills learned during military training can often apply to the civilian workforce. Individuals with military training and experience will be granted civilian professional licensure and/or certification when the service member has been awarded a military occupational specialty and performance in that specialty that is at a level equal to or exceeding the requirements for said license and/or certification. Provisions apply.

Education Benefits

Louisiana Title 29 Dependents' Educational Assistance. Louisiana offers education assistance to surviving spouses of deceased veterans as well as children of veterans rated with 90% or more service-connected disability and children of veterans rated with 100% service-connected disability due to unemployability.

Survivors and Dependents Education. This program provides education and training opportunities to dependents of veterans who are permanently and totally disabled due to a service-related condition or who died while on active duty or as a result of a service-related condition. Eligibility requirements apply.

Honor Medals

Louisiana Veterans Honor Medals are available to all honorably discharged Louisiana veterans and to the families of those killed in action, with a blue ribbon for honorable discharge, a purple ribbon for Purple Heart recipients, a black ribbon for prisoners of war, and a yellow ribbon for those killed in action.

Recreational Discounts, Licenses, and Passes

Hunting and Fishing Licenses. Louisiana veterans can enjoy discounts and fee waivers for hunting and fishing licenses. Certain qualifications apply.

Louisiana State Parks Benefits for Veterans and Service Members. Louisiana state parks offer several benefits. Disabled veterans are eligible for a free Louisiana state parks pass. Service members serving on active duty in the US Armed Forces and one immediate family member receive a 50% discount for day use. Service members serving in an active or reserve component of the US Armed Forces and retired service members receive 15% off all rentable facilities.

MISSISSIPPI
Veteran population: 6.2% (182,774)

Financial Benefits

Privilege Tax. Persons who are sixty-five years of age or older, blind, deaf, or mute; who have lost a hand or foot; or who can provide documentation that they are 50% disabled to perform physical labor and whose annual gross income is $900 or less are exempt from payment of privilege tax for specified businesses.

Ad Valorem Tax. Any veteran who has a service-connected, total disability and who has been honorably discharged from military service is exempt from all ad valorem taxes on the assessed value of homestead property, and the exemption extends to unremarried surviving spouses of such veterans.

Income Tax. Military retired pay and SBP payments are tax-free.

Housing and Healthcare Benefits

Veterans Homes. The Mississippi VA aims to provide all Mississippi veterans with assistance when they are in need through veterans homes that provide aging and chronically disabled veterans quality care in a complete living environment. They offer veterans access to trained specialists in a variety of healthcare disciplines, advanced medical technology and equipment, full support services, and nearby amenities. Mississippi veterans homes include Collins Veterans Home, Jackson Veterans Home, Martha Jo Leslie State Veterans Home (in Kosciusko), and Oxford Veterans Home. Each of the four state veterans nursing homes has 150 beds and provides skilled nursing home care for eligible veterans and spouses.

Applicants must have a medical need for nursing home care and must be able to pay the applicable daily charge for care in the home. A portion of the cost of care in a Mississippi State Veterans Home is covered by the VA, with the remaining cost paid by the veteran or their family; from available funding sources, such as military or civilian retirement; VA compensation or nonservice-connected pension; or social security benefits for personal funds. Indigent veterans may qualify for financial assistance.

Veterans' Home Purchase Board. The Veterans' Home Purchase Board provides low-interest mortgage loans for eligible veterans and unmarried surviving spouses to purchase an existing single-family home or to construct a new home. The unmarried surviving spouse of an eligible person who died as a result of service or service-connected injuries qualifies, as does the unremarried spouse of any eligible veteran who has not purchased a home since the veteran's death.

Employment Benefits

State Retirement. Members of the Public Employees' Retirement System (PERS) who served in the US Armed Forces or in maritime service during periods of hostility in World War II are entitled to up to four years of credit for active duty, provided they entered state service after discharge from the armed forces or after completion of such maritime service. PERS is a defined benefit plan designed to provide a monthly retirement benefit to employees at time of retirement.

Mississippi Employment Security Commission. Veterans seeking assistance regarding employment or unemployment insurance benefits should contact their local Mississippi Employment Security Commission Office for assistance. Offices are located in larger cities and towns across the state.

Education Benefits

Children and Spouses of POW, MIA, KIA, and Disabled Veterans. Children of any member of the US Armed Services whose official home of record and residence is within the state of Mississippi and who is officially reported as being either a prisoner of a foreign government or missing in action can receive an eight-semester scholarship, without cost, at any state-supported college or university within the state, exclusive of books, food, school supplies, materials, and dues or fees for extra-curricular activities. Tuition waivers at in-state schools are available for children or spouses of disabled veterans or service members who have died in action.

National Guard. The adjutant general is authorized to pay the tuition for any member in good standing with the active Mississippi National

Guard who is enrolled within the state of Mississippi at an accredited institution of higher learning, who is not eligible for GI Bill educational assistance, and who meets requirements specified in Mississippi law. In addition, the Mississippi Education Assistance Program pays tuition up to $250 per credit hour, maximum $4,500 per year for eligible National Guard members to obtain associates and bachelor's degrees.

In-State Tuition. Nonresident active duty military personnel and National Guard members stationed in Mississippi are classified as state residents for the purposes of payment of tuition at state colleges and universities. Any person who served in the active military, naval, or air service, and who was discharged or released therefrom under conditions other than dishonorable, is considered a veteran for in-state tuition.

University of Southern Mississippi's (USM) Center for Military Veterans, Service Members, and Families. USM's Center for Military Veterans, Service Members, and Families provides full support for service members and veterans and their families who are pursuing a higher education degree at the university. Learn more at *USM.edu/military-veterans*.

Recreational Discounts, Licenses, and Passes

Hunting and Fishing. Veterans who have a total service-connected disability from the VA are not required to purchase a hunting or fishing license but must have on their person proof of age, residency, and disability status while engaged in hunting or fishing.

Concealed Weapon Permit. Any veteran with a service-connected disability is exempt from concealed weapon permit fees and renewal fees.

NORTH CAROLINA

Veteran population: 6.5% (688,259)

Financial Benefits

Income Tax. Any amount up to $4,000 received by a taxpayer during any year as retired or retainer pay as a result of service in any of the US Armed Forces is exempt from income taxation. All disability payments to veterans by reason of service in the US Armed Forces are not reportable as income for income taxation purposes.

Homestead Exemption. To qualify as a disabled veteran and be eligible for a homestead property tax exemption under North Carolina law, the property owner must be a veteran of any branch of the US Armed Forces with an honorable discharge and must have a permanent and total service-connected disability of 100% from the VA. If in receipt of DIC, a surviving spouse of a disabled veteran may also qualify for a tax exemption. The disabled veteran homestead exemption exempts the first $45,000 of assessed real property value from tax abatement.

Housing and Healthcare Benefits

Veterans Homes. The VA runs five full-service state veterans homes with 449 skilled care beds and employs over 750 North Carolinians at locations in Fayetteville (150 beds), Salisbury (99 beds), Black Mountain (100 beds), Kinston (100 beds), and Kernersville (120 private rooms). Depending on the location, provided services may include semiprivate or private rooms (additional cost), twenty-four-hour nursing, IV therapy, oxygen therapy, physical therapy, occupational therapy, speech therapy, aquatic therapy, wound care and pain management, full-time dietitian, nourishment care, activity programming, hospice, counseling services, family group meetings, laundry, pharmacy, volunteer

medication management, psychiatry, MSW social worker, and barber/
beauty shop services.

Camp Lejeune and MCAS New River. The VA has established a pre-
sumption of service connection for eight diseases associated with exposure to contaminants in the water supply at Marine Corps Base Camp
Lejeune and MCAS New River in Jacksonville. Active duty, reserve, and
National Guard members who served at either location for a cumulative
minimum of thirty days between August 1, 1953 and December 31, 1987
may be eligible for disability benefits.

Housing Assistance. The federal and state governments have resources
available to aid veterans with their housing needs, from immediate assistance for those currently struggling with homelessness to tax credits and
exemptions for current homeowners. If you are currently homeless and
need assistance, please contact the National Call Center for Homeless
Veterans today at 1-877-4AID-VET. This is a free service and does not
require enrollment in any VA health program or registration with the VA.

Education Benefits

Scholarship for Children of Wartime Veterans. The North Carolina
Scholarship for Children of Wartime Veterans was created to show the
state's appreciation for the service and sacrifices of its war veterans.
The scholarship program applies to North Carolina schools and is for
eight academic semesters, which the recipient has eight years to utilize.
The scholarship program has been established for children of certain
class categories of deceased, disabled, combat, or POW/MIA veterans.
Applicants must be under the age of twenty-five at the time of application. The veteran's qualifying criteria must have occurred during
a period of war. At time of application, applicants must be domiciled

residents of North Carolina. In addition, the veteran parent must have been a legal resident of North Carolina at the time of entering service in the US Armed Forces during the eligibility period, or the veteran's child must have been born in North Carolina and been a resident of North Carolina continuously since birth.

Recreational Discounts, Licenses, and Passes

Hunting and Fishing License. All 50% or more disabled veterans can get a lifetime hunting and fishing license for $11 to $117, depending on the type of license.

State Parks. Discounted entry fees are available for disabled veterans. Contact the park for details.

OKLAHOMA
Veteran population: 7.3% (290,266)

Financial Benefits

Property Tax. Oklahoma law creates a property tax exemption for eligible 100% permanent disabled service-connected veterans, certain injured veterans, and surviving spouses. The exemption is for the full fair cash value of the homestead.

Income Tax. One hundred percent of income received as salary or compensation in any form by an Oklahoma resident as a member of any component of the US Armed Forces can be deducted from taxable income.

Exemption for Sales Tax. Sales of tangible personal property or services are exempt from sales tax when made to persons who have been honorably discharged from active service in any branch of the US Armed

Forces or Oklahoma National Guard, and who have been certified by the VA, or its successor, to be in receipt of compensation at the 100% rate for a permanent disability sustained through military action or accident or resulting from a disease contracted while in such service. The exemption includes sales to the spouse of such veteran or to a household member where the veteran resides and who is authorized to make purchases on behalf of the veteran in the veteran's absence, so long as the purchase is for the benefit of the qualified veteran.

Exemption for Retirement Benefits. Retirement benefits received by an individual from any component of the US Armed Forces are exempt from taxable income in an amount not to exceed the greater of 75% of such benefits or $10,000.

Housing and Healthcare Benefits

Veterans Centers. Oklahoma Veterans Centers are long-term, skilled nursing care facilities for veterans that are operated by the state of Oklahoma and approved by the federal Department of Veterans Affairs. ODVA administers the following veterans centers: Ardmore, Claremore, Clinton, Lawton, Norman, Sulphur, Talihina, and Sallisaw. The homes are open to honorably discharged Oklahoma veterans in need of nursing care. There is a fee for care; some spouses may be eligible for admission.

Fisher House Foundation. The Fisher House Foundation is best known for a network of comfort homes where military and veterans' families can stay at no cost while a loved one is receiving treatment at military and VA medical centers. The foundation also manages a grant program that supports other military charities and the Hero Miles program that uses donated frequent flyer points to bring family members to the bedside of injured service members.

Employment Benefits

Oklahoma Employment Security Commission. The Oklahoma Employment Security Commission has local Disabled Veterans' Outreach Program Specialists (DVOPs) at many Workforce Oklahoma Center locations. Local Veterans' Employment Representatives (LVERs) help disabled veterans with counseling, testing, and identifying training and employment opportunities.

CareerTech (CT) for Vets. The Oklahoma Department of Career and Technology Education is committed to helping Oklahoma's transitioning military members. Veterans will find resources on the Oklahoma Military Connection Partners site.

The Oklahoma Military Connection Partners. Oklahoma Military Connection connects civilian employers with Oklahoma veterans, service members, and their families. It is a cooperation between the Oklahoma Employment Security Commission, Oklahoma Department of Commerce (Office of Workforce Development), Oklahoma Department of Career and Technology Education (CareerTech for Vets), Oklahoma Military Department (Employment Coordination Program), and Citizen Soldier for Life.

Education Benefits

University of Central Oklahoma Veteran Student Support. The University of Central Oklahoma provides a full-time Veteran Student Support Office to assist students who are eligible to receive education benefits from the VA. All degree plans offered by the university have been approved by the State Accrediting Agency for payment of federal benefits.

VetHERO. VetHERO is a department of Veteran Support Services and is designed to support veteran students and military dependents succeed in postsecondary education by coordinating services to address the academic, financial, physical, and social needs of veterans and veteran dependent students. VetHERO is run entirely by students participating in the VA work-study program.

Fisher House Military Scholarship Tool. The Fisher House Foundation manages scholarship funds for military children, spouses, and children of fallen and disabled veterans and provides a scholarship search tool at *fisherhouse.org/programs/scholarship-programs.*

Southern Nazarene University VETS Center. The Veterans Educational Transitions Success (VETS) Center at Southern Nazarene University serves as a single point of contact to coordinate veteran student support services on campus for both graduate and undergraduate students, assisting veteran students with transitioning to campus life—including through orientations, academic and career counseling, and connecting to community support. The VETS Center serves traditional, professional studies, and graduate student veterans.

Transportation Assistance

Oklahoma Veterans Rural Transportation (OVRT) Program. The OVRT Program will provide safe, caring, and quality transportation services to and from the veteran's VA facility of record or healthcare provider to which the veteran has been appropriately referred in order to eliminate transportation barriers and afford veterans access to the care and health benefits they need. The Oklahoma Department of Veterans Affairs will use funding provided by the Grants for Transportation of Veterans in Highly Rural Areas program to provide transportation services over a multicounty area. The OVRT Program will cover the following counties: Beaver, Cimarron, Dewey, Ellis, Grant, Harmon, Harper, and Roger Mills.

Recreational Discounts, Licenses, and Passes

Admission to State Parks. All honorably discharged veterans who are currently Oklahoma residents are allowed free admission to all state-owned or state-operated parks and museums.

Hunting and Fishing Licenses. Disabled veterans who are legal residents and have proper certification of disability from the VA may purchase a lifetime disabled veteran combination hunting/fishing license. The fees for the license are $200 for veterans having a disability of less than 60% or $25 for veterans having a disability of 60% or more.

People with proper certification of 100% disability from the VA are exempt from the fees for:

- the deer gun hunting license
- the deer archery hunting license
- the primitive firearms license
- a bonus, special, or second deer gun hunting license

Legal resident veterans having a disability of 60% or more are exempt from the Wildlife Land Stamp requirements.

SOUTH CAROLINA
Veteran population: 7.6% (393,792)

Financial Benefits

Income Tax. South Carolina does not tax federal monies paid as a pension, disability pay from the military, or VA compensation.

Property Taxes for Disabled Veterans. Permanently and totally disabled veterans are eligible for a homestead tax deduction and a total exemption of property tax on their homes. This exemption can transfer to a surviving spouse and may also transfer to a new home.

Specially Adapted Housing Tax Exemption. Veterans who are paralyzed in the lower half of their bodies or who have lateral half paralysis can receive a tax exemption at the city, county, and state levels for their adaptive residences.

Housing and Healthcare Benefits

South Carolina has five veterans' homes in Anderson, Columbia, Florence, Gaffney and Walterboro. Honorably discharged South Carolina resident veterans in need of skilled or intermediate nursing home care are eligible for admission.

Employment Benefits

State Retirement Credit for Military Service. State employees called or returning to active duty may continue with the state's retirement program if they continue to make payments as normal. State employees can buy credit toward state retirement based on their military time.

SC Works Centers. To assist veterans transitioning into the civilian workforce, local veteran outreach specialists are trained to provide career coaching, job referrals, résumé preparation, and priority placement services.

Operation Palmetto Employment. Operation Palmetto Employment is a statewide initiative supported by the South Carolina Department of Employment and Workforce to help military members, veterans, and their families find meaningful careers after military service. Assistance includes access to education, training, job fairs, and more.

Education Benefits

Free Tuition for Children of Veterans. Some children may receive tuition benefits at South Carolina's state-funded postsecondary schools free of charge. Both student and veteran must meet residency requirements and other stipulations, and there are limits to benefits. The dependent children of resident veterans who meet additional criteria are eligible. The qualifying veteran must meet one of the following criteria:

- Died while serving our country
- Died as a result of injuries or disabilities received while serving our country
- Was awarded the Purple Heart or the Medal of Honor
- Is rated by the VA to be 100% permanently and totally disabled

Recreational Discounts, Licenses, and Passes

Hunting and Fishing License. Disabled South Carolina veterans who meet the residency requirement of having been domiciled in the state for at least 365 days at time of application are eligible for a three-year combination hunting and fishing license at no charge.

Palmetto Passport. The state offers the Palmetto Passport at a reduced price to 100% disabled veterans, the legally blind, active state National Guard members, and other residents who are sixty-five years of age or older. This annual pass secures free entrance to state parks for the pass holder and others in their vehicle. Passes must be purchased in person and do not guarantee admission, depending on park occupancy. Additional use fees may apply.

TENNESSEE

Veteran population: 6.4% (449,263)

Financial Benefits

Property Tax Relief for Disabled Veterans. To receive tax relief as a disabled veteran, one of the following criteria must be met: a service-connected disability that resulted in paraplegia, permanent paralysis from traumatic injury, disease to the spinal cord or brain, loss or loss of use of two or more limbs, or legal blindness; a service-connected permanent and total disability or disabilities; or a 100% total and permanent disability rating from being a prisoner of war. The veteran must own and use the property as their primary residence, and the maximum market value on which tax relief is calculated is $175,000.

Property Tax Relief for Surviving Spouses. Surviving spouses of disabled veterans are eligible for relief if the veteran would have qualified under later amendments to the law. The tax relief is in an amount necessary to pay or reimburse such taxpayers for all or part of the local property taxes paid for a given tax year on that property that the disabled veteran owned and used as their primary residence. The surviving spouse must own and use the property as their primary residence, and the maximum market value on which tax relief is calculated is $100,000.

Housing and Healthcare Benefits

Tennessee State Veterans' Homes. Tennessee offers four state veterans' homes in Clarksville, Humboldt, Knoxville, and Murfreesboro. Tennessee resident veterans are eligible for admission. Spouses, surviving spouses, and Gold Star parents may also be eligible.

Employment Benefits

Tennessee State Employment. The following employment benefits are available in Tennessee:

- Credit for military service in state employment
- Reemployment rights of public employees

Commercial Driver License (CDL) Program for Service Members and Veterans. The road skills test may be waived for qualified military personnel applying for a Tennessee CDL. Applicants are, however, required to pass the applicable CDL knowledge test.

Education Benefits

Tennessee Veteran Dependent Education Benefits. This program covers the full cost of college at Tennessee state colleges for survivors of veterans who were killed in action or who died as a result of injuries suffered in war. Children must be under the age of twenty-three.

Samsung American Legion Scholarship. Samsung scholarships may be used for undergraduate studies and applied toward tuition, books, fees, and room and board. Winners are selected according to academic record, involvement in school, and community service.

Recreational Discounts, Licenses, and Passes

Free State Park Day. In order to honor Tennessee veterans and encourage the use of natural parks across the state, the Department of Environment and Conservation designates Veterans Day as Free State Park Day for veterans, during which access to and use of all state parks—including but not limited to campgrounds and golf courses—is free of charge.

Discounted Camping Fees. All Tennessee resident veterans with a 100% total service-connected disability can receive 50% off camping fees. Premium campsites are excluded.

Hunting and Fishing Licenses. Veterans with a 100% permanent and total disability rating, or who are 30% or more disabled from service in any war, qualify for a sportfishing and hunting license with a one-time $10 fee. Applicants must be Tennessee residents.

TEXAS
Veteran population: 5.3% (1,562,560)

The Texas Veterans Commission (TVC) administers a wide range of disabled veteran benefits programs in Texas, including for claims assistance, education, employment, entrepreneurs and small business owners, grants, healthcare advocacy, mental health, and women veterans. For more information, visit tvc.texas.gov. Another fantastic resource is the new TexVet website, which provides a comprehensive listing of Texas Disabled Veteran Benefits by county: *TexVet.org*.

Financial Assistance

Property Tax Exemption. Property taxes in Texas are assessed and administered by each county. Disabled veterans in Texas with a 10%–90% VA disability rating can get a reduction of their home's assessed value in an amount ranging from $5,000 to $12,000 depending on disability percentage. One hundred percent disabled veterans are exempt from all property taxes. Surviving spouses also qualify. Disabled veterans or surviving families are required each year to apply for residence homesteads they own.

Disabled Veteran Discounts and Free Services

Thanks to the generous donations of for-profit entities as well as various nonprofit organizations, Texas offers disabled veterans a ton of discounts and free services. For a complete list of discounts and free offerings for Texas disabled veterans, visit *TexVet.org*.

- **Freedom Hunters** offers Texas disabled veterans outdoor adventures and hunting for military, veterans, and their families. Learn more at *FreedomHunters.org*.

- The **Gratitude Initiative** provides educational support and college scholarships to disabled veterans in Texas as well as the children and families of military service members, veterans, disabled veterans, and those killed in defense of our country. The initiative works with children and their parents around the globe and throughout the United States at *no cost*, and offerings include online college and career counseling, test prep, and financial aid counseling through the GI College Success Academy. Learn more at *GratitudeInitiative.org*.

Education Benefits

The Hazlewood Act. Texas's Hazlewood Act provides qualified veterans, spouses, and dependent children with an education benefit of up to 150 hours of tuition exemption, including most fee charges, at public institutions of higher education in the state. This benefit does not include living expenses, books, or supply fees. Learn more at *TVC.Texas. gov/education/hazlewood*.

On-the-Job Training. On-the-job training programs allow veterans to learn a trade or skill through training on the job rather than by attending a formal program of classroom-based instruction yielding a degree or certificate. Learn more on the Texas Veterans Commission website, *TVC.Texas.gov*.

Employment Benefits

WorkInTexas.com. WorkInTexas.com helps Texas veterans translate their military skills to jobs in the civilian world. The Military Occupation Code (MOC) Crosswalk function allows veterans to enter the type of work they performed in the US Armed Forces and receive a list of civilian jobs that require those skills. The system also translates MOCs into skills that employers are looking for in potential employees.

Veterans Employment Preference. Texas employers value your service to our country. Many employers recognize the skills and dedication that veterans bring to the workforce and therefore give employment preference to veterans when making hiring decisions. Talk to your local job coach or career advisor about veteran preference job opportunities.

Texas State Retirement Military Service Credit. Nonretired veterans may claim their active duty military time toward state retirement. After a veteran's first retirement contribution has been posted with the Employees Retirement System (ERS) of Texas, they can buy up to sixty months of eligible active duty service in the US Armed Forces to establish service credit.

Veteran Entrepreneur Program (VEP). VEP assists veterans with starting businesses and growing existing veteran-owned businesses through business planning, securing capital, and development of business fundamentals. VEP provides veterans with business tools, resources, and direct support that can be leveraged toward business success. The program continuously observes the Texas market landscape to create programs that enhance the scope of services it delivers to veterans. Veteran business consultants travel across the state to conduct and facilitate training and informational seminars.

Home Loans

Veterans Land Loan Program. The Veterans Land Loan Program is the only one of its kind in the nation, giving Texas veterans and military members the opportunity to borrow up to $150,000 to purchase land at competitive interest rates while typically requiring a minimum 5% down payment for tracts of one acre or more. Learn more at the Veterans Land Board (VLB) website: *VLB.Texas.gov.*

Veterans Housing Assistance Program (VHAP). In 1983, the state legislature created a VLB program called VHAP to aid Texas veterans in purchasing a home. Eligible Texas veterans and military members have an opportunity to purchase a home with a competitive, low-interest loan and little or no down payment. Veterans, military members, and their spouses may receive up to $647,200 on a fixed-rate loan for fifteen-, twenty-, twenty-five-, or thirty-year terms. Veterans with a VA service-connected disability rating of 30% or greater qualify for a discounted interest rate.

Land Loans Financing. The VLB offers loans up to $50,000 for a two- to twenty-year term or loans from $7,500 to $10,000 for a two- to ten-year term. Veterans with a VA service-connected disability rating of 30% or greater qualify for a discounted interest rate. No down payment is required; however, the program does require a $10 flood certification fee, required at time of application; a $125 title search fee, required at time of application; and closing costs. This program was introduced in 1986 to provide below-market interest rate loans to qualified Texas veterans for home repairs and improvement to their existing homes.

Veterans Homes

Texas State Veterans Homes provide affordable long-term care for Texas veterans, their spouses, and Gold Star parents. Conveniently located across Texas, each first-class facility is designed to enhance quality of life with a clean, caring, and dignified setting appropriate to those who have served our country with honor. There are homes for disabled Texas veterans in the following Texas cities: Amarillo, Big Spring, Bonham, El Paso, Floresville, Houston, McAllen, Temple, and Tyler.

Because the VA subsidizes much of a veteran's cost to stay at a veterans home, daily out-of-pocket rates are well below average and include the cost of medications for veterans. Residents can choose between a spacious private or semiprivate room based on availability. Memory care units at each home provide highly specialized care including beautifully landscaped, secure courtyards.

Like all VLB programs, Texas State Veterans Homes are self-supporting and cost Texas taxpayers virtually nothing.

Recreational Discounts, Licenses, and Passes

Driver's License or ID Card. Disabled veterans in Texas with at least a 60% VA disability rating and an honorable discharge can get a Texas driver's license or ID card for free.

Hunting and Fishing Licenses. Disabled veterans in Texas with an honorable discharge and a 50% or greater VA disability rating, or who have suffered the loss of use of a foot or leg because of service can get a free Super Combo Hunting and All-Water Fishing License Package each year. The package includes a variety of licenses and endorsements.

State Parks. The Disabled Veteran's Passport allows free entry to Texas state parks for Texas disabled veterans with a 60% or more service-connected disability or loss of lower extremity. One additional person may assist the pass holder at a reduced rate of 50% of the standard entry fee. Learn more at *TPWD.Texas.gov/state-parks/park-information/passes*.

VIRGINIA
Veteran population: 8.3% (713,344)

Financial Benefits

Income Tax. Up to $15,000 of military basic pay may be exempted from Virginia income tax.

Virginia Taxable Income Subtraction for Military Retired Pay. The Virginia State Budget for 2022 authorized a graduated income subtraction for military retired pay. For the 2023 tax year, veterans aged fifty-five and over who are receiving military retired pay can deduct $20,000 from their Virginia taxable income. This subtraction will increase each year by $10,000 until the 2025 tax year, for a maximum subtraction of $40,000.

Disabled Veterans Real Estate Tax Exemption. Veterans with a VA 100% disability are exempt from property taxes on their home. The surviving spouse may also be eligible.

Housing and Healthcare Benefits

Virginia State Veterans Homes. The Virginia Department of Veterans Services (DVS) State Veterans Homes provide affordable long-term nursing care for Virginia's veterans. The veterans care centers in Richmond and Roanoke are first-class facilities designed to enhance quality of life with a clean, caring, and dignified setting. Two additional care centers are under construction.

- The **Sitter & Barfoot Veterans Care Center** (SBVCC) in Richmond is a single-level facility featuring 200 single-occupancy rooms in four nursing units: two sixty-bed skilled nursing care units, one forty-bed skilled nursing care unit, and one forty-bed secure Alzheimer's dementia unit with enclosed courtyards. SBVCC accepts payment from private insurers, Medicare, and Medicaid. Most veterans also qualify for the VA per diem facility credit.

- **Virginia Veterans Care Center** in Roanoke has 224 beds in the facility and provides comprehensive high-quality care with on-site laboratory work, X-rays, physical therapy, podiatry care, and many other ancillary healthcare services. The Salem VA Medical Center is also located next door for additional services for those qualified. Additionally, the building and grounds offer an array of amenities to include wheelchair accessible nature trails and a deck, library, chapel, barber shop, and billiard room.

- The new **Jones & Cabacoy Veterans Care Center** is being built in the Princess Anne section of Virginia Beach on a twenty-five-acre site adjacent to Nimmo Parkway, West Neck Rd, and N. Landing Rd. The land for the site was donated by the City of Virginia Beach. The 128-bed facility will feature all private rooms that will be organized into eight sixteen-bed households that surround a central community center.

- The new **Puller Veterans Care Center** is being built on the former Vint Hill Farms Station in Fauquier County, which previously served as a United States Army and National Security Agency facility. The site played a critical role in eavesdropping on enemy communications during World War II, when it intercepted a message that helped lead to the D-Day invasion of Normandy. The new care center will deliver top-quality care to Virginia veterans in a homelike setting. The 128-bed facility will feature all private rooms that will be organized into households and neighborhoods that surround a central community center.

Employment Benefits

Virginia Values Veterans (V3) Program. V3 is a program of the Commonwealth of Virginia Department of Veterans Services, whose mission is to educate and train employers throughout the commonwealth on the value of Virginia's veterans and to help employers connect with these personnel assets to maximize the productivity of their workforce.

Education Benefits

Virginia Military Survivors and Dependents Education Program (VMSDEP). VMSDEP provides education benefits to spouses and children of military service members who were killed, are missing in action, were taken prisoner, or became at least 90% disabled as a result of military service in an armed conflict. This program may pay for tuition and fees at any state-supported college or university in Virginia. Benefits are available for up to thirty-six months.

Virginia HIRE VETS NOW Fellowship Program. The Virginia Department of Veterans Services SkillBridge/HIRE VETS NOW Fellowship Program offers six- to twelve-week internships with Virginia Values Veterans Certified Companies for transitioning service members. With commander approval, service members can participate in a fellowship up to six months prior to separation, helping them gain marketable skills and experience to enhance their civilian career opportunities.

Recreational Discounts, Licenses, and Passes

Hunting and Fishing Licenses. Virginia offers a free lifetime hunting and fishing license as well as a discounted saltwater license for Virginia resident veterans who are permanently and totally service-connected disabled. Veterans with at least 70% VA disability can get discounted hunting and freshwater fishing licenses.

State Parks. Veterans with 100% VA disability are eligible for free admission and parking for the pass holder and anyone needed to assist them at Virginia state parks. The pass also covers boat launch and horse trailer parking and a 50% discount on camping, swimming, shelters, and equipment rental.

WEST VIRGINIA
Veteran population: 7.6% (136,123)

Financial Benefits

State Income Tax Exemption. For taxable years beginning after December 31, 2017, military retirement income—including retirement income from the regular Armed Forces, Army Reserve, and National Guard paid by the United States or the state of West Virginia—is exempt from state income tax.

Disabled Veterans Homestead Exemption. Veterans with 100% permanent and total service-connected disabilities may be exempt from certain property taxes.

Veteran Bonus. House Bill 2285, passed in 2005, provides for the payment of a $400 veteran bonus to qualified eligible veterans of the Kosovo, Iraq, and Afghanistan conflicts who served during the designated time frame outside of the combat zone—and a maximum $600 bonus to those who served in the combat zone.

Jack Bennett Fund. Families of deceased veterans may be provided grave markers for their loved one free of charge by the VA. For families unable to cover the cost of installing these grave markers, the Jack Bennett Fund provides applicants up to $380 to offset the cost. A family's need for financial assistance may be used to determine eligibility and is based on the "means test threshold" as published by the federal VA. Any family member of a deceased veteran as well as licensed funeral directors and cemeteries may apply.

Veterans Home

The West Virginia Veterans Home is a 150-bed facility located on a twenty-three-acre plot that overlooks downtown Barboursville. A nursing department is staffed at all hours to provide for the health and well-being of residents. Services include first aid, preventive care, and assistance with medications. Facility staff provide regular transportation to the nearby Veterans Affairs Medical Center, through which all advanced medical care is provided.

The facility employs a recreation supervisor and five recreation specialists who plan events that encourage participation and self-improvement. A well-provisioned library facilitates learning, and several lounges throughout the facility encourage social interaction.

The home is not a treatment facility and cannot accommodate veterans in need of daily care or skilled assistance. Rooms available for occupancy accommodate two, three, or four people. A person's income is not a factor in gaining admission, although residents are required to contribute one-half of their monthly income as their maintenance contribution.

Employment Benefits

Military Incentive Program. The West Virginia Military Incentive Credit encourages the employment of veterans and service members in the private sector by providing tax credits to qualified businesses that employ economically disadvantaged veterans and unemployed members of the West Virginia National Guard and US Army Reserve forces.

Education Benefits

War Orphan Education Program. Students who qualify for the War Orphan Education Program will not be charged tuition and fees by a West Virginia postsecondary education or training institution. Award amounts administered by the West Virginia Department of Veterans Assistance are to cover costs associated with room, board, books, and other living expenses. This amount fluctuates according to the number of applications received each semester. No more than $1,000 will be awarded to a student in any one semester, and no more than $2,000 will be awarded to a student in any one year.

High School Diplomas for Veterans. West Virginia veterans who served in World War II, Korea, or Vietnam and did not graduate from high school may be awarded a high school diploma. The diploma may be granted by the veteran's current county of residence or by the county in which the school they attended is located.

Medal of Honor and Purple Heart Tuition Waivers. All public institutions of higher education waive tuition and mandatory fee charges for

West Virginia residents who have been awarded the Medal of Honor or Purple Heart.

In-State Tuition Rates for Nonresident Veterans. All public higher education institutions will assess tuition at the in-state rate for nonresident recipients of the GI Bill who enroll within three years of their discharge.

Veterans Re-education Assistance. Since fiscal year 1997, the West Virginia legislature has included in the annual budget various amounts of funding for postsecondary education. This program offers up to a $500 per semester stipend to veterans who are enrolled in a certified postsecondary class. Additionally, this program can assist veterans with vocational and nontraditional education endeavors on a case-by-case basis.

Veterans Upward Bound (VUB). The VUB program supports the efforts of public institutions to be veteran-friendly by providing academic and student support services that address the unique needs of student veterans.

Transportation Assistance

Disabled American Veterans (DAV) Transportation Network. The DAV Transportation Network provides transportation for medical appointments to veterans in rural areas or who have no other transportation. With more than 3,500 vehicles, volunteer drivers have donated nearly 1.5 million hours, providing more than 625,000 rides to transport veterans to and from their appointments at no cost to the veteran.

Becoming a volunteer driver can be a rewarding experience; it is a chance for veterans to help their fellow veterans. To schedule a ride or to volunteer to be a driver, call your local Veterans Affairs Medical Center Voluntary Services Office.

Recreational Discounts, Licenses, and Passes

Veteran Hunting and Fishing Licenses. Resident veterans who qualify for federal VA auto grant benefits or who have a 100% permanent and total service-connected disability qualify for free West Virginia hunting and fishing licenses. While on leave or furlough, service members who are on active duty in the US Armed Forces are permitted to hunt, fish, and trap without a license. Leave or furlough papers serve in lieu of any required licenses.

West Virginia State Parks "Veterans Salute" Discount. Veterans and active duty military personnel are provided a year-round 10% discount on all standard lodge rooms, cabins, and campsites operated by West Virginia state parks. Additional discounts and offers for veterans and military members are available seasonally. Visit *WVStateParks.com* for more information.

CHAPTER TWELVE

THE WEST REGION

ALASKA

Veteran population: 9.2% (67,388)

Housing Benefits

Veterans Homes. The Alaska Veterans and Pioneers Home, located in Palmer, strives to assist older Alaskans to have the highest possible quality of life by providing assisted living in a safe home setting that promotes independence, positive relationships, meaningful activities, and physical, emotional, and spiritual growth. Seventy-five percent of bed capacity is designated for veterans. Qualifying veterans are eligible for a per diem from the VA to help offset the costs of their care. Honorably separated veterans ages sixty-five or older who require assisted living care are eligible for admission. Veterans must have resided in Alaska for one year or more prior to application.

Alaska Housing Finance Corporation (AHFC) Mortgage Program. The AHFC administers the Veterans Mortgage Program, which offers financing for qualified veterans at lower interest rates. Active duty members in the US Armed Forces, public health service, or NOAA—or those with service as a cadet at the US Military, Air Force, Coast Guard, or Naval Academy—may qualify. Loans are generally processed rapidly, require little or no down payment, and often include lower interest.

AHFC also offers a veterans interest rate preference in which a veteran may receive a 1% lower interest rate on the first $50,000 of a bank loan when purchasing a new home. Ask the bank handling the financing to implement this program for you. AHFC also grants a preference to veterans for the rent or sale of a portion of its low-cost housing units.

Land Discount and Purchase Preference. The Veterans Land Discount program allows certain veterans a 20% discount on the purchase price of state residential or recreational land. The discount may be used only once during the veteran's lifetime and may not be used in conjunction with the veterans preference.

Under the Veterans Land Sale Preference, before offering to the general public any unoccupied residential land by auction, a veteran has the exclusive opportunity to purchase the land at a restricted sale at fair appraised market value. Parcels that are offered under this preference must be five acres or less, classified as settlement land, and zoned for residential use only.

Property Tax Exemptions. Real property owned and occupied as the primary residence and permanent place of abode by a qualified disabled veteran whose disability was incurred or aggravated in the line of duty and whose disability has been rated as 50% or more by the military service or the VA is exempt from taxation on the first $150,000 of assessed valuation. The exemption transfers to a spouse if the veteran passes away and the spouse is at least sixty years of age.

Employment Benefits

Employment Resources. The Alaska Department of Labor and Workforce Development has twenty-one job centers across the state. The Anchorage (Midtown and Muldoon), Fairbanks, and Wasilla Job Centers have on-site veteran representatives. All job centers provide priority services to qualified veterans and their eligible spouses, including:

- Priority job referral
- Career counseling
- Career assessment
- Employment assessment
- Job development
- Labor market information
- Job search workshops
- Special programs
- Testing
- Referral to educational services
- Résumé assistance

Visit *Jobs.Alaska.gov* for more information.

Recreational Discounts, Licenses, and Passes

Resident Military Hunting Licenses. Members of the military service or the US Coast Guard who are on active duty permanently stationed in Alaska and their dependents who have met the residency requirements may apply for military licenses at the time of license application and pay the same rate as a resident.

Free Hunting and Fishing Licenses for Alaska Guard and Army Reserve Members. Active members of the Alaska National Guard and Alaska military reserves stationed in the state of Alaska who have met the residency requirements may receive a free hunting and sportfishing license.

Disabled Veteran Hunting and Fishing Licenses. Disabled veteran resident hunting and sportfishing licenses are available at no charge to honorably discharged veterans with a 50% or greater service-connected disability and Alaska residency. Applicants must have lived in Alaska for twelve consecutive months immediately preceding the application.

Alaska Marine Highway System (AMHS). A reduced-fare pass is available for travel on AMHS vessels for US veterans with a service-connected disability. The pass entitles the disabled veteran and an attendant (if required by a physician) to travel at half the regular passenger fare.

Disabled Veterans (DAV) Camping Pass. The legislature granted DAV the right to receive one Alaska State Park Camping Pass free of charge. The DAV Camping Pass, which is valid in all developed Alaska state park campgrounds, is good for two years.

Vehicle Privileges

Alaska Driver's License Extension. Effective in June 1997, Alaska adopted a military extension policy that makes noncommercial driver's licenses valid for ninety days after discharge or return to the state of Alaska, whichever occurs first. The policy extends to military spouses.

Waiver of Commercial Driver's License (CDL) Test. The DMV may waive the commercial motor vehicle driving test for certain drivers with recent military commercial motor vehicle experience.

ARIZONA

Veteran population: 6.8% (493,453)

Financial Benefits

Income Tax. As permanent law, Arizona provides a full individual income tax exemption for benefits, annuities, and pensions received by military retirees, beginning in the year 2021.

Property Tax. The property tax of widow(er)s and disabled people may be waived in certain cases. Contact your county assessor office for eligibility.

Vehicle License Tax and Registration Fees. No license tax or registration fee is collected from any 100% service-connected disabled veteran for a personally owned vehicle. A veteran residing in Arizona is exempt from a vehicle license tax on a vehicle acquired by the veteran through financial aid from the VA. This exemption also applies to the unremarried surviving spouse.

Arizona Military Family Relief Fund (MFRF). The MFRF provides financial assistance to eligible families of currently deployed service members and post-9/11 military and veteran families for hardships caused by the service member's deployment after September 11, 2001.

Financial assistance from the Arizona MFRF is determined by MFRF Advisory Committees, which are composed of twelve members appointed by the governor, as well as the Arizona Department of Veterans' Services (ADVS) director or the director's designee. The pre-9/11 and post-9/11 MFRF have separate advisory committees. One-time emergency financial assistance is available for first-time applicants through the applicable MFRF Emergency Committee, which is composed of five of the advisory committee members.

Housing and Healthcare Benefits

Veteran Homes. Arizona State Veteran Home, Phoenix (SVH-PHX) is a 200-bed Medicare-certified, skilled nursing care facility for eligible Arizona veterans. SVH-PHX serves the long-term care and rehabilitative needs of the veterans of Arizona with energetic and caring staff, whose members provide nursing, therapeutic recreation, and social services to those who have served our nation.

Arizona State Veteran Home, Tucson is a 120-bed skilled nursing facility offering many amenities to Arizona's veterans, such as all private rooms, full baths, and selective dining in a homelike environment.

Community Resource and Referral Center (CRRC). CRRC provides veterans who are homeless or at risk of homelessness with one-stop access to community-based, multi-agency services to promote permanent housing, health and mental health care, career development, and access to VA and non-VA benefits.

Employment Benefits

ADVS Veteran Toolkit Program. The ADVS created the Veteran Toolkit Program to help unemployed veterans get the supplies they need to start working. Surveyed veterans repeatedly said they were ready to work but needed a few things to get them there, ranging from boots and tools to bicycles.

Education Benefits

Arizona Purple Heart Tuition Waiver. This scholarship is available to post-9/11 veterans with at least a 50% VA disability and a Purple Heart medal who were Arizona residents during their service; dependent children under age thirty and unremarried spouses of Arizona military members who were killed in the line of duty on or after September 11, 2001; and post-9/11 Arizona Guard members who were medically discharged or received a Purple Heart.

Arizona Veteran Supportive Campuses (**VSCs**). ADVS provides VSC certification to Arizona postsecondary institutions that meet specific requirements. Certified VSCs better understand the needs of military and veteran students and are continually responsive to those needs. For more information on VSCs, including a list of certified schools, visit *bit.ly/ArizonaVSC* or call 602-255-3373.

Recreational Discounts, Licenses, and Passes

Hunting and Fishing Licenses. Active duty members stationed in Arizona can get hunting and fishing licenses at the resident rate. Free hunting/fishing combination licenses are available for 100% service-connected disabled veterans who have been an Arizona resident for at least twelve months.

State Parks. Arizona offers the following discounts to state parks:

- 50% day-use discount to all active duty, guard, and reserve military members and up to three accompanying adult family members
- 50% day-use discount to all resident military retirees
- 50% off day-use pass to all disabled military
- Free day-use pass to all resident 100% service-connected disabled veterans

CALIFORNIA

Veteran population: 4.1% (1,615,957)

Financial Benefits

Disabled Veterans Property Tax Exemption. California offers a property tax exemption for the home of a disabled veteran or an unmarried spouse of a deceased disabled veteran. There is a basic $161,083 exemption or a low-income $241,627 exemption available to a disabled veteran who is blind in both eyes, has lost the use of two or more limbs, or is rated totally disabled by the VA or military. An unmarried surviving spouse may also be eligible if the service person died as the result of service-connected injury, a disease incurred while on active duty, or as the result of active duty.

The exemption and low-income amount are compounded annually by an inflation factor. This exemption has no personal wealth restriction. The exemption is only available on a principal residence. The home may only receive one property exemption. The issues regarding these exemptions are complex, and the eligibility requirements are specific. Consult the local assessor's office for detailed requirements regarding these exemptions.

California Military Families Financial Relief Act. The California Military Families Relief Act allows reserve component service members who are called to state or federal active duty for thirty days or more to defer certain payments until the end of their period on active duty.

These payments include:

- Mortgages
- Credit card payments
- Retail installment contracts

- Property taxes on the service member's primary residence
- Utility company bills
- Student loans

Deferrals can be for up to 180 days in a 365-day period, or for the duration of the service member's active duty plus sixty calendar days, whichever is less.

California Military Family Relief Fund (CMFRF). CMFRF was established to provide short-term financial assistance in the form of grants to California National Guard members and families impacted by mobilization and deployment.

Housing and Healthcare Benefits

California State Veterans Homes. The eight current veterans homes are a system of live-in residential care facilities offering a comprehensive plan of medical, dental, pharmacy, rehabilitation services, and social activities within a homelike, small community environment. Residents engage in a wide range of activities, including social events, dances, patriotic programs, volunteer activities, arts and crafts, computer access, shopping trips, and other off-site excursions. Residents live in an atmosphere of dignity and respect.

The homes range in size from sixty residents on a twenty-acre site to over 1,000 residents on 500 acres. Facilities are located in Barstow, Chula Vista, Fresno, Lancaster, Redding, Ventura, West Los Angeles, and Yountville. Veterans who are age fifty-five and above and discharged from active military service under honorable conditions are eligible to apply for admission. The age requirement is waived for disabled or homeless veterans needing long-term care.

CalVet Farm and Home Loans. The state of California offers farm, home, mobile home, construction, home improvement, and rehabilitation loans to honorably discharged veterans. The loans have highly competitive rates and quick processing, as well as flood, earthquake, and disaster coverage. Veterans with an honorable discharge and at least ninety days of active service may be eligible.

Employment Benefits

Business License, Tax, and Fee Waiver. Honorably discharged veterans who hawk, peddle, or vend any goods from a fixed location may be eligible for a waiver of municipal, county, and state business license fees, as well as other taxes and fees. This waiver doesn't apply to the sale of alcoholic beverages.

Disabled Veteran Business Enterprise (DVBE) Opportunities. Certified veteran-owned businesses can participate in the state goal of awarding 3% of all state contracts to disabled veterans through the DVBE program. Veterans with a service-connected disability rated at 10% or greater who own at least 51% of a business and who meet other criteria may be eligible.

Education Benefits

California National Guard Education Assistance. The California National Guard Education Assistance Award Program covers all or a portion of costs at select state universities and community colleges. Guard members must remain in an active status while attending school. There are some GPA, academic program, and enrollment requirements.

California College Tuition Fee Waiver for Veterans' Dependents. This tuition benefit waives mandatory system-wide tuition and fees at any state of California community college, California state university, or University of California campus. The program does not cover the expense of books, parking, or room and board. There are four plans under which dependents of veterans may be eligible.

Recreational Discounts, Licenses, and Passes

Hunting and Fishing Licenses. Any veteran with a 50% or greater service-connected disability may be eligible for reduced annual fees for fishing and hunting licenses. Veterans do not have to be California residents to receive this benefit.

State Parks. Any honorably discharged California resident war veteran who has a 50% or greater service-connected disability, is a former POW, or is a Medal of Honor recipient can get a free pass to all California state parks, including both camping and day use. The pass is not valid at units operated by local government, private agencies, or concessionaires, nor is it valid for special events, group campsites, commercial use, or supplemental fees. There may be a convenience fee to make online reservations.

Vehicle Privileges

Motor Vehicle Registration Fees Waived. Medal of Honor recipients, ex-POWs, and some permanently and totally disabled veterans may be eligible for a waiver of registration fees as well as free license plates for one passenger motor vehicle, motorcycle, or commercial motor vehicle of less than 8,001 pounds unladen weight.

COLORADO

Veteran population: 6.7% (387,617)

Financial Benefits

Property Tax Exemption. There is a property tax exemption for 50% of the first $200,000 of a home's value for 100% permanently and totally disabled service-connected veterans. Veterans receiving 100% disability solely as a result of an individual unemployability rating do not qualify. The exemption is for a primary residence only.

Income Tax on Retired Military Pay. Military retirees ages fifty-five to sixty-four can exclude up to $20,000 retired military pay from their taxable income, while those sixty-five and over can exclude up to $24,000. The same rules apply for SBP payments.

Military Family Relief Fund. Colorado may provide grants for families of reservists or guard members called to active duty or to families of active duty members serving in a combat zone. These grants are intended to help families defray the costs of food, housing, utilities, medical services, and other expenses.

The Colorado Veterans Trust Fund and Veterans Assistance Grants. The Colorado Department of Military and Veterans Affairs provides grants to help organizations that support veterans. Programs may include transportation, food and shelter for homeless veterans and their families, offerings for incarcerated veterans, homeless stand downs, job assistance, and other worthwhile "direct service" to veterans.

Housing and Healthcare Benefits

Colorado Veterans Community Living Centers. Colorado Veterans Community Living Centers serve honorably discharged veterans, their spouses or widow(er)s, and Gold Star parents, any of whose children died while serving in the US Armed Forces. Each location provides twenty-four-hour nursing care, meals, physician services and restorative therapy, transportation, and diversified activities at an all-inclusive rate. Additionally, the following services are offered: long-term care, short-term rehabilitation, domiciliary cottages (similar to assisted living), memory care services, short-term "respite" care, and end-of-life/hospice services. These facilities are located in Fitzsimons, Florence, Homelake, Rifle, and Walsenburg.

Education Benefits

Tuition Assistance. Any member of the Colorado National Guard is eligible for up to 100% tuition paid at any Colorado state-funded school, depending on funding availability. State funding can be used in conjunction with Federal Tuition Assistance. Colorado National Guard members must serve two years for each tuition year granted.

Operation Recognition. Operation Recognition awards high school diplomas to deserving and qualified World War II, Korea-, and Vietnam-era veterans. The program is authorized by Colorado state law and offered by the Colorado Board of Veterans Affairs in cooperation with the Colorado Department of Education and the Colorado Association of School Boards.

Recreational Discounts, Licenses, and Passes

Fishing License. There is no fishing license fee for members of the US Armed Forces stationed as resident patients at a military hospital or convalescent station, resident patients at a USDVA hospital located within the state, or veterans who are permanently and totally disabled.

Small-Game Hunting and Fishing License. Resident veterans with a service-connected disability of 60% or more are eligible for a free lifetime combination small-game hunting and fishing license.

State Parks. Veterans with a disabled veteran's license plate receive free admission to any state park or recreation area. Colorado resident disabled veterans with at least a 60% disability can get discounted admission to all Colorado state parks with a Columbine Pass.

HAWAII

Veteran population: 7.8% (112,756)

Financial Benefits

Property Tax Exemption. Property tax exemptions apply to real property owned and occupied as a first residence by a totally disabled veteran or their widow(er). Visit your local real property tax office for more information.

Income Tax. Veterans' disability compensation benefits and pension benefits are tax-free.

Housing and Healthcare Benefits

Hawaii State Veterans Home. The Yukio Okutsu State Veterans Home in Hilo is a state nursing home for honorably discharged Hawaii resident veterans over age fifty-five who require skilled nursing care and meet the VA requirements for eligibility. Veterans are responsible for any costs not covered by the VA or Medicare. Spouses may be eligible for admission, depending on the available space.

Special Housing for Disabled Veterans. Qualified totally disabled veterans may receive a payment by the state of up to $5,000 for the purpose of purchasing or remodeling a home to improve accessibility. Award of payment depends on the availability of state funds and VA approval. Contact your local OVS office for more information.

Education Benefits

Hawaii Army National Guard State Tuition Assistance Program (STAP). STAP offers tuition waivers for eligible members who have completed Basic Combat Training and Advanced Individual Training. The waiver covers 100% of community college tuition and 50% of four-year university tuition. It can be used in conjunction with GI Bill and Federal Tuition Assistance benefits.

Recreational Discounts, Licenses, and Passes

Hunting Licenses. Active duty military personnel and their dependents stationed in Hawaii are considered to be residents for the purposes of obtaining a hunting license.

Vehicle Privileges

Waived Vehicle Registration Fee. Permanently disabled veterans can receive a $45 discount on the state registration fee. To be eligible, you must have a service-connected 100% VA disability rating, be a Hawaii resident, and have an other-than-dishonorable discharge.

IDAHO
Veteran population: 6.4% (122,535)

Financial Benefits

State Income Tax Retired Military Pay Benefit Deduction. A veteran or their unremarried widow(er) aged sixty-five or older, or disabled and aged sixty-two or older, may deduct veterans' retirement benefits. The deductible amount of retirement benefits must be reduced by retirement benefits paid under the Federal Social Security Act or the Tier 1 Federal Railroad Retirement Act.

Tax Benefit. Veterans with a 100% service-connected disability may apply to reduce their property taxes by as much as $1,320.

Grocery Tax Credit. Veterans aged sixty-five or older, or disabled and aged sixty-two or older, may claim the Grocery Tax Credit even when not required to file an income tax return if VA disability benefits are the veteran's only income. See Income Tax Rule 771 by visiting *AdminRules. Idaho.gov.*

Idaho Veterans Support Fund. The policy of the Division of Veterans Services is to fund programs operated both within and outside state and local government that support Idaho veterans. Priority is given to proposals that serve the greatest number of veterans and for which there is no other source of funding. If you feel your program meets the criteria below and you would like to apply for funding, complete the application available at *Veterans.Idaho.gov/publications/idaho-veterans-support-fund.*

Eligible applicants include individuals, organizations, and governmental entities, including bureaus of the Idaho Division of Veterans Services. Eligible activities and costs include programs to inform veterans and the public of services and programs for veterans; programs providing career training to veterans, including those providing educational scholarships; programs providing training to individuals and organizations supporting veterans, including employees of public and private organizations assisting veterans with healthcare, education, and assistance in obtaining public benefits; the acquisition of equipment to support the health, rehabilitation, recreational activities, and care of veterans; financial support or sponsorship of ceremonies celebrating or honoring the service of veterans; and programs providing social, health, rehabilitation, recreational activities, or care to veterans.

Idaho Veterans Recognition Fund. The policy of the Division of Veterans Services is to fund programs operated both within and outside state and local government that solely benefit veterans in Idaho. Priority is given to activities that serve disabled veterans, as well as those that will serve the greatest number of veterans and for which there is no other source of funding. Individuals, organizations, and governmental entities, including bureaus of the division, may submit applications for funding from the program. If you feel your program meets the criteria below and you would like to apply for a Veterans Recognition Fund grant, complete the application available at *Veterans.Idaho.gov/publications/idaho-veterans-recognition-fund.*

Any purpose meeting the objective of supporting veterans of the US Armed Forces and not explicitly excluded is eligible for consideration to receive a grant under the program. Eligible activities and costs include programs to inform veterans and the public of services and programs for veterans, including those offered by the division; programs that may fill gaps in services; programs providing career training to veterans, including those providing educational scholarships; programs providing training to individuals and organizations supporting veterans, including employees of public and private organizations assisting veterans with healthcare, education, and assistance in obtaining public benefits; the acquisition of equipment supporting the health, rehabilitation, or recreational activities of veterans; and programs providing social, health, rehabilitation, or recreational activities or care to veterans.

Idaho Veteran's Emergency Relief Grant Application. Eligible individuals may receive relief grants for the purchase of food, fuel, shelter, and other necessities of daily living in a time of temporary emergency need. No grants will be made to residents of domiciliary or long-term care facilities or to a potential recipient who refuses to take advantage of available government benefits or federal, state, or local relief. Grant recipients may receive only one grant in a six-month period. In no case will a grant exceed $1,500, and the lifetime total of all grants awarded to a veteran and their dependents will not exceed $1,500.

Housing and Healthcare Benefits

Idaho State Veterans Homes. There are three skilled nursing facilities in Idaho for veterans, all of which are Medicare- and Medicaid certified. The Idaho State Veterans Home in Boise offers a 131-bed skilled nursing unit, a 36-bed residential unit, and a special care unit. The Idaho State Veterans Homes in Lewiston and Pocatello are both sixty-six-bed skilled nursing facilities.

Honorably discharged veterans and their spouses who require skilled nursing care are eligible for admission to the nursing homes. Spouses are not eligible for admission to the residential/domiciliary unit at the Boise home. There are limits to the number of spouses who can reside in a home at any given time.

Employment Benefits

Professional Licenses. Anyone holding occupational or professional licenses issued by the state of Idaho and serving in the US Armed Forces is exempt from the payment of any professional or occupational license or renewal fee required by state law while engaged in military service. Additionally, benefits include expedited processing of applications and credit for military training relevant to the occupational license or registration for which you are applying.

Recreational Discounts, Licenses, and Passes

Hunting Licenses and Tags. Resident disabled American veterans may be eligible for DAV reduced fees for licenses and tags. The DAV license ($5) allows the disabled veteran to purchase reduced-fee Disabled American Veteran tags for deer ($10.75), elk ($16.50), bear ($6.75), or turkey ($10.75).

Nonresident disabled American veterans with a VA disability rating of 40% or more are eligible for nonresident DAV reduced fees for licenses and tags. The nonresident DAV hunting with three-day fishing license ($31.75) allows the nonresident disabled veteran to purchase reduced-fee nonresident Disabled American Veteran tags for deer ($23.75), elk ($39.75), bear ($23.75), or turkey ($19.75).

State Parks. Idaho resident veterans who are 100% disabled with 100% service-related disabilities receive a free campsite while camping within Idaho's state parks and free day-use access.

MONTANA
Veteran population: 8.0% (88,352)

Financial Benefits

Montana Military Family Relief Fund (MMFRF). MMFRF provides monetary grants to families of Montana National Guard and reserve component members on active duty for federal service in a contingency operation on or after April 28, 2007. MMFRF grants are intended to help Montana families defray the costs of food, housing, utilities, medical services, and other expenses that become difficult to afford when a wage earner has temporarily left civilian employment to be placed on active military duty.

- Status-based grant: a flat rate of $250 per eligible dependent
- Need-based grant: up to $2,000 (maximum)
- Casualty-based grant: a flat rate of $2,000

Montana Disabled Veterans (MDV) Assistance Program. The MDV Assistance Program helps disabled veterans or their unmarried surviving spouse by reducing the property tax rate on their home. The veteran must have 100% disability from an injury related to service. The MDV reduction is based on income and marriage status, and the income ranges are updated each year for inflation.

Income Tax. Base pay, special pay, and incentive pay received by service members serving on active duty in the US Armed Forces; pay received by National Guard and reserve service members serving on active duty in support of a contingency operation or for homeland defense; combat zone pay; and military disability retirement pay received as a pension, annuity, or similar allowance for personal injury or sickness resulting from active service in the US Armed Forces should not be included in taxable income.

Housing Benefits

Veterans Homes. The state of Montana operates and manages the Montana Veterans' Nursing Home in Columbia Falls and oversees a contract for the operation of Eastern Montana Veterans' Nursing Home in Glendive. A sixty-bed skilled care facility at Southwest Montana Veterans' Home in Butte is also available. Facilities are restricted to honorably discharged veterans who have served in the US Armed Forces and their spouses. Spouses are admitted only if space is available.

Education Benefits

Nonresident Tuition Waiver. The Montana Board of Regents may waive nonresident tuition for selected and approved nonresident students, not to exceed at any unit 2% of the full-time equivalent enrollment at that unit during the preceding year for eligible resident veterans and their children and spouses.

Montana National Guard Education Benefit. The regents may also waive tuition for up to 5,000 credits each academic year in accordance with the Montana National Guard education benefit program established by the department of military affairs. The waivers provided are intended to be available for up to five years after a person qualifies.

Recreational Discounts, Licenses, and Passes

Hunting Licenses. People with disabilities are entitled to fish and to hunt game birds, not including turkeys, with only a conservation license if they are residents of Montana not residing in an institution and are certified as disabled as prescribed by departmental rule.

A person who has purchased a conservation license and a resident fishing license or game bird license for a particular license year and who is subsequently certified as disabled is entitled to a refund for the fishing license or game bird license previously purchased for that license year.

A person who is certified as disabled and who was issued a permit to hunt from a vehicle for license year 2000 or later is automatically entitled to a permit to hunt from a vehicle for subsequent license years if the criteria for obtaining a permit does not change.

Other Privileges

Veterans' Cemetery Fee Waivers. Eligible veterans are exempt from the veterans' cemetery fee.

Vehicle Registration Fee. Veterans may be eligible for two sets of special veteran license plates and exemption from all motor vehicle registration fees for two motor vehicles that are not used for commercial purposes.

NEVADA
Veteran population: 6.9% (218,049)

Education Benefits

Operation Recognition. This Nevada legislative act allows Nevada school districts to issue a standard high school diploma to veterans who served in the US Armed Forces sometime between September 16, 1940, and May 7, 1975. A veteran, a guardian of a disabled veteran, or a member of a deceased veteran's family on behalf of the deceased veteran may submit an application.

Nonresident Tuition Exemption. Any active duty member of the US Armed Forces who is stationed in Nevada and any active duty service member who has a permanent change of duty station to a state other than Nevada, as well as their spouses and dependent children, will remain classified as Nevada residents for tuition purposes as long as they remain continuously enrolled at a Nevada System of Higher Education institution.

Purple Heart Recipients. Purple Heart recipients can receive a tuition waiver at all public institutions once they have exhausted all their education benefits. More information is available at *nshe.nevada. edu/wp-content/uploads/Academic-Affairs/NSHEPurpleHeartFeeWaiver_ 20191008.pdf.*

POW/MIA Benefits for Children and Spouse. The child of a veteran identified as a prisoner of war or missing in action may receive a tuition waiver, which can be used for ten years after they reach the age of eighteen or ten years after the date of enrollment, whichever is earlier. Surviving spouses may use this benefit for up to ten years from the date on which the service member was identified as a prisoner of war or missing in action.

Nevada National Guard Tuition Waiver. Nevada National Guard service members can attend public institutions with a tuition waiver, and some fees may also be waived, depending on the institution. Contact the school's Veteran Office for more information.

Employment Benefits

Veteran Hiring Program. A veteran's coordinator works within the Division of Human Resource Management to oversee a veteran hiring program and match veterans with job opportunities at the state of Nevada. The veteran program helps bridge the gap between military and civilian employment and is available to anyone who has served in the US military, National Guard, or Army Reserve. The program provides individual assistance to veterans in the following ways:

- Identifies current openings and state positions that match well with the veteran's skills, education, and experience
- Answers questions about state employment and its hiring processes

- Advises and assists veterans with completing state job
  applications to best represent themselves

Additionally, program staff collaborates with nonprofit organizations and local, state, and federal agencies to better connect veterans to available resources and services throughout Nevada.

Work for Warriors. Work for Warriors assists veterans, service members, and their families in the employment process from start to finish to gain employment on track with their career goals. It helps with résumés, interview preparation, mock interviews, job placement, application assistance, and certifications to enhance career options. For more information, visit *WorkforWarriorsNV.org*.

Patriot Employer Program. The Patriot Employer Program provides businesses with education and support to hire employees who've already proven to be successful. The program explains where to find veterans, how to retain them, the tax credits available, and other benefits to hiring people who have served our country. Engaging in this key talent pool benefits a company in immeasurable ways. More information is available at *Veterans.NV.gov/employers/patriot-employer-program*.

Housing Benefits

Veterans Affairs Supportive Housing (VASH) Program. The Department of Housing Services wants to help homeless US military veterans obtain, and retain, permanent housing. To help us meet this goal, it offers rental assistance through a unique new program called VASH, which provides rental assistance vouchers specifically targeted to homeless veterans. Public housing authorities work closely with veteran affairs centers to manage the program. In addition to the rental assistance, VA

Health Care for Homeless Veterans Centers provide supportive services and case management to eligible homeless veterans.

The Southern Nevada Regional Housing Authority has received an award for 630 VASH vouchers during the last seven years to serve homeless veteran households. If you are a homeless veteran, consider enrolling in this program by contacting the local veteran office at 702-791-9077. Veterans cannot apply directly with the housing authority; all applicants must be referred by the veteran's administration staff.

Housing Choice Voucher Program (HCVP). The HCVP allows participants to utilize rental vouchers to find privately rented units in whatever neighborhood they wish. Families who meet eligibility and income requirements, which include a criminal history check, are entered onto a wait list based on the preferences they are eligible for and the date of application. As families reach the top of the waitlist, they are offered a voucher based on funding restrictions. The total amount of assistance to each family for rent and utilities is based on the family's income, composition, and unit selected as well as the Regional Housing Authority's (RHA's) payment standards. RHA has a minimum rent of $75.

Help USA Las Vegas. Renaissance Apartments has fifty apartments for veterans and their families. Learn more at helpusa.org.

U.S. VETS. The Las Vegas location of U.S. VETS operates transitional and permanent housing for more than 330 veterans at a time. Employment services are provided through a workforce program that helps over 110 veterans return to employment each year. Additionally, over 400 veteran households are provided rapid rehousing and homeless prevention services annually. For more information, visit *USVets.org/locations/las-vegas*.

SHARE Village. Dedicated to the creation of an environment that is home to US veterans, SHARE Village is a unique and innovative approach to holistic and comprehensive housing with 24/7/365 crisis-intervention and intensive support services. Public and private collaborative partnerships provide supplies and services to residents, including housing, medical and mental health services, employment training, referrals and placements, food pantry and nutrition programs, and transportation to the VA hospital and primary care clinics. Learn more at *SHARELasVegas.org*.

Capitol Hill Building Veterans Outreach Center. This center in Reno provides food, showers, and other free resources. Call 775-786-7200 or 1-877-222-VETS (8387) for more information.

Volunteers of America. In northern Nevada, Volunteers of America offers access to affordable housing communities, ReStart, The Resource Center, shelters, the Village on Sage Street, and Reno Works:

- The **Resource Center** provides homeless individuals access to computers, telephones, and mail delivery to help move toward greater self-sufficiency, obtain and maintain employment, and access additional community resources in a safe, welcoming environment.

- **Reno Works** provides job training and income while holistically addressing and treating other factors that contribute to homelessness. Through the intensive life skills classes, participants receive the tools necessary to gain sustained employment, housing, and self-sufficiency.

- The **Men's Shelter** offers emergency shelter for up to 159 single men and also provides support services, such as referrals for permanent housing, healthcare, education, and career opportunities.

- The **Village on Sage Street** is a unique co-ed, dorm-style facility consisting of eight modular buildings with 216 small single-occupancy units for individuals who are at least eighteen years of age. The village is primarily designed to serve working people earning minimum wage or those with other income sources such as social security or disability as a low-income housing option.

Home Is Possible for Heroes Program. This program gives honorably discharged veterans, active duty military personnel, and surviving spouses more buying power and even more opportunities to experience the joys of homeownership for less. Key benefits include:

- Below-market fixed interest rate for a thirty-year loan
- Reduced monthly mortgage payment
- No first-time homebuyer requirement
- Eligible to combine with the mortgage credit
- Certificate (MCC) with program fees waived
- Available statewide

To qualify, veterans must meet these criteria:

- Income below $98,500 (in 2020)
- Home price below $400,000
- Government-insured loans only (no conventional loans)
- Minimum credit score of 640 (in 2020)

- Must live in home as primary residence
- Homebuyer education course required
- Must meet standard underwriting requirements
- One-time fee applies

Learn more at *HomeIsPossibleNV.org*.

Legal Assistance

Nevada Attorney General's Office of Military Legal Assistance (OMLA). OMLA provides pro bono legal assistance and representation to active duty, reserve, and National Guard service members in a wide area of civil law matters as well as with wills and powers of attorney. Additionally, the program seeks to educate Nevada's communities and create policies aimed at addressing issues affecting the state's military families. OMLA is a comprehensive, statewide program combining the joint efforts of legal aid organizations, private sponsors, and the State Bar of Nevada to address the need for affordable legal representation in military communities. Visit *nvagomla.nv.gov* to learn more.

Nevada Veterans Court. Veterans Court is a multijurisdictional court that accepts clients with misdemeanor, gross misdemeanor, and felony charges. To be eligible, the defendant needs to have been, or currently be, in the military. A substance abuse or mental health diagnosis and a relation between criminal behavior and military experiences is also necessary. Referrals may come from the Public Defenders' Office, law enforcement, judges, pretrial officers, jail staff, or family members.

A public defender is assigned to all clients. Clients on probation will be assigned the same probation officer. There is also a Veterans Justice Outreach representative from the VA, a therapist from the VA, and a representative from the Nevada Department of Veterans Services. The

Veterans Court program lasts a minimum of one year. There are no fees for Veterans Court. Fees ordered by the original court, such as restitution or supervision fees, still apply and must be paid in full before graduation from Veterans Court. For more information and referral forms, visit *WashoeCourts.com/SpecialtyCourts/Veterans*. (Note: Not all counties in Nevada participate in the Veterans Court Program.)

Nevada Department of Veteran Services (NDVS) Veteran Justice Reintegration Program. NDVS supports veterans in the criminal justice system by partnering with government and private organizations. The NDVS Veteran Justice Reintegration Program aims to ensure that veterans involved in the criminal justice system have access to services, programs, and resources that will enable them to return to society as productive members with promising futures. A new "Veterans Reintegration Checklist" begins the process of matching incarcerated veterans with benefits, services, and resources before their release. Veterans can learn more here: *veterans.nv.gov/benefits-and-services*.

NEW MEXICO
Veteran population: 7.0% (148,377)

Financial Benefits

Income Tax. Active duty military pay is tax-free. Beginning in 2022, up to $10,000 of military retirement is tax-free, and the amount will increase to $20,000 in 2023 and to $30,000 after that.

Disabled Veteran Property Tax Exemption. Up to $4,000 of the taxable value of property, including the community or joint property of spouses, is exempt from the imposition of the tax if the property is owned by a New Mexico resident veteran or resident unmarried surviving spouse. Certain discharges may render a veteran ineligible for this benefit.

Exemption from Excise Taxes on Vehicle Purchases. Residents of New Mexico who served in the US Armed Forces are exempt from the Motor Vehicle Excise Tax if they suffered, while serving in the armed forces or from a service-connected cause, the loss or complete and total loss of use of (1) one or both legs at or above the ankle, or (2) one or both arms at or above the wrist.

5% Procurement Advantage for Veteran-Owned Businesses or Contractors. The state of New Mexico sets aside an additional 5% hiring preference for veteran-owned businesses or contractors over the existing 5% preference currently established for locally owned businesses during the bidding process for state contracts and jobs.

Housing and Healthcare Benefits

New Mexico State Veterans' Home (NMSVH). NMSVH is New Mexico's only nursing facility for veterans. It is centrally located in the town of Truth or Consequences, halfway between Albuquerque and El Paso, and is nestled in the Rio Grande Valley and situated on twelve beautifully landscaped acres. Subject to availability, any veteran with an honorable discharge from the US Armed Forces is eligible for admission.

Education Benefits

Wartime Veteran Scholarship. This scholarship may be available to any veteran who has served in combat; was awarded the Southwest Asia Service Medal, Global War on Terrorism Expeditionary Medal, Iraq Campaign Medal, Afghanistan Campaign Medal, or any other medal issued for service in the Armed Forces of the United States in support of any US military campaign or armed conflict as defined by Congress or presidential executive order for service after August 1, 1990; and has exhausted all available federal GI Bill education benefits. This scholarship allows eligible veterans to complete their education without worrying about GI Bill deadlines that may not fit their time frame.

In-State Tuition for Veterans. Veterans, their spouses, and their children do not need to wait to establish in-state residency status when applying for college. Those who wish to use their GI Bill benefits can immediately take advantage of less expensive resident in-state tuition rates at any state-funded college, university, vocational school, or vocational training program.

World War II and Korean War Veterans' High School Diploma. Any veteran who left a New Mexico high school before graduating to serve in World War II or the Korean War will be awarded a valid high school diploma issued from the high school they attended.

Vietnam Veteran Scholarship. The Vietnam Veteran Scholarship will pay tuition at any state-funded postsecondary school, and reimbursement is available for books and fees. For any nonstate institution, tuition reimbursement will not exceed the highest resident tuition charged at a state institution, and the fees and costs of books will not exceed financial aid guidelines. All billing is directed to the New Mexico Higher Education Department. Eligible veterans must have been honorably discharged from the US Armed Forces, have been a resident of New Mexico at original time of entry into the US Armed Forces or have lived in New Mexico for ten years or more, and have been awarded a Vietnam Campaign Medal for service in Vietnam between August 5, 1964 and the official termination of the Vietnam conflict as designated by executive order of the president of the United States.

Children of Deceased Veterans. This scholarship applies to matricular fees, board and room rent, and books and supplies for the use and benefit of the children, not under sixteen and not over twenty-six years of age, of (1) those persons who were residents of New Mexico at the time of entry into US military service during World War I, World War II, or any action in which the military forces of the United States are engaged in armed conflict, and who were killed in action or died of another cause during the conflict or as a result of such military service; (2) deceased members of the New Mexico National Guard who were killed while on active duty in the service of the state after having been called to active duty by the governor; and (3) deceased members of the New Mexico state police who were killed while on active duty in the service of the state. Eligible children may be admitted to state educational institutions free of tuition. In addition to the free tuition, the scholarship pays up to a maximum of $300 in fees for any child for one year.

On-the-Job Training (OJT). State OJT programs typically last between six months and two years. Participating veterans work under a skilled worker's supervision and draw monthly benefits from the US Veterans' Administration. Upon completion, the veteran is awarded a certificate by the employer, indicating the successful completion of that training program. Some of the programs offered include heating and air-conditioning repair, law enforcement, security and corrections officer training, warehouse operations, shipping and receiving, landscaping, welding, commercial painting, auto mechanics, and food and beverage industry training.

Recreational Discounts, Licenses, and Passes

State Parks. Every Veterans Day holiday, any New Mexico resident who was honorably discharged from the US Armed Forces or is currently on active duty—along with their spouse and children—is entitled to free use of any New Mexico state park. Admission fees will also be waived for campsites, the Museum of New Mexico, the New Mexico Museum of Natural History, and the New Mexico Museum of Space History.

Any veteran rated 50% or higher service-connected disabled may obtain an annual free day-use pass and three free nights of camping for personal use only.

Any veteran rated 50% or higher service-connected disabled may obtain a free state monument and museum pass for personal use only.

Hunting and Fishing Licenses. Any veteran rated 100% service-connected disabled is eligible for a free lifetime New Mexico small-game hunting and fishing license.

New Mexico's 41,646 service-connected disabled veterans may apply for a reduced-fee $10 small-game and fishing license—no matter what age their disability.

Hunting licenses for deer, antelope, elk, javelina, and turkey may be sold to nonresident disabled US military members or veterans at resident license-fee rates if the applicant is undergoing a rehabilitation program utilizing hunting activities supported by the VA or an authorized nonprofit organization.

OREGON

Veteran population: 6.8% (290,035)

Financial Benefits

Property Tax Exemption. If you are a disabled veteran with a 40% or higher disability rating, you may be entitled to exempt $24,071 or $28,886 of your homestead property's assessed value from property taxes. The exemption amount increases by 3% each year. The exemption is first applied to your home and then to your taxable personal property.

Conservatorship Program. This financial management program is available to certain veterans, their dependents, and survivors to help meet their current and future needs. Visit the Oregon Department of Veterans Affairs website for contact information and benefits assistance.

Oregon Veterans' Emergency Financial Assistance Program (OVEFAP). When funds are available, this financial assistance program is available for veterans and their immediate family (spouse, unremarried surviving spouse, child, or stepchild) who are in need of emergency financial assistance. Assistance needs include, but are not limited to, emergency or temporary housing and related housing expenses, such as expenses for utilities, insurance, house repairs, rent assistance or food; emergency medical or dental expenses; emergency transportation; expenses related to starting a business, such as business licenses or occupational licenses; temporary income after military discharge; and legal assistance. *Note:* This program is funded quarterly and often runs out of funds. Veterans are encouraged to contact the ODVA for assistance and to find out if funds are currently available.

Housing and Healthcare Benefits

Veterans' Homes. Oregon runs two veteran's homes: one in The Dalles and the other in Lebanon. Admission is open to all veterans with an other-than-dishonorable discharge, their spouses, and Gold Star parents. Applicants must need skilled nursing care and be able to pay their share of the cost of care.

Education Benefits

Oregon National Guard State Tuition Assistance (ONGSTA). ONGSTA provides funding for tuition at Oregon community colleges (up to ninety quarter credits), public universities, Oregon Health & Science University (up to 180 quarter credits), eligible postsecondary private institutions (up to 180 quarter credits or 120 semester credits), and certificate programs for current Oregon National Guard service members. Tuition is funded up to the average of the in-state resident tuition rate at the seven Oregon public universities. ONGSTA also provides a book allowance up to $1,000 per academic year.

Oregon In-State Tuition and Fees for Student Veterans. Public universities listed in ORS 352.002 and community colleges charge the resident rate for enrolled undergraduates and graduates who meet these criteria:

- Served in the US Armed Forces
- Were relieved or discharged from that service with either an honorable discharge or a general discharge under honorable conditions
- Are undergraduate students newly enrolled after September 15, 2013, or graduate students newly enrolled after September 15, 2014
- Provide proof that they have established a physical presence in Oregon within twelve months of being enrolled at the public university or community college

Voyager Tuition Assistance Program for Oregon Resident Reserve Component Service Members. This program is offered to Oregon resident service members who served on active duty in the Oregon National Guard or the US Armed Forces Reserve in a combat zone on or after September 11, 2001. Voyager is a "last dollar award," meaning it pays after all other federal military education benefits are used. The typical maximum length of the award is four years for undergraduate programs (a fifth year may be approved under certain programs). This benefit is only available to those seeking their initial bachelor's degree, and it carries a maximum credit limit of fifteen course credits beyond the minimum needed for degree completion. It does not cover e-campus or distance courses and is not transferable to a spouse or dependents. For more information, students should contact the admissions office at the school they plan to attend.

Benefit for Dependents of Deceased, Disabled Oregon Veterans. A full tuition waiver for a bachelor's or master's degree at any Oregon University System institution may be available for children or spouses of service members who died on active duty, became 100% disabled in connection with military service, or died as a result of a disability sustained on active duty.

Recreational Discounts, Licenses, and Passes

Hunting and Angling Licenses. Service-connected disabled veterans rated 25% or more are eligible for a free lifetime Oregon hunting and angling license. Disabled veterans are eligible for an Oregon elk tag at a reduced cost. Active members of the US Armed Forces or veterans who retired within twelve months of the date of application may apply to the Oregon Military Department for reimbursement for the cost of a resident annual hunting and angling license.

State Parks. Service-connected disabled veterans and active duty military personnel on leave may receive free day-use parking and free overnight rental of RV and tent campsites for up to five consecutive days and no more than ten days total in a calendar month.

UTAH

Veteran population: 3.4% (132,120)

Financial Benefits

Utah Disabled Veteran and Survivors Property Tax Exemption. Utah offers a property tax exemption of up to $283,964 of the taxable value of the residence or personal property of disabled veterans, who must have a 10% or greater service-connected disability. The amount of the exemption is based on the disability percentage of the veteran. Veterans with 100% disability can claim the entire amount of the authorized exemption. If the percentage of disability is less than 100%, the veteran will receive a percentage of the total exemption allowable that is equal to their disability percentage. The surviving spouse or minor orphans of a service member who was killed in action or died in the line of duty are eligible for an exemption of the total value of their primary residence and all personal property not used for trade or business.

Military Leave. Utah state, county, city, or other municipal government employees who are members of the organized army reserve or National Guard are allowed full pay (some exceptions apply) for fifteen days of military leave per year for annual military encampments. This military leave is in addition to and distinguished from the annual accrued vacation leave with pay.

Housing and Healthcare Benefits

Utah Veteran First-Time Homebuyer Grant Program. This program offers veterans and service members who are first-time homebuyers a $2,500 grant toward the purchase of their first home in Utah. Homes must be occupied as their primary residence within thirty days of execution of the mortgage closing documents.

Utah State Veterans Homes. Quality nursing and healthcare services are provided for Utah veterans with US military service during peacetime or wartime. Although wartime service is not a requirement for admission to the homes, wartime veterans with one day or more of wartime service, as recognized by state and federal laws, receive priority. A veteran's spouse or surviving spouse may also be eligible for admission, provided that the marriage to the veteran occurred no less than one year before the application. There are currently four Veterans Homes in Utah for eligible veterans, spouses, and Gold Star parents:

- William E. Christoffersen Salt Lake Veterans Home
- George E. Wahlen Ogden Veterans Home
- Southern Utah Veterans Home
- Mervyn Sharp Bennion Central Utah Veterans Home

Homeless Veterans Fellowship. The Homeless Veterans Fellowship provides veterans with up to eighteen months of transitional housing as well as emergency food bags and personal hygiene items. Coffee and doughnuts are provided during open hours. Learn more at 541 23rd Street Ogden, UT 84401 or by calling 801-392-7662.

Valor House. Located on the VA campus in Salt Lake City, Valor House provides homeless veterans with up to two years of transitional housing. There are a total of sixty beds available. For more information regarding this program, call 801-582-1565 ext. 2703 or 1-800-613-4012 ext. 2703.

State-Sponsored Life Insurance (SSLI) for Utah National Guard Service Members. The National Guard Association of Utah offers SSLI to Utah National Guard service members. This program coordinates several voluntary group life policies designed to help meet the needs of service members and their families. Every member of the Utah National Guard is covered with $1,000 SSLI at no cost.

Employment Benefits

Veterans' Job Preference. Eligible veterans, spouses, or unremarried widow(er)s are granted either five or ten additional points for employment preference. These points are added to the results of any written or oral exam, other related qualifying technique, or examinations by any Utah government entity (e.g., state, county, local municipality, etc.).

Veterans Hiring Priority. Applicants must belong to one of the following categories to be eligible for hiring priority:

- Veteran who served on active duty in the US Armed Forces for 180 consecutive days or more (active duty for training does not qualify) and received an honorable discharge
- Current or former service member in a reserve component of the US Armed Forces who served on active duty in a campaign or expedition for which a campaign medal has been authorized and received an honorable discharge
- Veteran who received a disability rating from the VA or a branch of the US Armed Forces
- Spouse or unremarried surviving spouse of an eligible veteran
- Purple Heart recipient
- Service member who retired from the US Armed Forces

Any officers, agents, or representatives of the state or any contractors performing work for the Utah state government who willfully fail to give preference to an eligible veteran are guilty of a misdemeanor.

Veterans' Employment Representatives. Disabled Veterans Outreach Program representatives and Local Veterans Employment Representatives are located statewide in various employment centers of the Utah Department of Workforce Services. They provide intensive employment-related services and aid for veterans, including referrals to employment opportunities, help with résumé writing and referral letters, ensuring that veterans hiring preference is adhered to, and employment counseling.

Accelerated Credentialing to Employment (ACE). The ACE program assists Utah veterans, actively drilling members of the National Guard and army reserve, and their respective spouses in overcoming most barriers to employment or even better employment. This program offers short-term training as well as assistance in attaining certificates and licenses using their military experience.

Veterans Business Resource Center. This program ensures that veteran entrepreneurs and their family members have the best resources available to start or grow a business in Utah. The program works closely with the Utah Veteran-Owned Business Partnership to help serve the 17,000 veteran-owned businesses and veteran entrepreneurs throughout the state. Learn more about free services for veterans, military personnel, and their immediate families by contacting 801-957-5288 or visiting *Veterans.Utah.gov/business*.

Utah Veterans Employment Opportunity Program (VEOP). VEOP gives eligible veterans and their spouses or surviving spouses the option to be hired into designated career-service positions with a six-month on-the-job examination period instead of a competitive hiring process. Applicants must upload the veteran's DD 214 to the Utah Job Seeker website and indicate that they would like to be considered for hire under this program. Hiring officials may choose to interview and hire a qualified applicant who has opted into this program separately from other candidates.

Extension of Utah Professional Licenses for Service Members in the National Guard and US Armed Forces Reserve. Any professional license held by a service member serving in a reserve component of the US Armed Forces that expires while they are serving on active duty may be extended until ninety days after they are discharged from active duty status.

Education Benefits

Purple Heart Tuition Waiver. Utah resident Purple Heart recipients are eligible for a tuition waiver in all Utah System of Higher Education schools. This benefit can be used toward a degree up to and including a master's degree. For more information, students should contact the admissions office at the educational institution they plan to attend.

In-State Tuition Rates. Any institution in the Utah System of Higher Education will grant residency for tuition purposes to:

- Nonresident service members and their immediate family members who are stationed in Utah
- Nonresident US Armed Forces veterans who received an honorable discharge within twelve months of applying and their immediate family (must demonstrate intent to become a Utah resident)
- Service members and veterans who were Utah residents for one year prior to active duty service in the US Armed Forces
- Service members in the Utah National Guard or a US Armed Forces reserve unit in Utah

Veterans Tuition Gap Program. This program enables qualifying Utah resident military veterans to receive tuition assistance for the last school year at state institutions of higher education if they are eligible under applicable chapters of the post-9/11 GI Bill. It is for tuition only and does not include housing, books, or other fees. They must not have earned previous degrees, must make satisfactory academic progress, and must have three or fewer semesters left to graduate.

Scott B. Lundell Tuition Waiver for Surviving Dependents. This benefit waives the undergraduate tuition at state institutions of higher education for the surviving dependents of a Utah resident military member killed in the line of duty after September 11, 2001. This waiver does not apply to fees, books, or housing expenses. The Utah Department of Veterans and Military Affairs is the administering agency for this benefit.

Honorary High School Diplomas. Veterans of World War II, the Korean War, or the Vietnam War who left high school for military service during those conflicts may be eligible to receive honorary high school diplomas from the particular school they attended. Contact the local school district for information on how to receive the diploma.

Veterans Upward Bound (VUB). VUB is funded by the Department of Education and sponsored by Weber State University. It provides an invaluable service by assisting veterans in obtaining admission to the state's postsecondary schools. Veterans can receive free instruction and tutorial assistance in mathematics, English, and basic computer applications. These services are provided to veterans in the counties of Salt Lake, Davis, and Weber. For more information, call 801-626-7173.

Recreational Discounts, Licenses, and Passes

Bus and TRAX Reduced-Fare Cards. Utah Transit Authority (UTA) offers reduced-fare cards for riding UTA buses, TRAX light-rail systems, and FrontRunner commuter rail to veterans meeting one of the following criteria by having a disability that causes difficulty getting on or off a system, standing in a moving system, reading system schedules and understanding signs, or hearing announcements by system operators. To be eligible for the reduced fare, you must provide one of the following documents, along with a completed application form:

- Proof of age (sixty-five years or older) and photo ID (may be same item), e.g., a state driver's license, pictured VA card, or passport
- Medicare card and photo ID
- Healthcare provider statement form from one of the following approved providers: physician, optometrist, audiologist, psychologist, psychiatrist, physician's assistant, Advanced Practice Registered Nurse, Nurse Practitioner, Licensed Clinical Social Worker

Upon approval of your eligibility, the $2.00 card fee is due. FAREPAY cards are $2.00 plus a $5.00 load. FrontRunner connects Salt Lake, Davis, and Weber counties and has stations in Salt Lake City, Woods Cross, Farmington, Clearfield, Roy, Layton, and Ogden. Each station has connections to UTA's bus system and park-and-ride lots.

Fishing License Privilege. Veterans with a 20% or higher service-connected disability rating with the federal VA can purchase a fishing license at a reduced cost of $12.00 per year. To verify eligibility, provide a summary of benefits letter obtained from the VA. You can apply for a license on the Utah Division of Wildlife Resources website, by calling 1-800-827-1000, or by visiting the regional VA Salt Lake City Public Contact Office.

Free Use of Armories. Per Utah Code 71-3-1, federally chartered veteran's organizations have the right to the free use of armories owned or leased by the state of Utah, provided that such use does not interfere with their use by the National Guard or organized militia of the state.

Veterans with Disabilities Honor Pass for State Parks. Veterans with a 50% or greater service-connected disability can provide a current summary of benefits letter issued by the VA to obtain the Honor Pass at select locations across Utah. For locations, call 801-538-7220 or visit the Utah State Parks website at *stateparks.utah.gov/resources/ contact-our-regional-offices.*

Vehicles, Licenses, Plates, and Privileges

Disabled Veteran License Plates. A disabled veteran license plate is available for all veterans with a service-connected disability. This plate has a one-time $15.00 fee and no additional renewal fees. To prove eligibility, present a military ID card or other documentation and a VA Summary of Benefits Letter. This plate does not qualify for disabled parking privileges.

Veteran Status on Utah Driver's License and Utah ID Card. Veterans can now have "Veteran" printed on their state-issued driver's license or ID card by going to any state driver's license or ID office and indicating veteran status on the application. Eligible veterans must have served on active duty and have an honorable or general discharge. Veterans must provide a DD 214 or a report of separation to have their status verified. All renewal fees are still applicable.

Purple Heart Fee Exemption. Recipients of the Purple Heart with a Purple Heart license plate are exempt from paying the fees related to motor vehicle license and registration, excluding property taxes and age-based fees, which are still applicable.

WASHINGTON
Veteran population: 7.1% (546,892)

Financial Benefits

Property Tax Exemption. Income-based exemptions and deferrals are available to seniors, those retired due to disability, and veterans compensated at the 80% service-connected rate. Widow(er)s of 80% disabled veterans may also qualify for assistance. Contact your county assessor for more information.

Washington State Property Tax Assistance Program for Surviving Spouses of Veterans. Surviving spouses of eligible veterans can receive a grant to help pay their property taxes. The grant amount is based on the applicant's income, the value of the residence, and the local levy rates. The grant does not have to be repaid if the applicant continues to live in the residence until at least December 15 in the year a grant is received. The surviving spouse must own and occupy a primary residence in Washington and have a combined disposable income of $40,000 or less.

Washington State VA Veterans Innovations Program (VIP). VIP provides financial assistance to veterans who served on or after September 11, 2001 and are facing financial hardships. Eligible veterans must be

Washington residents, have served under honorable conditions, be experiencing financial hardship where income is not sufficient to meet basic needs, present a discernable positive outcome, and make a request that is within the grant funding capabilities.

Housing Benefits

State Veterans Homes. The Washington State Department of Veterans Affairs serves veterans in four veterans homes, all of which are Medicare- and Medicaid-certified facilities where veterans are treated with the dignity and respect they deserve in settings that provide a sense of belonging unique to veterans. Each home provides twenty-four-hour nursing care, medical care, and pharmacy services as well as a number of supportive programs and services, including physical therapy, occupational therapy, recreational activities, social services, hospice, religious programs, and transportation. Veterans rated 70%–100% service-connected disabled or whose service-connected disability is the reason nursing care is needed may have their nursing home care paid by the federal VA.

Veterans Transitional Housing Program. The Veterans Transitional Housing Program is in Port Orchard and Orting, Washington. Transitional housing facilities assist those in need of stable housing, vocational rehabilitation, and increased income potential. Veterans are surrounded with supportive staff and wraparound services designed to lead to their successful completion of the program and a successful return to the community.

- On-Site Chemical Dependency Services: Veterans in the program have access to individual and group chemical dependency services, including AA and NA groups. The program is a zero-tolerance environment, with random drug and alcohol testing.

- On-Site Mental Health Services: Veterans in the program have access to mental health services to identify issues that need to be addressed and to develop a course of treatment. The treatment plan may include individual and/or group mental health services. Part of the treatment may include life skills training and community volunteer work.

- On-Site Job Center: An on-site job center is available to veterans in the program, providing access to computers, internet, email, voicemail, and fax services. Employment and training services are provided collaboratively by program staff, WorkSource, volunteers, community providers, and the local business community. Employment services include vocational guidance, job-readiness skills, computer familiarity, computer-assisted job search, internet and email guidance, résumé development, and job referrals.

- Transportation: There is a van to transport veterans in the program to case-management-related appointments. The Port Orchard facility is also located on bus lines and is accessible from the Seattle area by ferry.

- Women Veterans Wing: The Women Veterans Wing provides more privacy and security for women veterans participating in the Transitional Housing Program.

Washington State Housing Finance Commission Veterans Down Payment Assistance Loan Program. The Veterans Down Payment Assistance Loan Program is a down payment assistance, second mortgage program with a 3% interest rate and payments deferred for up to thirty years for Washington veterans. The program combines with the Home Advantage first mortgage loan program. Eligible households may qualify for a maximum loan amount of up to $10,000.

Employment Benefits

Veteran-Owned Business Certification. State-based businesses at least 51% owned by veterans are eligible for certification. Public agencies are encouraged to increase contracts with veteran-owned businesses.

Washington State Employment Military Service Credit in Retirement System. State employees who participate in the Washington State Department of Retirement Systems (DRS) who leave their state employment to serve in the US Armed Forces may be eligible to receive up to ten years of what is called interruptive military service credit for the time they served. Service credit is one of the factors used in computing state retirement pay, and increasing service credit increases future retirement benefits. Service members can receive five years of service credit free for service during a wartime period or for service when a campaign medal was authorized. Service members can purchase five additional years of credit by paying any required employee contributions. Credit for wartime service must be requested within five years of returning to their DRS-covered employment.

Washington State Department of Labor and Industries Apprenticeship Programs. Some apprenticeships in Washington offer direct entry into their programs for veterans. Apprenticeships combine on-the-job training with related classroom instruction under the supervision of a journey-level professional. Apprentices are paid while they learn and develop knowledge, skills, and abilities in a new career field. Veterans may be eligible for VA education benefits to pay for books, supplies, and housing expenses. After completing a registered apprenticeship program, apprentices receive a professional credential that is recognized nationwide.

Washington State Department of Health Military Licensure Benefits. The Washington State Department of Health offers expedited licensing for the spouse or domestic partner of service members in the US Armed Forces who are stationed in Washington. In addition, the department will accept military education, training, and experience toward meeting the license requirements for service members and veterans for certain entry-level health professions.

Washington State Employee Leave for Military Service. State employees who are service members in a reserve component of the US Armed Forces can receive military leave with pay for up to twenty-one working days during each fiscal year. This leave can be used for required military duty, training, or drills. Service members are charged military leave only for the days they are scheduled to work.

Washington State Employment Veterans' Hiring Preference. Washington offers veteran hiring preference for eligible veterans and their spouses or surviving spouses. Applicants must meet the requirements for the position and be able to perform the duties required.

Education Benefits

Free or Reduced Tuition. State colleges and universities may provide reduced tuition for veterans. Dependents of 100% disabled or veterans who died in service may be eligible for a full tuition waiver.

High School Diplomas for Wartime Veterans. Washington's Operation Recognition will award high school diplomas to veterans who left high school before they received their diploma to serve in the US Armed Forces during World War II, the Korean War, or the Vietnam War. Veterans who have received a GED are also eligible.

Military Interstate Children's Compact Commission (MIC3) on Educational Opportunity. The purpose of this compact is to remove barriers to educational success imposed on children of military families because of frequent moves and deployment of their parents.

Recreational Discounts, Licenses, and Passes

Hunting and Fishing Licenses. The Department of Fish and Wildlife offers reduced license fees for veterans rated 30% service connected or more. Permits are also available for companion assisted hunting and fishing. Service members in the Washington National Guard are eligible for a free annual hunting license package that includes a big-game license (deer, elk, bear, and cougar with tags) and a small game license with a migratory bird permit.

State Parks. Free camping and day-use entry is offered to Washington veterans with a service-connected disability of at least 30%.

State Ferries and Other Transit. State ferries and local transit authorities may offer reduced rates for disabled veterans.

WYOMING
Veteran population: 8.1% (46,844)

Financial Benefits and Resources

Veterans Property Tax Exemption. Eligible resident veterans and their spouses receive an exemption that applies to taxes on a primary residence, lowering the assessed value by $3,000. If the exemption is not used on property, it may be applied to a vehicle's licensing fee.·

Personal Financial Counselor. The Wyoming Personal Financial Advisor Program provides free, confidential, personal financial counseling and group presentations to Wyoming National Guard members, veterans, and their families. This program includes advice about resolving financial problems, budgeting and spending planning, retirement planning, major purchases (home, auto, college), identity theft, and Thrift Savings Plan planning. The personal financial advisor can help with debt issues, credit management, insurance, security clearance concerns related to financial issues, and most other issues that are financial in nature.

Housing Benefits

Veterans' Home of Wyoming (VHW). The VHW is a 117-bed assisted living facility situated in the beautiful foothills of the Bighorn Mountains. Built on the grounds of the former Fort McKinney, the home is located three miles west of Buffalo on US Highway 16. The facility offers two-room suites for married couples and private rooms for single residents.

Wyoming Military Assistance Trust Fund. This fund provides financial assistance for service members and their dependents in times of financial hardship or emergencies that are directly related to state or federal active duty service. All grant applications will be forwarded to the service member's unit for consideration.

Education Benefits

Wyoming Tuition Assistance for Veterans and Surviving Dependents. Wyoming will pay tuition at community colleges or the University of Wyoming for overseas combat veterans, surviving spouses, and dependents. Students can receive financial assistance for eight semesters within an eight-year period.

Wyoming Tuition Assistance for Surviving Dependents of a Wyoming National Guard Service Member. Wyoming will pay the matriculation fees and tuition at any university, community college, or vocational training institution in Wyoming for the children and spouse of any member of the Wyoming National Guard who dies or sustains a permanent total disability while serving on state active duty or any authorized training duty.

Wyoming National Guard (WYNG) Educational Assistance Plan. The WYNG Educational Assistance Plan pays 100% resident rate tuition and mandatory fees at state-sponsored community colleges and the University of Wyoming toward the completion of a specialized certificate, bachelor's, master's, or doctoral degree.

High School Diplomas for Wartime Veterans. Through Operation Recognition, wartime veterans who left high school to serve in the US Armed Forces may be eligible for a high school diploma if they served between December 8, 1941 and December 31, 1946; June 27, 1950 and January 31, 1955; or February 28, 1961 and May 7, 1975.

Military Interstate Children's Compact Commission (MIC3) on Educational Opportunity. The purpose of this compact is to remove barriers to educational success imposed on children of military families because of frequent moves and deployment of their parents.

Employment Benefits

Wyoming Department of Workforce Services (DWS) Veterans Program. DWS Employment and Training Workforce Centers offer employment and training services to veterans who served on active duty in the US Armed Forces and eligible spouses on a priority of service basis.

Wyoming Veterans Hiring Preference in State Employment. Wyoming offers a hiring preference to eligible veterans and their surviving spouses when they apply for state employment. Applicants must meet the requirements for the position and be able to accomplish the duties of that position.

Paid Military Leave for Wyoming State Employees Who Are Reserve Component Service Members. State employees receive fifteen days of paid military leave per calendar year without loss of seniority, status, efficiency rating, vacation, sick leave, or other benefits. National Guard and US Armed Forces reserve service members who have been state employees for at least one year and are on orders for drill, annual training, or active duty are eligible.

Other Benefits, Resources, and Records

Wyoming Veterans Commission. The Wyoming Veterans Commission works diligently to assist veterans with benefits, whether by trying to pass legislation, establishing programs, or providing information on available benefits. If you need further assistance, don't hesitate to contact one of the VSOs located around the state. A comprehensive guide to Wyoming veteran benefits is published biennially and can be found at *WyoMilitary.Wyo.gov.*

Military Records. The Wyoming Military Department Records Office stores and can provide copies the DD 214 for all veterans who listed Wyoming as their home of record at the time of their separation and military service, and records for veterans and retirees of the Wyoming Army and Air National Guard.

Transition Assistance Advisor (TAA). The TAA Skyline Team primarily supports uniformed service members and their families by ensuring they understand the services available through the VA and the military health system. Additionally, TAAs coordinate resources for these members and their families with the myriad service programs provided by the VA and DOD, including TRICARE, Veterans Service Organizations, and other supporting agencies. The office is located in Cheyenne and can be reached at 307-772-5163.

Recreational Discounts, Licenses, and Passes

Hunting and Fishing Licenses. Wyoming resident veterans with at least a 50% disability can get a lifetime fishing license for free. Wyoming resident veterans with 100% disability can get a lifetime gamebird, small-game, and fishing license for free. Wyoming resident Purple Heart recipients can get a free lifetime bird hunting, small game hunting and fishing license. Any Wyoming veteran who is sixty-five years of age or older and has lived in Wyoming for thirty or more continuous years can receive a pioneer-bird, small-game, and fishing license for free.

State Parks. A free lifetime day-use and camping pass to all Wyoming state parks, recreation areas, archaeological sites, and historic sites is available to Wyoming resident veterans with at least a 50% disability.

PART 3

OTHER BENEFITS

You've probably heard businesses talk about offering discounts to veterans. Whenever I did, I certainly took advantage of them! But I was never sure who offered what. I always wished there were a comprehensive list to help me decide how and where to shop. So my team and I created one.

In this section, we will go beyond federal and state government benefits to learn about the ways in which civilians are offering help. It is all part of this book's holistic approach to connecting veterans and their families with the best resources. Chapter 13 takes a deep dive into services offered by nonprofit organizations, running the gamut from mental health treatment centers to recreational excursions. Many of these are geared toward helping veterans reintegrate after discharge, which is a big part of our mission at VA Claims Insider, too. Take advantage of these opportunities! Take your kids on a free week-long fishing trip—it's a no-brainer.

Note that a lot of the specifics we mention were accurate at the time of the book's publication but may have changed by the time you read this. We recommend checking each resource directly for the most up-to-date information.

The same disclaimer applies to Chapter 14 in which we will tell you about a truly insane number of discounts for-profit businesses want to give disabled veterans and their families as a way of saying thank you for wearing the uniform. While reading this chapter, maybe you'll find a few ways to say, "You're welcome." *Boom!*

How to Approach Part 3

The chapters in this section give you a laundry list of possible benefits, support, services, and discounts. Read through them and note which ones interest you. Then use the contact information and follow the instructions to access those benefits.

★ ★ ★

CHAPTER THIRTEEN

NONPROFIT RESOURCE LIST

This list provides information about groups that offer support and resources to veterans.

GENERAL SERVICES

Cell Phones for Soldiers

Cell Phones for Soldiers is a national nonprofit dedicated to providing cost-free communication services to active duty military members and veterans. Since 2004, the charity has provided more than 400 million minutes of airtime to service members deployed around the world, by recycling more than 25 million cell phones and reducing the impact on landfills.

Code of Support Foundation

The Code of Support Foundation supports PATRIOTlink, a cloud-based resource solution that provides access to cost-free veteran's services for service members, veterans, caregivers, and their families. Service agencies and government organizations that support veterans and the caregiver population can also use this service.

Consumer Financial Protection Bureau
Office of Servicemember Affairs

Service members should be able to accomplish their mission without worrying about illegal or harmful financial practices. The Office of Servicemember Affairs helps ensure that military personnel and their families have a voice at the Consumer Financial Protection Bureau. Military life can have some extra challenges with sometimes powerful financial repercussions. For more information, call 1-855-411-CFPB (2372).

Green Beret Foundation

This foundation serves the army's special forces, our nation's most elite soldiers. It provides help for wounded Green Berets and their families, as well as the families of those who gave their lives for our country. The foundation believes Green Berets are our nation's greatest assets. Every day, it connects them with the right resources to prosper and thrive, because given the opportunity, our nation's most elite soldiers become our nation's best leaders.

Iraq and Afghanistan Veterans of America (IAVA)

IAVA's mission is to serve and empower our post-9/11 veteran's community: "We believe these dynamic men and women represent America's future—our next greatest generation. They are our true north, and everything we do is designed to focus on them and the positive future they bring to the world."

Just Our Soldiers' Helpers (JOSH)

Founded in 2011, JOSH is an IRS-approved 501(c)(3) nonprofit organization that is volunteer led and operated. Located in Florida, it ships care packages to troops deployed around the world. Everyone associated with JOSH volunteers their time and resources to accomplish its mission.

Military Mama Network

The network's main mission is to support our troops and their families by providing supply boxes for deployed troops, moral support and information for trainees and families, and recognition and appreciation for veterans' needs. According to the organization, "over 90% of what we raise goes to our troops, veterans, and their families; the remaining 10% of our funds is used for administrative, outreach, and training costs for our large team of volunteers."

Military OneSource (MOS)

MOS is a one-stop shop for military families. It provides information on health, career planning, parenting, finances, legal issues, recreation, special needs, and more. The site also provides podcasts, webinars, discussion boards, moderated chats, and current news feeds. MOS staff will research local community resources on a case-by-case basis for any need a family may have, from counseling to childcare to auto repair. Counselors are trained at the master's level or higher and licensed to practice independently. They are available 24/7 at 1-800-342-9647 and can provide up to twelve free confidential counseling sessions per issue.

Operation: Care and Comfort (OCC)

Americans support our troops serving in times of war in many ways: by writing letters, mailing care packages, organizing welcome-home events, or showing support for a deployed service member or veteran's family. OCC provides support and comfort to "adopted" units of deployed US military service members serving in Iraq, Afghanistan, and other conflict regions. Working within communities and through donations received from all over the country, OCC assembles and ships care packages to adopted units every month until they return home. They currently support up to 200 units monthly.

Operation Gratitude

Operation Gratitude's mission is to forge strong bonds between Americans and their military and first responder heroes through volunteer services projects, acts of gratitude, and meaningful engagement in communities nationwide.

Operation Homefront

This accredited national nonprofit aims to help military families become "strong, stable, and secure" by providing valued programs and aid to veterans.

Operation Troop Appreciation (OTA)

OTA provides wish-list items for deployed military units around the globe, with a special focus on those serving in Afghanistan, the Middle East, and Africa. The wish-list items are intended to ease the burden of deployment, contribute to safety, and enable our troops to perform more effectively. OTA has provided items for over 190,000 troops since 2004. And since 2014, the Welcome Home Program has been helping to prevent homelessness and provide a hand-up for veterans experiencing poverty today.

Tragedy Assistance Program for Survivors (TAPS)

TAPS is a national organization that provides peer-based emotional support and compassionate care for anyone grieving the loss of someone who died during or as a result of military service to the United States. TAPS has assisted more than 100,000 surviving family members as well as casualty assistance officers, chaplains, and others supporting bereaved military families since 1994.

United Service Organizations (USO)

With over 250 centers worldwide, the USO works to support the military and vets with a variety of programs and services—from entertaining our troops and helping soldiers stay connected with their families to assisting vets with transitioning back into their communities.

Veterans Advantage

Veterans Advantage provides access to hundreds of offers and military discounts from Continental, United Airlines, Amtrak, Eastbay, Wendy's, Footlocker, Dell, Greyhound, car rental companies, Verizon, and many other businesses.

Veterans of Foreign Wars (VFW) Foundation

The VFW Foundation seeks to provide unique and urgently needed services that improve the lives of veterans, military personnel, and their families, all the while supporting positive citizen involvement for the betterment of US communities. One of the VFW's main services is to operate as your VSO. They offer free VA claims services, representing vets to the VA.

Vietnam Veterans of America (VVA)

VVA's goals are to promote and support the full range of issues important to Vietnam veterans, to create a new identity for this generation of veterans, and to change public perception of Vietnam veterans. Founded in 1978, VVA is a national nonprofit organization that advocates for

Vietnam vets through legislation, community support, and local and national events that recognize veterans from all service eras. Its mission is to ensure that Vietnam vets get the care and respect they have earned.

Yellow Ribbon Network

Those who have worn the uniform and their spouses, family members, and caregivers can use the Yellow Ribbon Network as a tool to simplify their search for support. One request can lead to a plethora of nonprofits that can help.

EDUCATION AND SCHOLARSHIPS

Blue Star Families (BSF)

BSF strengthens military families every day. Through career development, caregiving, and leading research on military family life, they strive to better understand and provide solutions to the challenges facing today's military families. Founded by military spouses in 2009, the organization has engaged tens of thousands of volunteers and served more than 1.5 million military family members annually, including wounded and transitioning service members and their loved ones. Free BSF worldwide membership includes military spouses, children, parents, and friends, as well as service members, veterans, and civilians.

Bob Woodruff Foundation

Bob Woodruff, a journalist, was critically injured while reporting for ABC's *World News Tonight* in 2006. He spent thirty-six days in a medically induced coma, and his wife, Lee, was introduced to many families of service members dealing with post-traumatic stress and traumatic brain injuries. Although Bob eventually recovered, the Woodruff family made it their mission to help the military and veterans struggling with these issues and many more. Today, the foundation has invested more than $125 million, awarded more than 585 grants, and reached more than 12 million vets and military families.

Children of Fallen Patriots Foundation

As a scholarship program for children who have lost a parent in the line of duty, the Children of Fallen Patriots Foundation provides much-needed support for struggling military kids and surviving spouses.

Folds of Honor

Since 2007, Folds of Honor has carried forth a singular, noble mission: to provide educational scholarships to spouses and children of America's fallen and disabled service members. It is truly one of the best veteran charities and grants up to $5,000 per year in academic scholarships for the dependents of eligible disabled veterans.

Freedom Alliance

Freedom Alliance's mission is to advance the American heritage of freedom by honoring and encouraging military service, supporting our troops, defending the freedom and sovereignty of the United States, and promoting a strong national defense. They help provide college scholarships to the children of fallen American heroes.

Gary Sinise Foundation

The Gary Sinise Foundation was established under the philanthropic direction of a forty-year advocate for our nation's defenders, actor Gary Sinise. Its outreach supports those who sacrifice to defend our country: active duty service members, veterans, first responders, and their loved ones. Although their mission is broad, the organization has created nine key programs to show gratitude for our American heroes through entertainment, family support, and acts of appreciation. The foundation works to ensure that the sacrifices of America's defenders and their families are never forgotten.

Intrepid Family of Foundations and Museum

Intrepid promotes awareness and understanding of history, science, and service through collections, exhibitions, and programming to honor our heroes, educate the public, and inspire young people. The Intrepid Family of Foundations funds the Intrepid Sea, Air & Space Museum; the Fisher House Foundation; the Intrepid Fallen Heroes Fund; and the Intrepid Relief Fund, making a difference in the lives of countless military service members, veterans, and their families through aid and educational experiences.

Pat Tillman Foundation

Since 2008, the Pat Tillman Foundation has provided academic scholarships, professional development opportunities, and a national network to empower the Tillman Scholar community. These scholars are making a difference in the fields of healthcare, business, public service, STEM, education, and the humanities.

Starfish Foundation

This foundation raises funds for scholarships to assist individuals to attend programs for emotional healing, including providing programs for military veterans to heal the emotional wounds of war. They aim to provide funds for those unable to pay for participation in Taking It Lightly and Renewal, programs designed for emotional healing and trauma recovery, and Healing Warrior Hearts, free retreats for veterans.

ThanksUSA

ThanksUSA provides need-based college, technical, and vocational school scholarships and pathways to employment for children and spouses of our troops.

EMPLOYMENT AND JOB TRAINING

FourBlock

FourBlock helps veterans build professional networks, and relationship building is at the core of all the programs and content. Everything they do supports the opportunity for a transitioning veteran to have a conversation with a hiring manager, so they both can learn from each other, discuss career opportunities, and begin to build a relationship that may lead to meaningful employment.

Hero2Hired (H2H) Program

The Department of Defense created H2H through the Yellow Ribbon Reintegration Program to make it easy for reserve component service members to connect to and find jobs with military-friendly companies. H2H offers career exploration tools, military-to-civilian skills translations, education and training resources, and a mobile app. Visit *YellowRibbon.mil* for more information.

Hire Heroes USA

Hire Heroes USA provides free job search assistance to US military members, veterans, and military spouses, while helping companies connect with opportunities to hire them.

HireVeterans.com

HireVeterans.com is the world's most trusted marketplace to search for and find top jobs for veterans. Since 2003, the site has offered a free job seeker profile for military service members, veterans, and military spouses. Note: VA Claims Insider, LLC, owns and operates this website.

The Mission Continues

The Mission Continues is dedicated to the empowerment of veterans as community-based leaders. This national organization invests in veterans and underresourced communities, developing new skillsets and equipping a growing veteran volunteer movement with the tools to drive positive change.

Train Our Troops

The vision of Train Our Troops is to provide each US veteran and their spouse with skillsets that will give them a competitive advantage in the crowded marketplace, whether they want to start a brand-new career or simply build their existing résumé to make themselves more professionally valuable. Train Our Troops focuses on getting veterans and their spouses trained, prepared, and engaged in the marketplace to obtain solid positions, allowing them to better support their families and excel in their individual careers.

USA Cares

USA Cares provides financial and advocacy assistance to post-9/11 active duty US military service personnel, veterans, and their families. They have assisted thousands of veterans and military families facing hardships related to service.

FITNESS, SPORTS, AND ENTERTAINMENT

Bikersinc

Through the Bikers Helping Veterans program, Bikersinc helps bridge the gap between the battlefield and the home front by assisting returning veterans. Started in 2012 by a veteran with a passion for motorcycles and for helping other people, the organization has mainly focused on fellow veterans from the start. As time went on, a few friends stepped in to assist with program ideas and additional funding.

Team Red, White & Blue (RWB)

Team RWB exists to guide veterans through a journey with real-life and virtual opportunities focused on building a healthier lifestyle, because a strong focus on mental and physical health is critical to ensuring veterans' best days are ahead. Their mission is to enrich the lives of America's veterans by connecting them to their community through physical and social activity.

Veteran Tickets Foundation (Vet Tix)

Vet Tix supports military personnel, veterans, and their families by providing free tickets to sporting events, concerts, and family activities (with a small delivery fee). The Tickets for Troops program is dedicated to giving back to those who have given so much. By teaming up with major sports teams, leagues, promoters, organizations, venues, and everyday event ticket holders, the organization provides free tickets to military members and veterans. To date, more than 15 million event tickets have been given out in all fifty states and Washington, DC, to service members, veterans, and their families. You can submit a wish list for tickets! Vet Tix accepts tax deductible ticket donations from individuals and companies, then donates them to veterans for free through the

Hero's Wish program. Other discounts are available as well. To learn more, visit *VetTix.org*.

XSports4Vets

XSports4Vets is dedicated to helping our nation's heroes through extreme sports, saying, "We utilize as many veteran extreme sports as we can to take the edge out of civilian life. Some of us have wounds left over from combat; others can't be seen—but we all benefit from getting out and meeting people that have been in our shoes."

HOMELESSNESS AND HOUSING

Alpha Omega Veterans Services

Alpha Omega is a 501(c)(3) nonprofit charitable organization that provides displaced and homeless veterans with the social services needed to totally reintegrate them back into society. Services include food, shelter, and clothing; referrals for training in vocational, educational, and job placement goals; community service referrals; individual and group counseling; and other offerings and facilities designed to meet their physical, social, and psychological needs. The organization promotes veterans' health, security, happiness, and usefulness in society. During their program, every veteran receives intensive counseling on both an individual and group basis to deal with combat or service-related conditions such as anger management, substance abuse, combat stress, PTSD, and other mental health disorders.

Fisher House Foundation

The Fisher House Foundation is a national not-for-profit organization established to provide support for the Fisher House program that provides free housing and "a home away from home" for the families of patients receiving medical care at major military and VA medical centers. Since its founding in 1990 by Zachary and Elizabeth Fisher, the organization has helped more than 430,000 families, saving them more than $547 million in out-of-pocket costs for housing and transportation.

Genesis Joy House Homeless Shelter

This organization facilitates social change and empowers veterans and community by providing enrichment programs and counseling services to improve quality of life. Their supportive transitional housing programs offer homeless female veterans a chance to realize their potential and achieve their dreams.

Homes for Our Troops (HFOT)

HFOT is a publicly funded 501(c)(3) nonprofit organization that builds and donates specially adapted custom homes nationwide for severely injured post-9/11 veterans with conditions such as multiple limb amputations, partial or full paralysis, and/or severe traumatic brain injury. The homes restore some of the freedom and independence veterans sacrificed while defending our country and enable them to focus on their family, recovery, and rebuilding their lives. Since its inception in 2004, nearly 90% of the organization's expenditures have gone directly to program services for veterans. HFOT builds homes where veterans choose to live and provides ongoing assistance after home delivery.

Military Warriors Support Foundation

The Military Warriors Support Foundation is a 501(c)(3) nonprofit charity founded by Lieutenant General Leroy Sisco (Ret) in 2007. Its mission is to provide support and programs that facilitate a smooth and successful transition for combat-wounded heroes and Gold Star families.

Programs focus on housing and homeownership, recreational activities, transportation assistance, and leadership development. The organization awards mortgage-free homes and payment-free vehicles to combat-wounded heroes and Gold Star spouses. In addition to the home or vehicle, the families receive family and financial mentoring.

New England Center and Home for Veterans (NECHV)

NECHV was founded in 1989 and is one of the nation's largest private resource providers for veterans of every era who face challenges or are at risk of homelessness.

Swords to Plowshares

A community-based nonprofit 501(c)(3) organization, Swords to Plowshares is dedicated to supporting nearly 3,000 homeless, low-income, and at-risk veterans in the Bay Area every year. They offer employment and job training, supportive housing programs, permanent housing placement, counseling and case management, and legal services.

HUNTING, FISHING, AND OUTDOORS

America the Beautiful National Park Pass for Military Members and Their Families

An America the Beautiful National Park Pass is your ticket to more than 2,000 federal recreation sites. Each pass covers entrance fees at national parks and national wildlife refuges as well as standard amenity fees at national forests and grasslands, and at lands managed by the Bureau of Land Management and Bureau of Reclamation. A pass covers entrance and standard amenity fees for a driver and all passengers in a personal vehicle at per-vehicle-fee areas (or up to four adults at sites that charge per person). The pass is available free of charge to US military members and dependents in the army, navy, air force, marines, and Coast Guard as well as army reserve and National Guard members.

Freedom Hunters

Freedom Hunters is a 501(c)(3) military outreach program dedicated to honoring those who protect our freedoms. Freedom Hunters reflects the outdoor community's appreciation for our troops by taking select active duty and combat veterans, families of fallen heroes, children of the deployed, and those wounded or injured on outdoor adventures. The organization's mission is empowered by the generous support of many sportsmen, conservation groups, state agencies, outfitters, corporations, and landowners.

Sierra Club's Military Outdoors (SCMO)

SCMO is at the forefront of a national movement to ensure every veteran in America has an opportunity to get outdoors when they return home after service. SCMO organizes outdoor trips for veterans, other service members, and their families because time spent in nature provides a unique experience to foster mental and physical health, emotional resilience, and leadership development.

Trinity Oaks

Trinity Oaks is a 501(c)(3) nonprofit organization founded on the premise that active participation in the outdoors is a powerful, healing, and fundamentally life-changing experience. Its mission is to use hunting, fishing, and outdoor activities to give back and make a meaningful difference in the lives of others. Outdoor activities cause a philosophical change within participants, profoundly impacting the wellness of our society. Since 2007, Trinity Oaks has impacted thousands of people who otherwise would not be able to afford the experience of the outdoors.

Veterans Expeditions

Veterans Expeditions empowers veterans to overcome challenges associated with military service through outdoor training and leadership. The goal is to create an outdoor community that builds trust, comradeship, and support networks among veterans during trips and in their home communities. The organization creates opportunities for employment in the outdoor industry and related fields and improve veterans' quality of life.

PTSD AND MENTAL HEALTH

Boot Campaign

At Boot Campaign, the mission is to unite Americans to honor and restore the lives of veterans and military families through individualized life-improving programs. Fewer than 50% of military personnel and veterans who experience invisible wounds receive care, compared to 83% who have visible wounds. Boot Campaign's comprehensive health and wellness program targets the five most common invisible wounds: PTSD, traumatic brain injury, chronic pain, self-medication, and insomnia.

BR Soldier Outreach

The fundamental purpose of BR Soldier Outreach is to provide comfort items from home to deployed military personnel serving selflessly around the globe. Since 2017, the organization has overseen the gathering, packing, and shipping of thousands of pounds of comfort items.

Courage Foundation

The Courage Foundation's mission is to foster post-traumatic growth, restore purpose, and transform lives through integrative self-awareness, physical health, mental toughness, emotional resilience, and spiritual well-being. The foundation educates, equips, and empowers veterans living with post-traumatic stress (PTS) with the skills, resources, and training to thrive. It seeks to restore a sense of purpose, hope, and connection for veterans with PTS who desire to cultivate more meaningful and courageous lives.

Give an Hour

Give an Hour's mission is to develop national networks of volunteers capable of responding to both acute and chronic conditions in our society. Harnessing the skill and expertise of volunteer professionals increases the likelihood that those in need will receive the support and care they deserve. The organization works to match military personnel and veterans struggling with mental health and well-being with volunteer health professionals who can help them recover and has provided more than 389,000 hours of service.

Operation: Heal Our Heroes (HOH)

HOH supports veterans by raising awareness and funds to combat PTSD and eradicate the staggering suicide epidemic. The nonprofit partners with organizations that can effectively provide the attention and care required for the thousands of service members who have endured and continue to bear the psychological burdens associated with our country's time at war.

H.E.R.O.E.S. Care

H.E.R.O.E.S. Care is a collaborative effort among well-established non-governmental organizations designed to provide complete and proactive support for members of all branches of the military and their families through pre-deployment, deployment, family reintegration, and post-deployment. The program consists of a network of tens of thousands of trained caregivers and thousands of professional mental health care and service providers working together to provide an unprecedented system of support for military members and their families.

Operation Second Chance (OSC)

OSC is an organization of patriotic citizens committed to serving our wounded, injured, and ill veterans. They support veterans and their families by building relationships and identifying and supporting immediate needs and interests, and they are dedicated to promoting public awareness of the many sacrifices made by our armed forces.

Permission to Start Dreaming Foundation

This foundation's mission is to help veterans and first responders throughout the Pacific Northwest access effective long-term solutions to transform post-traumatic stress into post-traumatic growth.

Project Healing Waters Fly Fishing

Project Healing Waters Fly Fishing is dedicated to the physical and emotional rehabilitation of disabled active military service personnel and disabled veterans through fly fishing and associated activities, including education and outings. The organization brings a high-quality, full-spectrum fly-fishing program to an ever-expanding number of disabled active military service personnel across the VA healthcare system, military hospitals, and the Warrior Transition Command.

Project Sanctuary

Believing that when one person serves, the whole family serves, Project Sanctuary takes a human-centered, solutions-based approach to helping military families heal and move forward in life. Through innovative long-term programming focused on connectedness, they restore hope and empower families to recover and thrive.

Soldiers' Angels

Soldier's Angels is a national nonprofit organization providing aid and comfort to the men and women of the United States Army, Marines, Navy, Air Force, and Coast Guard as well as their families and a growing veteran population. A team of volunteers assists veterans, wounded and deployed personnel, and their families in a variety of unique and effective ways.

Stop Soldier Suicide

Stop Soldier Suicide is a national nonprofit organization leading the fight to end military and veteran suicide. They serve all service members, veterans, and military families from every branch and every generation, regardless of discharge status. They have a unique, proactive, and disruptive approach, focused on meeting at-risk individuals where they are. Their team provides personalized care and continued case management to help identify specific needs. Whether it's mental health support, housing assistance, or any other service, they work tirelessly to find the right and most effective tools. When you reach out to Stop Soldier Suicide, you'll be connected with a wellness coordinator who will provide personalized attention, support, and assistance.

Veteran's PATH

Veteran's PATH enables returning veterans to discover meaning, purpose, and joy in their lives through mindfulness, meditation, and a safe community. Through practical tools of meditation and mindfulness, physical and outdoor experiences, and a community of camaraderie, veterans rediscover peace, acceptance, transformation, and honor in a new journey forward. The Chopra Foundation and Veteran's PATH are now partnering to provide 1 million veterans with access to proven mind-body tools and support via classes, workshops, and other programs. Additionally, the partnership will use innovative technologies to provide immediate, confidential 24/7 support—for veterans by veterans.

Warrior Bonfire Program

The Warrior Bonfire Program provides opportunities that improve the lives of Purple Heart recipients on their lifelong journey of recovery and healing. The program creates activity-based stress-free environments that promote camaraderie and therapeutic healing.

SERVICE DOGS

Guardian Angels Medical Service Dogs

Guardian Angels Medical Service Dogs was established for the charitable purposes of rescuing, raising, and training the highest caliber medical service and assistance dogs; pairing highly trained dogs with individuals afflicted by disabilities, including a focus on veterans with combat wounds; building and restoring independence and improving quality of life for both the recipient and the dog, while minimizing reliance on government, communities, caregivers, and families; advancing successful service dog training practices by promoting appropriate trainer education and contributing to related research studies; and pursuing increased public awareness and education regarding current disability laws and contributing to new and enhanced laws regarding service dogs.

Healing4Heroes

Healing4Heroes focuses on rescuing dogs from local shelters, pairing them with veterans at no cost to the veteran, and providing all the training to help them become ADA compliant. The dogs are trained to help veterans through inhibitive situations in their daily lives.

K9s for Warriors

Determined to end veteran suicide, K9s for Warriors is the nation's largest provider of trained service dogs to military veterans suffering from PTSD, traumatic brain injury, and/or military sexual trauma. The organization supports veterans by using a scientifically proven process, pairing them with a trained service dog, and supporting them during and after the program.

MK9s Service Dogs

MK9s Service Dogs provides highly trained service dogs to meet specific veteran needs at no cost to the qualified and deserving veteran.

NEADS

NEADS World Class Service Dogs (formerly known as National Education for Assistance Dog Services and Dogs for Deaf and Disabled Americans) was established in 1976 and has trained over 1,900 service dog teams since its founding. The organization offers fully trained service dogs for United States veterans who have a permanent physical disability, hearing loss, MS, or other progressive conditions. These disabilities do not need to be service related.

Patriot PAWS

Patriot PAWS trains service dogs of the highest quality and provides them at no cost to disabled American veterans and others with mobile disabilities to help restore their physical and emotional independence. Patriot PAWS intends to build partnerships with state and community organizations to help develop and support this goal.

Pets for Vets

This nonprofit's mission is to help veterans and pets create new beginnings together, healing emotional wounds of military veterans by pairing them with a shelter dog specially selected to match their personality.

Semper K9 Assistance Dogs

Semper K9 rescues dogs from shelters and trains them to be service dogs at no cost for disabled service members.

Southeastern Guide Dogs

This service dog program provides dogs to veterans living with PTSD and other challenges, such as hearing loss, seizures, and balance issues.

Working Dogs for Vets

Working Dogs for Vets is one of the nation's largest service dog providers, offering service dogs and training to disabled heroes in need, empowering them as they return to civilian life with newfound independence, and reducing suicide and overcrowding in animal shelters. They have volunteers and heroes in every state and continue to grow daily. Contact them if you are a disabled veteran in need of a service dog.

TRANSITIONING VETERAN CHARITIES

Backpacks for Life

Backpacks for Life's mission is to provide a unique and personalized support system for homeless and at-risk veterans who are struggling to reintegrate back into civilian life. They want veterans of all eras to be able to seamlessly and confidently reintegrate and thrive—equipped with the right tools and solutions to do so. Through two main programs, they effectively support and empower veterans, reigniting the flame inside of them.

The Honor Foundation (THF)

THF is a unique transition institute created exclusively for the US Special Operations community. They provide a clear process for professional development and a diverse ecosystem of world-class support and technology. Every step is dedicated to preparing these outstanding men and women to continue to realize their maximum potential during and after their service career. THF exists to serve others with honor for life so that their next mission is always clear and continues to impact the world.

Hope for the Warriors

Hope for the Warriors, founded in 2006, has several areas of focused aid to benefit different needs of veterans, including sports and recreation, community development and engagement, transition services, and health and wellness.

Navy SEAL Foundation

The Navy SEAL Foundation provides immediate and ongoing support and assistance to the Naval Special Warfare community and its families.

Operation Supply Drop (OSD)

Since 2010, OSD's Veteran Support Ecosystem has impacted over 1 million veterans, active duty military personnel, and family members through award-winning programs emphasizing social connectivity, professional development, and community service. Working together with community members, OSD creates and nurtures an environment with the goal of improving local communities and assisting veterans as they transition to civilian life.

Semper Fi & America's Fund

Serving all branches of the military, this fund provides emergency financial assistance to vets who are wounded, are critically ill, or were injured during their service. The nonprofit also supports vets and their families to smoothly transition back into their communities.

CHAPTER FOURTEEN

FOR-PROFIT VETERANS' DISCOUNTS

In this chapter, we will explore discounts available to veterans from for-profit companies, broken into categories.

APPAREL DISCOUNTS FOR VETERANS '

Abercrombie & Fitch

Receive 10%–15% off when you show your valid military ID card. Military veteran discounts are only offered in store. Please check with your local Abercrombie & Fitch for participation.

Adidas

Adidas offers a 30% discount online and in store, as well as 20% off at factory outlets, for military members and veterans. Verify eligibility and identity through the ID.me page to claim the discount.

Allen Edmonds

With proof of military service, veterans can receive 15% off eligible merchandise. Online verification is completed through ID.me. Once verified, your discount will be applied to eligible items in your cart. To shop in store, bring your valid ID for verification. This offer is valid on full-priced products only and cannot be combined with factory second pricing, promotions, or any other discounts.

Alpha Industries

All active duty, retired, and reservist members of the US Armed Forces are eligible to receive 15% off all orders. Product exclusions apply.

American Giant

American Giant offers a 25% discount to all members of the military community, which includes active duty, reservists, National Guard, veterans, and military family members. The discount applies to the first $500 of any order. Verify eligibility through SheerID.

Armed Forces Gear

Past and present military, their spouses, and immediate family members receive 10% off. Eligible parties include active duty, inactive reserves, National Guard, veterans, retirees, spouses, and dependents. To receive your discount, shop as you normally would, then verify your eligibility during the shopping process using the GovX widget on the checkout page. This offer cannot be combined with any other promotional codes and cannot be applied to gift card purchases.

Ashley Stewart

Military members receive 10% off when verified through *ID.me*.

Bates Footwear

Active duty and retired military personnel and their dependents are eligible to receive generous discounts of up to 15% off after verifying their military affiliation through *ID.me*. To redeem the discount, add items to the cart, click the red button that says "Military" under the "ID.me Discounts" section to verify your ID, and proceed to checkout.

BN3TH

BN3TH offers active duty, retired, and veteran military personnel 20% off their entire purchase. Follow these three steps to receive your discount:

1. Verify your ID by using the ID.me button at checkout.
2. Upon verification, you will be redirected to *BN3TH.com*.
3. Your discount will be applied at checkout, with no promo code necessary.

Bonobos

Active duty service members and veterans can receive a 20% discount for five orders over the course of a year. Verify that you are active duty or a veteran by visiting the SheerID link. When verified, you will receive an immediate pop-up and an email with your unique code that works for five orders.

Brides across America Military Bride Wedding Gown Giveaway

Multiple bridal retailers and wedding dress designers work with this organization to provide free wedding dresses to military brides (or brides of military members), including veterans who have served within the last five years. Special events are held twice a year to give away wedding dresses. Check out their site for a listing of upcoming free wedding dress events in a city near you.

Buckle

Active duty and veteran shoppers can receive 10% off their purchase after completing verification through SheerID. Select the "Military Discount" link on the shopping bag page.

Carhartt

Active duty service members, veterans, retirees, military spouses, and military family members receive a 25% discount on apparel and accessories. You must be verified through ID.me before completing your order. If you're shopping in a Carhartt-owned retail location, show your validated ID.me eligibility card during checkout, and the discount will be applied to your purchase.

Champion.com

All members of the military community, including veterans, can save an additional 10% off at Champion with identification once they have verified themselves online.

Champs Sports

Service members and veterans can receive 10% off most purchases. During checkout, under "Payment Method," click on the "Use military discount" link and follow the instructions provided. You may be asked to upload documents to help verify your service through SheerID.

Chubbies Shorts

Active duty and veteran members of the US Armed Forces receive an exclusive 10% discount. Just click the "Claim your discount" button on their website and verify your service status through GovX ID. After you verify, you'll receive a single-use discount code to apply at checkout.

Clarks Shoes

Clarks offers a 10% discount on purchases made by active duty service members, retirees, veterans, military spouses, and military family members. Discounts may be greater during promotional time frames. Verification is done through *ID.me*.

Cole Haan

Active duty military, guard, and reserve members as well as retirees and veterans receive a 20% discount on all orders at ColeHaan.com. Verify via SheerID to claim the discount.

Columbia Sportswear

Columbia offers a 10% military discount on online orders. The offer is valid for active duty military, retirees, veterans, military spouses, and dependents. Verification is completed via ID.me. Upon verification, you will be redirected to Columbia.com. Your discount will be automatically applied at checkout, with no promo code necessary. Veterans may also present a valid military ID to receive a discount in store.

Dickies

Military members enjoy a 10% discount on their total purchase. Click "Verify Now" on the landing page to access a pop-up form.

Dirt Cheap Stores

Every Monday, active, reserve, and retired military members as well as dependents and veterans receive 10% off with ID.

Dockers

Active and retired military members who verify their service are eligible to receive a 25% discount on purchases at Dockers. Simply click the "Unlock Discount" button on the landing page.

Express

Military members can receive 5% off entire in-store purchases.

Fanatics

All military personnel, including veterans, their spouses, and immediate family members, receive 15% off plus free shipping. This military discount is good on most products sold on Fanatics.com, except for gift cards. Verify your eligibility with the *ID.me* button at check out.

Footaction

Active duty personnel, veterans, and retired service members may qualify for a 10% discount on most purchases. During checkout, under "Payment Method," click on the "Use military discount" link and follow the instructions provided. You may be asked to upload documents to help verify your service via SheerID.

Foot Locker

Active military and veterans receive 10% off most purchases. During checkout, under "Payment Method," click on the "Use military discount" link and follow the instructions provided. You may be asked to upload documents to verify your status via SheerID.

Gap Factory

Receive 10% off purchases when you present your valid military ID, in store only. Check with your local store for participation.

GelPro

GelPro offers a 25% discount off online purchase year-round to those who honorably served or are currently serving our country.

Hanes.com

Active duty personnel, military veterans, and their dependents may receive 10% off their order after verifying their military affiliation through Troop ID. This offer applies to all Hanes brands, including FAN Shop, Champion, One Hanes Place, Just My Size, and Maidenform.

Hari Mari

Current and former military and responders receive 20% off full-priced items for online purchases only after verifying eligibility through VerifyPass.

Huckberry

A 10% military discount is available for active duty personnel, retirees, veterans, military spouses, and military family members.

HYLETE

Military service members and veterans receive special discounts on the retail value on all HYLETE orders year-round. Once verified, you'll be prompted to create your HYLETE Service League account. Your "Team Pricing" will be reflected across all eligible HYLETE products once you're logged in. Get verified through GovX ID to be eligible.

JackThreads

Active duty service members, veterans, and their spouses receive 15% off sitewide.

Jockey

Active military personnel, veterans, and their families receive 10% off. Verify your military affiliation by clicking the designated ID button during checkout on Jockey.com, click "Join," and follow the prompts to complete your verification via *ID.me*.

Karen Kane

Active duty personnel, veterans, and their families receive 20% off with verification. Fill out the required fields for your corresponding category on the website to verify your eligibility.

KEEN Footwear

KEEN offers discounts to active duty military personnel, veterans, and military spouses through the KEEN Pro program. Apply on the website and follow the prompts to verify your eligibility and receive a discount.

Kohl's

On Mondays, Kohl's offers a 15% discount for active military personnel, veterans, retirees, and their immediate family members who present a valid US military ID in select branches nationwide (in store only).

Lacoste

Military members receive 10% off. Verify your eligibility through *ID.me*.

L.L.Bean

Active duty service members and veterans can receive 10% off via a promo code by verifying eligibility through SheerID.

Moosejaw

Military members, including active duty personnel, retirees, and veterans, receive 20% off after verification through *ID.me*.

Merrell

Members of the US Armed Forces, veterans, and their families can receive a 20% discount on every order by verifying military status through *ID.me* at checkout.

MLB Shop

MLB offers a 15% discount for military members, which includes active duty service members of the US Armed Forces, veterans of all branches, National Guard members, reservists, and their spouses and immediate family members. Verify eligibility through ID.me.

Mountain Khakis

Active duty military personnel, veterans, and their dependents can receive a unique discount code for 40% off all purchases after verifying eligibility through VerifyPass.

Murse World

Active duty personnel, National Guard and army reserve members, retirees, veterans, and military spouses receive a 10% discount. Click the "Troop ID" button at checkout to verify your eligibility.

NASCAR Store

Active duty personnel, veterans, and their spouses and immediate family members receive a 10% discount when verified via *ID.me* at checkout.

NBA Store

Active duty personnel, veterans, and their spouses and immediate family members receive a 15% discount when verified via *ID.me* at checkout.

NFL Shop

Military members and their spouses and immediate family members receive a 15% discount when verified via *ID.me* at checkout.

Nike

Active, veteran, retired, and reservist US Army, Navy, Air Force, Marines, Space Force, and Coast Guard personnel are eligible to receive a 10% Nike military discount at Nike.com as well as Nike or Converse Stores in the United States (excluding Nike company/employee stores). Verify your eligibility through SheerID.

North Face

All active, reservist, veteran, and retired US military personnel, as well as the spouses and dependents of active personnel, receive a 10% discount after verifying eligibility through SheerID.

Old Navy

In store only, a discount of 10% off apparel is available to active duty personnel, retirees, army reserve or National Guard members, and dependents. Valid military ID is required to verify eligibility.

Orvis

US military veterans, active duty military personnel, National Guard and army reserve members, and their families receive 10% off. You must be a Veterans Advantage member enrolled in VetRewards to enjoy this offer.

Puma

Active and veteran military personnel can take an additional 10% off purchases on the website after verifying eligibility via *ID.me*.

Quiksilver

Quiksilver gives a 15% discount to active military personnel and veterans. The discount is available online only and not at any corporate-owned stores, authorized dealers, or outlet stores.

Reebok

Reebok offers military personnel up to a 50% discount after verifying eligibility through *ID.me*.

Roxy

All active duty personnel, reservists, National Guard members, veterans, retirees, and registered dependents are eligible to receive a 15% discount when shopping with Roxy online through SheerID. This discount is available online only and not at any corporate-owned stores, authorized dealers, or outlet stores.

Saucony

Saucony shares exclusive deals on its VIP program with active duty military members and veterans, including 20% off purchases, first access to new products and exclusive offers, a special birthday gift, and news about local events.

TOMS

Active duty personnel, retired military, and family members who are verified with their ID can receive exclusive offers on TOMS purchases. Contact customer service and request a discount, which cannot be combined with any other offers.

Tread Labs

Tread Labs offers a 25% discount program for active service military personnel, veterans, and their families. Get verified and obtain your code through VerifyPass.

Under Armour

Under Armour offers a 20% discount to active duty service members and veterans sitewide and in all UA brand house stores. Just choose "military and first responder discount" and verify eligibility via *ID.me* at checkout.

UNTUCKit

All members of the US Armed Forces, veterans, and military family members receive a 25% discount after verifying eligibility via *ID.me* at checkout.

Vineyard Vines

Active duty military personnel, military spouses and dependents, National Guard and army reserve members, veterans, and retirees receive a 15% discount. Some exclusions apply. Verify your eligibility through SheerID.

Wrangler

Wrangler offers a 10% discount to active duty personnel and veterans using *ID.me*. Click the "Troop ID" button at checkout to verify your eligibility.

Zappos

Active, veteran, or retired members of the United States military (including reservists and the National Guard) and registered dependents of a member of the United States military receive 10% off every purchase at checkout. To claim the discount, you must log in to a Zappos account.

AUTO DISCOUNTS FOR VETERANS

Advance Auto Parts

Advance Auto Parts offers 10% off regularly priced items for in-store purchases (and online purchases by calling 1-877-ADVANCE prior to purchase) to customers who are currently active duty personnel, reservists, or retirees with twenty years or more of service. The discount also applies to veterans with a service-connected VA rating and immediate family members.

Amanda Products

Veterans and active duty personnel receive a 10% discount, subject to verification via *ID.me* on the Amanda Products website.

Anthem Off-Road

Anthem offers a 15% discount on any set of regularly priced Anthem wheels, including any applicable custom drill fees for US Armed Forces (active duty personnel, veterans, disabled veterans, and retirees). Fill out and submit the online form on their website to verify eligibility and receive a custom order link.

Auto Accessories Garage

Members of the US Armed Forces (active duty personnel, veterans, retirees, and reservists) receive discounts of 5%–20% not offered to the public. To receive the discount, email the company from an active military email address or send a copy of your DD Form 214 along with your contact information.

CARiD

Active duty members, reserves, veterans, and retirees—including their immediate families—of the US Air Force, Army, Coast Guard, Marine Corps, Navy, and National Guard receive a 10% discount.

CarParts.com

All active duty military members, reserves, retirees, and veterans of the US Armed Forces are eligible for a 5% discount on all products. To claim your special discount, email the company from an active military email address or send a copy of your DD Form 214 along with your contact information.

Chevrolet

Chevrolet offers special discounts to eligible military personnel, including active duty members, reservists, National Guard members, veterans within three years of discharge date, and retirees of the US Army, Navy, Air Force, Marine Corps, and Coast Guard. Eligible military personnel can sponsor their spouse and household members. To claim the discount, you must verify your identity and confirm eligibility via *ID.me*.

Chrysler

If you're active duty military, active reserve, retired military, retired military reserve, or an honorably discharged veteran within twelve months of your discharge date, you're eligible for a $500 military bonus cash on some Chrysler vehicles under the company's military incentive program.

Ford

Military Appreciation Cash is exclusively for active military personnel, National Guard members, reservists serving on active duty, members of the Delayed Entry/Enlistment Program, veterans within twenty-four months of separation, retirees, spouses and surviving spouses, and other household members who are residents of the United States. If you are a veteran separated by more than two years, you might still be eligible for bonus cash as a member of the DAV, PVA, or Veterans Advantage. Verify eligibility through *ID.me*.

General Motors

The GM military discount is the best military discount from any car company. It can also be combined with most current lease offers for an even greater deal. Sign in to the website with your *ID.me* information to see lease deals specific to your GM military discount.

Jiffy Lube

Jiffy Lube offers up to 15% off most services for veterans and active military members, only at participating Jiffy Lube locations.

Mazda

Active duty members, reserves, and veterans within two years of separation or retirees of the US Air Force, Army, Navy, Marines, National

Guard, or Coast Guard, as well as spouses and children living at the same address are eligible for $500 bonus cash toward the purchase or lease of a new and unused 2022 or 2023 Mazda vehicle.

Morris 4x4 Center

Morris 4x4 Center offers 5% off all orders for active members, veterans, and reserve members of the army, Marine Corps, US Air Force, Navy, Coast Guard, and National Guard. Simply fill out the form on their website to receive a discount code.

Nissan

The exclusive Nissan Military Program gives a discount between $500 and $1,000 and can be combined with all current national and regional incentives for US military personnel who are active, reserve, retired with twenty years of active or reserve duty, or veterans within twenty-four months of separation from active or reserve duty. Visit a dealership to take advantage of this offer.

O'Reilly Auto Parts

All O'Reilly Auto Parts stores provide a 10% discount on in-store purchases for active duty and reserve members of the military, retired service members, and veterans. The immediate family members of an active duty service member or veteran are also eligible to receive the discount. Valid ID is required. The online store is unable to offer a military discount at this time.

Pelagic Gear

Active duty personnel, veterans, and dependents receive 30% off, with access to exclusive discounts, after verifying eligibility through VerifyPass.

Pep Boys

Every day of the week, active duty and retired military customers can receive a 10% discount at local stores. Present a valid military ID to save (not valid for online orders).

Subaru

Subaru offers a special discount to active duty and reserve members of the US Air Force, Army, Navy, Marines, National Guard, and Coast Guard, as well as veterans and retirees within twelve months of separation. For complete program details and eligibility information, contact your local participating Subaru retailer or VIP Program Headquarters at vipprogram@subaru.com or 1-800-VIP-0933.

Take 5 Oil Change

Veterans and active military can receive 25% off any oil change by showing proof of service or military ID. Claim the offer via text or via email through the website.

Throtl

Current and former US military members, spouses, and dependents can save up to 7% after verifying through GovX ID. You will receive a unique discount code that you can use at checkout.

TireBuyer.com

Active duty military personnel, veterans, and their immediate family members (spouses, parents, and children) are all eligible to receive a 10% discount after verifying through *ID.me*.

TrueCar

TrueCar's Military Appreciation Package has additional savings and incentives customized to active duty military personnel, veterans, and their families. You can receive $500–$2,000 bonus cash from select manufacturers, dealer discounts on new and used vehicles, vehicle condition summaries on every used car, up to $4,000 worth of benefits for repair, and auto deductible reimbursement. There is also a dedicated Military Customer Service Hotline 1-866-850-8318. Report your completed purchase from a certified dealer within forty-five days to receive additional benefits that could be worth more than $4,000.

Urban Helmets

Urban Helmets offers a 15% discount to active duty military personnel and veterans. Verify with *ID.me* at checkout.

Volkswagen

Qualified active duty US military service members, US military veterans within twenty-four months of active duty, and US military retirees who have served twenty years in the military can receive a $500 bonus toward purchasing or leasing a select new Volkswagen.

Volvo

Volvo's US Military Affinity Bonus is exclusively offered for active duty members, reservists, National Guard members, and veterans within three years of discharge date. You will receive a $500 bonus incentive on the purchase or lease of a new Volvo or a $500 bonus incentive on a Certified by Volvo purchase.

CAR RENTAL DISCOUNTS FOR VETERANS

Avis Car Rental

Avis offers military-rate car rentals of up to 25% off base rates. The offer is valid for US military veterans, active duty military personnel, National Guard members, reservists, and their families who have enrolled in Veterans Advantage.

Budget

US military veterans, active duty military personnel, National Guard members, reservists, and their families receive a military discount on car rental up to 25% off simply by being a member of Veterans Advantage.

Dollar

If you're a veteran or active duty military, National Guard, or reserve service member who is also a member of VetRewards through Veterans Advantage, you can receive a 5% discount on all Dollar car rentals and a fee waiver for additional drivers or underage drivers.

Enterprise Rent-A-Car

Enterprise offers exclusive discounts for the military community (active duty, veterans, National Guard, reservists, and family).

ParkRideFly USA

Airport parking discounts are available to all veterans, US Armed Forces personnel, and their families. Prepay for three days in advance and receive up to one day free, all year long.

SIXT

Active military members and veterans can receive a 5% discount off car rentals. The special offer is available to those with a valid active military ID or veterans ID, which can include a valid driver's license with a veteran designation, a state veterans ID card, or the VA Veterans Identification Card.

Thrifty

Thrifty Car Rental gives 5% discounts to veterans, active duty military personnel, National Guard and reserve members, and their families who are Veterans Advantage members.

COMPUTER DISCOUNTS FOR VETERANS

Apple

The Apple Veterans and Military Purchase Program is available to current military personnel and veterans of the US military, National Guard, and Army Reserve, as well as for immediate family members who live in the same household. Veterans and military personnel receive a 10% discount on Apple products and accessories as a thank-you for service after verifying eligibility through *ID.me*.

Dell

Active duty military personnel and veterans receive 10% off. Obtain your coupon on their website by creating an account using your .mil email address.

Element Case

Active duty personnel, veterans, and dependents receive a 20% discount code to use at checkout by confirming their eligibility via VerifyPass.

Microsoft

Microsoft offers up to 10% off select products for active, former, and retired military personnel and their families on PCs, PC gaming, Office 365, Xbox One, accessories, and much more.

Lenovo

Lenovo offers 5% off almost all products, free shipping, and special discounts for active military, reservists, veterans, and immediate family members. Click the "Verify with *ID.me*" button at checkout to apply the discount.

Motorola

All active, veteran, retired, and reservist personnel are eligible to take 10% off Motorola products. Receive a discount code by verifying eligibility through *ID.me*.

RoboForm Password Manager

RoboForm Everywhere offers a 30% military discount for active duty, veterans, reservists, retirees, military spouses, and families. For only $16.70 per year, RoboForm organizes and encrypts passwords and personal data, increasing convenience and security of your online experience. Verify eligibility through *ID.me*.

Samsung

Samsung provides up to 30% discounts to active military personnel, veterans, and their families. Create a Samsung account and verify eligibility through ID.me. You must use an active military email address to register. If you have shopped on *Samsung.com* with a different email address, you will need to create a new account with this military email for the Samsung Military Discount Program.

Targus

Any member of the US Armed Forces (including veterans, active duty, reservists, National Guard, and their spouses and dependents) can receive 25% off laptops and tablets after verifying eligibility through the SheerID link.

EDUCATION AND TRAINING DISCOUNTS FOR VETERANS

Amazon AWS Educate

US service members, transitioning veterans, and military spouses have access to a free membership to AWS Educate, which includes cloud computing resources, AWS Educate promotional credits, and the option to learn skills based on a desired career path.

Berklee College of Music

Active duty and veteran military personnel receive a 30% tuition fee discount on top of available tuition assistance programs for military students or GI Bill benefits for veterans (up to sixty credits).

California Southern University

California Southern University offers active duty military personnel, veterans, military spouses, and their dependent children a discount of 15% per credit.

LinkedIn

LinkedIn offers a free one-year premium subscription to US service members and veterans who verify eligibility through *ID.me*.

Regent University

Regent University offers military and veteran college benefits in the form of tuition discounts and bookstore vouchers. A variety of special scholarships and awards programs are available to both undergraduate and graduate military and veteran students who are pursuing a certificate or degree program and are in good academic standing.

Rosetta Stone

Special veterans and military pricing and an extra 10% discount are available to current and former members of the US military, National Guard, and Army Reserve, as well immediate family members who reside in the same household. Verify identity and eligibility with *ID.me*.

Trident University

Trident University's Military Discount Program covers regular military personnel, drilling and active duty reservists, retired military personnel, and members of the National Guard. Military spouses may also qualify for discounts. Members of the armed services may be eligible for Trident's Military Education Grant, which provides service members with a tuition reduction of up to 43%, depending on the selected program.

ENTERTAINMENT DISCOUNTS
FOR VETERANS

AMC Theatres

Service members can show a valid photo military ID at the box office for a discount on tickets at participating theaters.

Caesars Entertainment

Caesars Entertainment provides year-round discounts worth up to 30% off hotel reservations made online by United States active duty military personnel and veterans who can verify their identity through ID.me.

Cinemark Movie Theatres

Active or retired military members may get discounted rates by presenting valid military ID at ticket booths nationwide. Different terms may apply at each location.

DISH

On top of the three-year TV Price Guarantee, DISH offers a free Stars & Stripes Pack upgrade to an existing TV package, providing one on-demand movie rental each month for free and all-day access to sports, local news, and other TV content straight to your mobile device.

Pandora

Pandora offers a Premium Military Plan for just $7.99 per month and a sixty-day free trial for qualified military personnel, including active duty service members, retirees, reservists, veterans, and military dependents. The Premium Military Plan is 20% off the regular plan price, and features include ad-free listening, searching and playing, creating and sharing playlists, unlimited skipping, offline listening, high-quality audio, and more.

Regal Cinemas

Regal Cinemas offer discounted ticket prices for active duty military personnel and retired military veterans. Present a valid military ID at the box office.

Sennheiser

Military veterans and their families can receive up to 30% off their Sennheiser headphones when they verify their military affiliation. The offer is only valid on headphones, not any other products.

Universal Orlando Resort

Active duty and retired military personnel receive a special rate from Universal Orlando Resort, with stays starting at $105 per adult per night, tax inclusive, depending on availability.

EYEWEAR AND EYE CARE DISCOUNTS FOR VETERANS

AC Lens

Active duty military members and veterans receive 10% off contact lenses purchased through AC Lens. To receive the discount, you must have active military ID or an active Veterans Advantage card and enter the promo code "MILITARY" during checkout.

Armed Forces Eyewear

Military members are eligible for an additional exclusive discount on sunglasses and prescription glasses. Verify eligibility through SheerID.

ContactsDirect

Military members are eligible for a 20% discount and free shipping. Click on "Military, First Responders, Teachers and Government Discount" at checkout and then the "Verify with *ID.me*" button to verify your military status.

Eyemart Express

Show your valid retired, active, nonactive, veterans, or dependent military ID at checkout to receive 20% off all purchases.

Glasses.com

Glasses.com provides special 60% off military discounts on new glasses and lenses for active military personnel and veterans. Click "Military, First Responders, Teachers and Government Discount" at checkout and then the "Verify with *ID.me*" button to verify your military status, and the discount will be applied to your cart.

Kaiser Permanente Eyecare

All federal employees and retirees, active US military personnel and retirees, veterans, and their dependents are eligible for 20% discounts on prescription eyeglasses and contact lenses. Show ID or paperwork to be eligible for these savings.

LasikPlus

A 20% discount for LASIK is available to military personnel and veterans at all fifty locations nationwide. Discount and price matching are available. Set up a free consultation to learn more.

Oakley

Oakley offers military personnel up to 60% off. Oakley SSI has elite products at extremely discounted prices only for veterans and service members around the country.

Ray-Ban

Ray-Ban offers a 15% military discount for active duty personnel and veterans after online verification via *ID.me*.

Sunglass Hut

Active duty personnel, retirees, veterans, military spouses, and military family members can receive a 15% discount while shopping online by verifying eligibility via ID.me. This discount cannot be combined with other promotional codes or applied to any gift card purchases.

FINANCIAL AND INSURANCE DISCOUNTS FOR VETERANS

AARP

Active duty service members, retired military personnel, and veterans receive up to a 30% discount off an annual AARP membership. Members are eligible for benefits carefully chosen for veterans, military service members, and their families.

Embrace Pet Insurance

Embrace offers a 5% military discount to active and former members of the US Air Force, Army, Marines, Navy, or Coast Guard.

GEICO

Pay 15% less than regular insurance premiums if you are an active duty or retired member of the military, or a member of the National Guard or army reserves. To take advantage of these discounts, call 1-800-MILITARY (645-4827).

Liberty Mutual

Active, retired, or reserve members in the US Armed Forces receive a military discount.

Navy Federal Credit Union (NFCU)

Active duty and retired military personnel may qualify for a 0.25% APR discount on loans. Call 1-888-842-6328 or visit your nearest NFCU branch. The offer is not available for online applications.

USAA

USAA provides discounted auto, home, and life insurance to military members and veterans.

FITNESS DISCOUNTS FOR VETERANS

24 Hour Fitness

Active, reserve, and retired military personnel and their spouses receive special discounts. Bring your military ID into any club to unlock the savings.

Atkins

Military veterans and active service members receive 15% off bars and shakes every day. Verify eligibility through SheerID.

Beachbody

Veterans, reservists, and active duty personnel are eligible for the military waiver program, which waives the Coach Business Service Fee. Qualifying coaches also get a reimbursement of the Business Starter Kit fee.

Bodybuilding.com

This site offers a 10% discount every day to the entire military community. Verify eligibility through ID.me.

Gold's Gym

Gold's Gym offers special discounts for members of the military and veterans. Complete verification through ID.me on the website to receive a special military discount offer.

PureFormulas

PureFormulas offers a 10% military discount for active duty members, retirees, veterans, spouses, and dependents. Receive your discount while shopping online by verifying your eligibility with ID.me.

Tommie Copper

Active or retired military personnel receive 15% off online orders with verification via VerifyPass. This discount can only be applied to online orders and cannot be combined with other Tommie Copper® promotions or offers.

Tonal Home Gym Equipment

Active duty personnel, veterans, and dependents can receive a one-time discount code by verifying eligibility through VerifyPass.

Tough Mudder Events

Verified active duty, reserve, and retired members of the US Armed Forces and related government agencies get up to a 25% discount off the participant registration price through GovX.

FLOWER AND GIFT DISCOUNTS FOR VETERANS

1-800-Flowers

Save 30% every day when you order from 1800Flowers.com or via the toll-free phone order line, 1-800-Flowers by using the Veterans Advantage military discount code combined with your Member ID. Family members with their own VetRewards Card are eligible to redeem 25% off.

FOOD, WINE, AND TOBACCO DISCOUNTS FOR VETERANS

Burger King

Receive 10% off your order with your Veterans Advantage card. Discounts vary by location; call your local Burger King for details.

Costco Wholesale

Active duty, veteran, and retired military members, as well as their spouses or dependents, who join Costco as new members can receive a $20 Costco Shop Card. Simply log in or verify your military status online through *ID.me* to complete a new registration and purchase a Costco membership.

Fred Meyer

Military members, their families, and veterans with ID receive an extra 10% off private brand groceries, including Fred Meyer, Kroger, Simple Truth, and more as well as discounts on apparel, shoes, accessories, and home items, including toys, sporting goods, auto and garden, most electronics, and Fred Meyer Jewelers.

Holt's Cigar Company

Active military personnel, veterans, retirees, National Guard members, and reservists may receive a 10% discount online and over the phone by verifying eligibility through SheerID and creating a *Holts.com* account.

JR Cigar

JR Cigar automatically gives all those who have served in the military, including inactive personnel and veterans, a 10% military discount on all orders shipped to APO and FPO addresses around the world. Including everything but gift cards, this offer extends to a vast assortment of handmade premium cigars, machine-made cigars, cigar samplers, cigar five-packs, pipe tobaccos, vapes, e-cigarettes, hookah tobacco, cigar accessories, and more. Sign in to your JR Cigar account and verify your eligibility through *ID.me* at checkout.

Omaha Steaks

Omaha Steaks offers a military discount for active duty military personnel, retirees, veterans, military spouses, and dependents. Verification is completed through ID.me, resulting in a Troop ID credential for eligible members of the military. Once your credentials are verified, you will immediately receive $10 off your order. Simply click on the Troop ID button to receive discounts on future orders.

Sam's Club

Active duty, retired military, and civilian military employees and their spouses receive a $10 gift card upon joining or renewing a Sam's Club membership and presenting a valid military ID or qualifying document.

Thrive Market

Veterans and low-income families can receive a free membership ($60 value), gain exclusive member savings of 25%–50%, and access the Thrive Market Health Hacks video series.

HEALTH AND BEAUTY DISCOUNTS FOR VETERANS

BURST Oral Care

Active duty personnel, veterans, and military families can save 25% off eligible BURST Oral Care products and services available through *ID.me*.

The Original Foot Alignment Socks

Active duty personnel, veterans, retirees, and military dependents are eligible to receive 50% off their order of foot alignment socks to help relieve foot pain. Qualify for discounts by providing a military email address, a quick DOD scan, or qualifying documents.

HOME AND GARDEN DISCOUNTS FOR VETERANS

Boscov's

Boscov's offers up to 15% off—even during sales—for US Armed Forces, including active and reserve members as well as veterans. The discount code is good for one full year and can be used in any store and online. Verify military credentials through Boscov's website.

Brooklyn Bedding

Brooklyn Bedding offers a 25% discount to all eligible military members, and the discount is applicable to all purchases, both online and in store.

Casper

Casper offers 20% off any order with a mattress for active duty personnel, retirees, veterans, military spouses, and military family members. Military affiliation must be verified on their website via *ID.me*.

Cove Smart

Cove offers an incredible discount on home security for military members and veterans. Receive equipment and six months of monitoring for $150, including a sixty-day risk-free trial, after verifying eligibility and identify through VerifyPass.

iRobot

Military members, veterans, and their families can save up to 15% on select robots, plus free shipping, after verifying eligibility through ID.me.

Joann Fabric and Crafts

Joann offers 15% off in-store and online purchases, every day on every purchase—even sale price and clearance items—to military members or veterans honorably discharged from the US Army, US Navy, US Air Force, US Marine Corps, US Coast Guard, army reserves, or the National Guard, as well as their spouses and/or dependent children. You must have a Joann account and present proof of your military service, past or present, or a military dependent ID upon checkout to receive a discount.

John Deere

Military service members, including veterans, are eligible for a complimentary John Deere Rewards upgrade (Platinum 1 status), which unlocks the best loyalty rewards, including valuable equipment discounts. Register today and explore all that the rewards have to offer.

McCoy's Building Supply

McCoy's offers two military discounts, a year-round military discount and a veteran holiday discount, worth 10% off purchases, with a $500 maximum discount per transaction and a daily discount limit of $500. Present a valid military ID card to verify that you belong to one of these eligible groups: active or reserve status members of the US Armed Services (Army, Navy, Air Force, Marine Corps, Coast Guard, or National Guard), retirees with over twenty years of service, Department of Veterans Affairs recipients, or immediate family members (spouse or dependent child).

Michaels

Currently serving military personnel, military retirees, and their immediate family members can receive 15% off every day, in store and online. To receive the discount, log in or create a Michaels rewards account and provide your military information.

Northern Tool + Equipment

All active, reservist, retired, and veteran military members receive 10% off purchases every day in stores nationwide with a valid military ID. The military discount is not currently available online, and the maximum discount is $500.

Overstock.com

Overstock.com offers free Club O Gold membership for military veterans or active duty service members. Membership benefits include 5% reward dollars on every purchase, free shipping every day of the year, and extra reward dollars on select products. Verification is through *ID.me.*

Pier 1 Imports

Active and retired military personnel receive a 10% discount off their entire purchase by showing valid military ID in store.

Sherwin-Williams

Current and former military service members, reservists, and their spouses can receive 15% off in-store purchases of paints, stains, and painting supplies.

Tuft & Needle

Verified active military personnel and veterans receive a 15% discount.

WellnessMats

All active and retired military personnel receive 25% off their purchases on WellnessMats.com or at any participating WellnessMats retailer location after verifying eligibility through SheerID.

WORX

All active US military service members and veterans receive a 10% discount on WORX lawn, garden, and power tools after verifying eligibility through SheerID.

Yankee Candle

Military personnel and immediate family members receive a 10% discount. Present a valid form of military ID at checkout in retail and outlet stores. For online orders, military members should reach out to the customer service team via the Contact Us form on the website, provide the order confirmation number, and reference the military discounts in the message.

Z Gallerie

Military and veterans receive a 25% discount on regular priced items in store only. Simply show a valid military or veteran ID.

JEWELRY DISCOUNTS FOR VETERANS

Alpine Rings

This veteran-owned and -operated company offers 15% off to all active duty, guard, and reserve members as well as veterans and family members. Verification through a GovX ID account is required to receive a discount code to apply to your shopping cart at checkout.

Antique Jewelry Mall

Current members and veterans of the US military are eligible for 10% off jewelry purchases of in-stock items. A valid US military ID, US military email address, or other proof of service is required.

Blue Nile

Verified military members in the United States can enjoy an exclusive discount of 15% off regularly priced jewelry after verifying eligibility via ID.me. Shipping is free on all Blue Nile orders, including those sent to

APO, FPO, and DPO addresses where a partnership with the military postal service ensures secure delivery.

Genesis Diamonds

Get your engagement rings with a 10% discount for members of the military. Participating designer brands include Bez Ambar, Christopher Designs, Genesis Designs, Henri Daussi, Tacori, Verragio, and more. Place your order over the phone at 1-888-OMG-RING and present your statement of service with a valid US military email address to receive your discount.

Glamour Life Diamonds

Glamour Life Diamonds offers a 15% discount on purchases for active duty military personnel, law enforcement, and military veterans. Those who are awarded 50%+ disability by Veterans Affairs and present a VA award letter are eligible for a 25% discount on purchases. Jewelry produced by Glamour Life Diamonds features lab-created simulated diamonds designed to protect the environment.

Helzberg Diamonds

Active duty service members, retirees, disabled veterans, and dependents of active duty and retirees receive a 10% discount on purchases made in store, online, or via 1-800-HELZBERG (435-9237). Once verified, those eligible will receive a one-time promotion code. The offer can't be combined with any other promotion and is not applicable toward loose diamonds from Create Your Own Helzberg Diamond Ring or custom gemstone jewelry.

QALO

Discounts are available for active duty, veteran, retired, and National Guard service members, as well as their spouses and immediate family members. QALO wedding rings are designed for people with an active lifestyle who are looking for both function and style. The brand also offers a selection of apparel and hats.

Robbins Brothers

Military members can get a discount code for 10% off product purchases, including loose diamonds, engagement rings, wedding bands, or fine jewelry. Military ID is required. Robbins Brothers is known as the engagement ring store and offers a large selection of rings from a variety of top designers and brands.

Samuels Jewelers

Samuels Jewelers offers a 10% in-store discount to all active duty and retired military personnel as well as their dependents. A valid Military ID must be presented at the time of purchase. Samuels Jewelers offers a variety of engagement and wedding rings, plus a selection of necklaces, bracelets, gemstone jewelry, and watches.

Sword & Plough

US active duty military personnel, National Guard members, reservists, veterans, retired personnel, spouses, and Gold Star family members are eligible to receive up to 20% off all orders from Sword & Plough, a boutique jewelry and accessory line created by military daughters. Details for accessing the military discount code are available on their website.

Rogers & Hollands

Save on your next jewelry purchase. Rogers & Hollands | Ashcroft & Oak salutes all active duty personnel, career-retired service members, and disabled veterans with the Everyday Hero discount of 10% off with the code HERO. Present valid military ID or other qualifying documentation to receive the discount.

Tiffany & Co.

Tiffany & Co. offers 10% off engagement rings and wedding bands for active duty service members, reservists, and veterans of the US Armed Forces. Fiancés, domestic partners, and spouses are eligible for the discount even if their US military partner is stationed overseas and not able to come into the store. The offer may not be extended to other family members, and the engagement discount is available in the United States only.

RESTAURANT DISCOUNTS FOR VETERANS

99 Restaurants

All military service members and veterans with military ID receive a 10% discount every day on both dine-in and to-go orders. Simply present your military ID to your server.

Bubba Gump Shrimp Co.

All military members receive a 15% discount on Memorial Day and 20% on Veterans Day. Simply present your military ID.

Chuck E. Cheese

Chuck E. Cheese has special food offers for active duty service members and their dependents; National Guard, reservists, and their dependents; and retired service members.

Cicis Pizza

Ask about the year-round discount for the military that varies from store to store, depending on the individual franchise owner's policy.

Outback Steakhouse

Outback Steakhouse offers a 10% discount all day, every day to service members who present valid state or federal service ID.

Texas de Brazil

Military members and veterans receive a 15% discount off the regular or salad-only dinner or lunch price. This offer is good for up to four guests per table or reservation with a valid ID, only at locations in the United States and not on holidays.

RETAIL DISCOUNTS FOR VETERANS

CVS

Active duty personnel, veterans, and eligible family members save 20% on online purchases at CVS.com and receive free shipping. Submit your Veterans Advantage card information to be approved for discounts.

QVC

Active duty personnel, reservists, retired, or disabled veterans with a valid military ID receive 10% off the total purchase at QVC Outlet Stores.

SHIPPING AND STORAGE DISCOUNTS FOR VETERANS

Penske Truck Rentals

Penske offers a 10% off military discount code for truck rentals at more than 2,500 convenient locations.

PODS

Active duty, retired, and veteran members of the military can receive a 10% off PODS military discount code.

U-Haul

U-Haul does not have an official military discount. However, some former customers claim they saved 10%–15% by contacting U-Haul over the phone and asking about a military discount. The best method is to contact their sales department at 1-800-GO-U-HAUL (468-4285).

SPORTING GOODS DISCOUNTS FOR VETERANS

Allen Fly Fishing

Active, retired, or former military personnel receive a special discount on fly-fishing products. Visit *AllenFlyFishing.com/us-military-purchase-program* for more information.

Ballistic Armor Co.

Military service members and veterans receive a 10% discount on all products after verifying eligibility through VerifyPass.

Bass Pro Shops

Bass Pro Shops offers active military personnel, veterans, retirees, National Guard service members, and reservists a 5% discount every day, in store and online, with valid ID.

Big 5 Sporting Goods

All active duty and reserve military personnel, retirees, veterans, and their spouses and dependent children receive 10% off with valid military ID or veteran status on driver's license. The discount is offered in store only and excludes gift cards and licenses.

Cabela's

Cabela's Legendary Salute offers a 5% discount every day to active military personnel, veterans, retirees, National Guard service members, and reservists with valid ID, both online and in store.

Callaway Golf

Receive 15% off orders upon verifying your active, reserve, or retired military status with *ID.me*. This discount cannot be combined with other promotional codes, and some exclusions may apply.

Camping World

Active military personnel, veterans, National Guard service members, and reservists receive 5% off at retail locations and at varying times throughout the year online. Make sure to bring your military ID, DD Form 214, or state-issued ID that indicates veteran status.

Cobra

Cobra offers 10% off as well as other exclusive offers and benefits for the active duty and veteran military community. Verify eligibility through *ID.me*.

Eastbay

Active duty personnel, veterans, National Guard service members, reservists, and registered dependents of active duty or retiree service members receive 10% off most purchases. Click the "Use Military Discount" link at checkout and verify eligibility through SheerID.

Evolve Skateboards

Evolve offers $100 off for active duty service members, veterans, and their dependents after verifying eligibility through VerifyPass.

E-Z UP

Active duty and veteran military personnel can qualify for up to 30% off by filling out the form on their website.

Gerber Gear

US military active duty personnel and veterans are eligible for the Pro Program, which includes discounted products, exclusive offers, and free shipping on orders of $50 and above.

JustBats/JustBallGloves

Active military members, veterans, retirees, National Guard service members, reservists, and their spouses can receive a 10% discount by emailing *experts@justbats.com* or *experts@justballgloves.com*, using the live chat feature, or calling 1-866-321-2287.

Lund Boats

Lund offers a military family discount on selected models for members of the US or Canadian military. Discounts are applied to purchase by the dealer at time of sale; ask the dealer for details.

Military Tee Times

All United States military members—including active duty, National Guard, army reserve, retired, and veteran—as well as their dependents receive 15% off at golf courses.

PING

PING offers a military rebate program to active, active reserve, or retired military personnel and their spouses with current ID. See the eligible equipment models and rebate amounts on the company's website, *PING.com.*

PROFOX Racing

Adrenaline junkies can get 10% discounts on regular-priced racing gear and accessories. This offer is available for active duty, veteran, reserve, Coast Guard, National Guard, and retired personnel as well as their families. Discounts are available on phone orders, or fill out the form on their website to receive a discount code via email.

S3 Power Sports

Active duty and former military personnel receive exclusive discounts after verifying eligibility through VerifyPass.

Scuba.com

Scuba.com (formerly Leisure Pro) offers a 6% discount for military personnel (including spouses and family members) and veterans. Verify eligibility and take advantage of the offer at checkout through *ID.me.*

Sunny Sports

Sunny Sports offers a 6% discount for military personnel, military spouses, and veterans. Verify eligibility at checkout through SheerID.

TacticalGear.com

Active duty personnel, retirees, veterans, military spouses, and military family members receive a 10% discount through *ID.me*, excluding products on clearance, products with promotional pricing, and shipping costs.

TaylorMade Golf

Active duty personnel, retirees, veterans, military spouses, and military family members receive 15% off the entire purchase from TaylorMade Golf, Adidas Golf, Ashworth Golf, or Adams Golf after verifying eligibility via *ID.me*. This discount cannot be combined with other promotional codes, and some exclusions may apply.

Throwback Sports

Veterans and active duty military personnel receive a 15% discount on every bag. Use the code "THROWVET" at checkout on Amazon.

VICIS

VICIS offers a significant military discount on tech, gear, and apparel for all active duty and retired military members as well as veterans. The discount is available through the website with verification of military service via VerifyPass. VICIS develops top-rated helmets, including the ZERO1 and ZERO1 Youth football helmets. Due to the outstanding quality of their products, in 2018 VICIS was awarded a contract with the US Army Natick Soldier Research, Development and Engineering Center to develop improved combat helmets for the army and Marine Corps.

Wilson

Military personnel and veterans are eligible to receive 15% off select merchandise. Once you have verified your eligibility through SheerID, you will see your 15% discount automatically applied to all eligible products every time you log in.

YETI

YETI offers special pricing for military service members, who go the extra mile in their jobs and deserve gear that does, too. After verifying eligibility via ID.me, you can purchase select YETI gear with special pricing. With a one-time verification, you may use your personal information, including your verified IDs, at hundreds of integrated partners across the *ID.me* network.

TRAVEL AND HOTEL DISCOUNTS FOR VETERANS

Allegiant Air

Allegiant Air offers select free benefits to US active and reserve duty military personnel and military veterans. To qualify for the benefits of the Allegiant Honors program, US military members of the seven uniformed services traveling on an Allegiant itinerary must show proof with a qualifying document or ID. See the company's website for a complete list of benefits and documents for verification.

American Forces Travel

Supported by Priceline, this discount travel site is especially for military members, eligible veterans, and caregivers. Find savings on cruises, hotels, flights, cars, and vacation packages.

Amtrak

Veterans of the United States military receive a 10% discount on the lowest available rail fare on most Amtrak trains. Additionally, Amtrak welcomes uniformed military personnel to the head of the ticket line.

Armed Forces Vacation Club (AFVC)

AFVC is a vacation deal club that offers free membership to active and retired military personnel. Sign up for a free club membership to book various vacation deals. Some exclusions may apply.

Beaches by Sandals

US and Canada military members and their families save an extra 10% on top of all their special promotions. Apply for a discount by filling out the form at the bottom of the web page.

Best Western

Military personnel and veterans enjoy discounts at or below per diem at hotels and resorts throughout North America. Present an official identification card or work order at time of check-in.

Castle Resorts & Hotels

Castle offers special discounts for active duty, reserve, and National Guard service members as well as veterans. Request "Military Friends & Family" rates.

Celebrity Cruises

All active and retired military members are eligible for reduced rates. The service member plus a guest will save $25 per person on inside or ocean view staterooms and $100 per person in Veranda, Concierge Class, Aqua Class, or Suite Class. Military offers are valid on cruises that are four nights or longer, and a valid military ID is required to receive the discounted rates.

Choice Hotels

Active duty and retired military members as well as their dependents receive a discount on leisure travel. The eligible person must occupy the room. Fill out the form on the Choice Hotels website to apply for eligibility.

Clipper Vacations

Special discounted rates are available for active and retired members of the US or Canadian military, military reserves, Coast Guard, National Guard, or Department of Defense and their immediate families. Military discounts must be mentioned at the time of booking.

Delta Vacations

Plan your next big trip anywhere in the world and save $50–$300 on your vacation package of choice. To redeem your discount, submit your military email address using the "Before You Book" form on the upper right side of the web page. You will receive a personal eCertificate number via the email address you provided, along with redemption instructions.

Disney Cruise Line

Disney Cruise Line offers special military rates on select Disney cruises. The discount is valid for new bookings only, and special military rates are limited to a maximum of one stateroom per military member, per sailing.

Divi Resorts

A 20% discount is available for those who have served their country and communities. Just enter the promo code MIL20 when booking online. To qualify, a valid military ID or service ID must be provided to make the reservation and then presented during check-in.

Great Wolf Lodge

Active, retired, and veteran military service personnel save up to 25% with the offer code "HEROES" and a valid ID.

Greyhound

Get a 10% discount on full-priced fares for yourself and your family if you are either active duty or retired US military personnel and present valid ID for purchases at the station. Or use your Veterans Advantage card when you purchase online or at the station. Other terms may apply.

Hale Koa Hotel

The Hale Koa is an incredible resort hotel with a great location, right on the beach in Honolulu, Hawaii. Veterans with 100% disability qualify for Category 2 priority throughout the year, which will give you a high-quality room at a reduced nightly rate. With the passage of the Disabled Veterans Equal Access Act of 2018, effective January 2020, veterans who are Purple Heart recipients, veterans who are former POWs, all veterans with any VA service-connected disability rating, and individuals assessed, approved, and designated as the primary family caregivers of eligible veterans under the VA Program of Comprehensive Assistance for Family Caregivers are eligible to use the Hale Koa in Honolulu, Hawaii.

Hilton Hotels

Active and retired military members and their families are eligible for exclusive discounts at participating hotels. You will be required to show a valid military ID at check-in.

Hotwire

Active, retired, and veteran members of the US military and their dependents get $100 or more off Hot Rate hotel bookings at Hotwire.

Jellystone Park Camp-Resorts

Active duty and retired military families who enjoy camping receive discounts of up to 15% off at most of Jellystone's campgrounds. Details vary by location. Present military ID at check-in.

JetBlue

JetBlue always offers special discounts and fares, airport assistance, and other unique services for veterans and active military personnel. JetBlue offers both military discounts and Veterans Advantage discounts, which are both typically 5%.

La Quinta Inn & Suites

Members of the military, veterans, and their families enjoy 12% off the best available rate at La Quinta hotels in the United States and Canada with a valid military ID presented at check-in. Veterans Advantage VetRewards members can also save up to 20% off the best available rate at participating locations worldwide.

Lufthansa

Veterans Advantage members receive a 5% discount on tickets. Restrictions apply.

Motel 6

All active and retired military personnel and their families are eligible for a 10% discount every stay, including at Studio 6 locations. When booking online, simply click "Military" in the drop-down menu to receive the discount.

Peter Pan Bus Lines

Active duty and retired military personnel as well as their dependents can request a discount off the standard terminal fare on Peter Pan schedules. A valid ID card must be presented upon request.

Princess Cruises

As part of the Military Cruise Benefit Program, active duty, retired, or disabled military personnel and veterans can receive up to $250 in free onboard spending money. This military benefit is available on any cruise, at any time of the year. To qualify, download the application form from their website and submit it directly to Princess Cruises via email, fax, or postal mail.

Red Lion Hotels

Participating Red Lion Hotels across the United States and Canada offer a 15% discounted rate to active duty and retired military personnel as well as their families. Book on RedLion.com and search with the promo code MIL.

Red Roof Inn

Military personnel, veterans, and retirees save 10% on all stays with Red Roof Inn with the code VP#606732 when booking. Use the Book Now section at the top of the page or call 1-800-RED-ROOF (733-7663).

Royal Caribbean

Take advantage of special cruise rates available for military personnel and veterans. Eligible military members must be in the same stateroom for dependents to qualify for discounted rates, and discounts are subject to terms.

Sandals Resorts Vacation Packages

Active military, retired, reserve, US National Guard, US veterans, US Department of Defense, and Canada Department of National Defense and their spouses receive 10% off the purchase of all-inclusive vacation packages from Sandals. The discount is on top of other promotions the company offers. Fill out the form on the web page to apply for qualifying discounts.

SeaWorld Parks & Entertainment

Waves of Honor offers one complimentary admission per year to SeaWorld, Busch Gardens, or Sesame Place for military personnel and as many as three direct dependents. Service members and their direct dependents must have a valid active military ID in order to participate. Inactive, standby, and retired reserve members, military retirees, US Merchant Marine, and civilian Department of Defense workers are ineligible for the program. SeaWorld Parks & Entertainment reserves the right to terminate the program.

Shades of Green at Walt Disney World Resort

Shades of Green is an incredible resort and hotel with a great location on Disney property which will also give you a high-quality room at a reduced nightly rate. With the passage of the Disabled Veterans Equal Access Act of 2018, effective January 2020, veterans who are Purple Heart recipients, veterans who are former POWs, all veterans with any VA service-connected disability rating, and individuals assessed, approved, and designated as the primary family caregivers of eligible veterans under the VA Program of Comprehensive Assistance for Family Caregivers are eligible to use the Shades of Green Resort in Orlando, Florida.

Through the Shades of Green "Salute to Our Veterans" program, all military veterans who have received an honorable discharge (with no VA service-connected disability rating) have an opportunity to vacation at Shades of Green during January and September. Reservations are subject to availability. Proof of honorable discharge is required with a copy of a current DD 214 form.

Southwest Airlines

Southwest Airlines offers a discount to active military personnel and their dependents. (However, note that the Wanna Get Away fare will usually be even less expensive.) This discount is available by contacting Southwest directly by phone, not online, and requires showing a valid military ID. Call Southwest at 1-800-I-FLY-SWA (435-9792).

Super 8

A discount of 15% is available for reservations for current and retired military personnel and their spouses as well as veterans and their families. Follow the "Book Now" link on the web page.

United Airlines

Active duty and retired service members and their families can get 5% off airline tickets through Veterans Advantage. The discount is valid on flights purchased through *United.com* and operated by United or United Express.

Wyndham Hotels & Resorts

Enjoy 15% off the best available rate at participating Wyndham Rewards Hotels across the United States and Canada when you present a valid military ID at check-in. This discount is available for members of the US or Canadian military with active, reserve, veteran, or retired status and their spouses.

WIRELESS AND INTERNET DISCOUNTS FOR VETERANS

AT&T Wireless

Active duty, reserve, and National Guard personnel as well as veterans and spouses receive 25% off mobile phone services. Just present identification or proof veteran status at any AT&T store.

T-Mobile

T-Mobile offers military discount wireless plans for up to half off family lines. Save $25 per line on up to four lines with the Magenta Military signature plan and $35 per line on up to four lines with the Magenta MAX Military premium plan. The military programs are available to active duty military personnel, veterans, retirees, and reservists.

Verizon Wireless

Military members, veterans, and their families can save up to $25 per month on wireless plans after verifying eligibility through ID.me.

PART 4

BONUS RESOURCES

Parts 1 through 3 of this book provide everything you need to put action plans in place and get the benefits you deserve. Still, at VA Claims Insider, we know that everybody learns differently. Some people prefer videos to print. Some people need a higher-level education or a deep dive into specific topics or conditions. Sometimes you want to talk to someone personally. And sometimes you need to be part of a community that's keeping you empowered and accountable.

The list of bonus resources in this section can provide you with all of those options. This section is different from the others: it gives you access to additional VA Claims Insider resources proven to help veterans get the benefits they deserve—fast.

★ ★ ★

How to Approach Part 4

- Pick and choose which resources best suit your needs or try them all.

- Take the webinar training for a more condensed overview of the disability claim and denial process.

- Join a personalized, full-service, education-based coaching and consulting program to carry you through the VA claim process from beginning to end.

- Poke around on the VA Claims Insider blog and YouTube channel to see what kinds of information are out there for you. You can also search by keyword for specific information.

- With the click of a mouse, answer any question you have about any of the 834 ratable disabilities on the VA's rating schedule.

★ ★ ★

CHAPTER FIFTEEN

BONUS RESOURCES

1. FREE "INSIDER" TIPS FOR VA DISABILITY

Join 600,000+ fellow veterans who come to our website each month to learn tips, strategies, and lessons on filing or refiling a winning VA disability claim so that you can get the VA rating you deserve by law. On our blog, we go way more in depth on each of the subjects specific to disability benefits and claims.

We post a new, high-value resource each week. There's always fresh content. The blog's topics include a combination of education, medical perspective, and case law. Precedent decisions change often, so our blog is where veterans can arm themselves with the best and most up-to-date information. For example, we may post a deep dive into sleep apnea: why it's so common among veterans, how to determine whether yours is service connected, how eligibility or ratings might have recently changed, and of course, how to successfully get a disability rating for it.

Our blog is pretty epic. I don't say that lightly. We could easily charge a monthly fee for access to this information. But we don't need to, so we don't. Learn more at *VAClaimsInsider.com/Blog*, or scan the QR code now.

2. FREE VA CLAIM "SECRETS" WEBINAR TRAINING

Many of the veterans in our community tell us they prefer to learn via video training. Whether that statement applies to you or not, I strongly recommend watching my free webinar training in which I'll teach you... drumroll, please...how to win your VA disability claim *and* get a higher rating—even if you've already filed or been denied.

In this master class, you'll learn a basic overview of the disability process as well as crucial insider tips. I've organized it by three expert "secrets":

- **Secret #1:** How to improve your VA disability claim, get an immediate rating increase (if warranted by law), and have it decided faster and more accurately

- **Secret #2:** How to legally and ethically get a 100% rating and more than $3,500 a month, tax-free, for life (this one is easier than you think!)

- **Secret #3:** How to structure your personal statements in the exact way VA raters want to see them so you can get the rating and compensation you deserve in less time

Now that you've read the book, this webinar will help reinforce the most essential pieces of information you need and motivate you to dig into your action plan. Register now! You can even watch the replay instantly at *VAClaimsInsider.com/auto-webinar-registration*.

Or scan the QR code now to access the free training.

3. START FREE: CONNECT WITH A VA CLAIM EXPERT

Since 2016, the company I'm blessed to lead has personally helped more than 25,000 fellow disabled veterans get the VA rating they deserve! Will you be next?

We do so through our flagship premier program, VA Claims Insider Elite. No one pays anything up front. You only pay a fee if you get a higher rating on your disability claim that results in an increase in your disability compensation from the VA. Otherwise, the service is free. Based on that business model, you can tell we are good at what we do, or our company wouldn't still be around! We follow our eight-step VA Claims Insider Elite process based on our three-part SEM Method:

Strategy + Education + Medical Evidence =
VA Rating You Deserve in Less Time!

VA Claims Insider is the world's largest community of Veterans Helping Veterans Worldwide. Here's how it works. You complete a three-step intake form online, and within minutes, you'll be contacted by a veteran coach (VC) who is trained in our process. You'll book a strategy session to talk about your disabilities and your claim. You'll also get access and permission to use the Elite Experience Portal Plus

(EEP+), which offers access to our high-value education-based resource library and 24/7/365 live support.

Once you have a strategy in place, we use our proprietary process to review your existing medical evidence of record and identify any gaps between your current rating and what you qualify for by law. Then, as a member, you'll receive reduced rates on visits to independent medical providers if you need medical examinations, disability evaluation, or Medical Nexus Letters, if and only if you want to use them. This step is optional, not required.

After you've submitted your claim, we'll provide some Compensation and Pension (C&P) exam preparation and coaching. Most veterans are very nervous about C&P exams. We calm nerves by demystifying the process and fully preparing veterans to tell their full, true story.

During the waiting period, we are in constant contact. The veteran is never alone, whether they are joining one of our webinars or Zoom calls, or just having coffee with the coaches and fellow veterans to talk. Community is key during this process. The community and level of engagement we offer and the availability of our team and resources are *unmatched*.

Change your life by joining us now. Complete our three-step intake to get started for *free*. You'll hear from a member of our team within minutes. Visit *VAClaimsInsider.com/Elite-Membership*, or scan the QR code.

4. FREE FOURTEEN-DAY TRIAL TO MILITARY DISABILITY MADE EASY'S ALL-ACCESS MEMBERSHIP

Having trouble understanding your DOD and VA disability rating schedule? Frustrated by the bureaucracy of the military disability system?

We understand. The web resource *MilitaryDisabilityMadeEasy.com* has simplified, categorized, and indexed the entire VA schedule for rating disabilities. Whether you want a general overview of the 834 medical conditions that can be service connected and compensated under the law, or you want to search for a very specific part of the law regarding one component of your claim, this is your resource.

The site breaks down each condition by name and medical lingo, and it includes pictures. Say you've had surgery on your left shoulder and can move it up to only a forty-five-degree angle. This website will tell you exactly what the rating should be for your level of disability.

This resource is also a way for us to be of service to the active duty community. If you're on active duty and are being med-boarded, we can help you understand what's happening and how to get the outcome you deserve. This site is the world's most comprehensive and intuitive resource for navigating the entire VA disability rat-  ing system. Don't get frustrated—get rated! Visit *MilitaryDisabilityMadeEasy.com*, or scan the QR code now to start your fourteen-day free trial of Military Disability Made Easy.

5. FREE ACCESS TO WEEKLY TRAINING VIDEOS

Our insider community of fellow disabled veterans have watched these videos more than 3 million times! We're one of the most trusted and watched YouTube channels for VA disability benefits. Our channel pro- vides two main resources. First, we produce free, expert-level, educational, deep-dive content each week. Second, our experts go live, offering veter- ans an opportunity to join an event, receive answers to questions about their own claims, and get to know our experts in a more personal way.

We developed this YouTube channel because we've found that community is one of the most important things we can provide to our veterans. People want to engage not only with the material but with each other to ask questions live and participate.

Join us to find out what we're all about! Subscribe now for *free* at *YouTube.com/VAClaimsInsider*, or scan the QR code now to watch us free on YouTube.

6. THE ULTIMATE GUIDE TO VA CLAIMS FOR PTSD

This is arguably the most comprehensive resource ever published regarding VA disability claims for PTSD. In this Ultimate Guide, you'll learn how to get a VA rating for PTSD even if you've already filed or been denied benefits in the past. You'll also unlock the top three ways to get a VA rating for PTSD as well as critical evidence requirements to include qualifying in-service stressor events.

Visit *VAClaimsInsider.com/VA-Rating-for-PTSD*, or scan the QR code now to read "Top Three Ways to Get a VA Rating for PTSD: The Ultimate Guide."

7. THE FIVE BEST STATES FOR DISABLED VETERANS

In this post, I break down the top five best states for disabled veterans, using a weighted average statistical analysis. We have compared metrics across five key financial measures that matter most to disabled veterans. If you're a disabled veteran, choosing where to live after leaving the military is an important decision for you and your family. And you might be wondering, what are the best states for disabled veterans? Well, here's the deal: some states are more friendly to disabled veterans than others, so selecting where to live could save (or cost) you thousands of dollars per year.

Visit *VAClaimsInsider.com/Best-States-for-Disabled-Veterans*, or scan the QR code now to read "Five Best States for Disabled Veterans (The Insider's Guide)."

8. EIGHTEEN STATES WITH FULL PROPERTY TAX EXEMPTION FOR 100% DISABLED VETERANS

In this high-value post, we list and give details on the eighteen states with full property tax exemption for 100% disabled veterans. (Typically, you must have a 100% P&T VA rating, with some limited exceptions.) Although all fifty states offer some form of property tax exemption for disabled veterans, our research and analysis uncovered eighteen states with no property tax for disabled veterans at all, meaning those eligible are exempt from paying *any* property tax on their primary residence.

Visit *VAClaimsInsider.com/Property-Tax-Exemption-for-100-Disabled-Veterans*, or scan the QR code now to read "Eighteen States with Full Property Tax Exemption for 100% Disabled Veterans (The Definitive Guide)."

9. THE THIRTY-FIVE BEST BENEFITS FOR 100% DISABLED VETERANS

In this guide, I reveal and explain the thirty-five top benefits for 100% VA disabled veterans. We've also compiled a complete list from A to Z of little-known 100% disabled veteran benefits for 2023 along with tips, strategies, and lessons learned so you'll know how to get them. And we even took the time to rank them by importance (in our opinion) and the amount of benefit you can receive for yourself and/or your dependents. In our experience helping more than 25,000 disabled veterans, we've discovered many with a 100% VA disability rating don't even realize the incredible benefits available to them at the federal and state levels, from various nonprofits, and in the form of everyday military and veteran discounts, among other sources. You could be missing out on thousands of dollars of benefits you deserve for yourself and your family!

Visit *VAClaimsInsider.com/Benefits-for-100-VA-Disability*, or scan the QR code now to read "Thirty-Five Best Benefits for 100% VA Disability: The Ultimate Guide."

10. FREE E-BOOK REVEALS THE 100+ MOST COMMON VA SECONDARY CLAIMS

I could probably sell this guide for $97 or more (worth it), but for a limited time, you can download the e-book version right here, right now, at no cost. Here's a sliver of what you'll learn:

- **Part 1:** The five types of service connection, explained from A to Z—simple answers make it clear exactly *why* secondary service connection might be key for you (even if you don't know where to start).

- **Part 2:** The definitive list of the top VA secondary claims for secondary service connection of over 100 conditions, listed in detail—you'll learn *how* to make a secondary claim. Plus, we've included medical research studies and BVA examples for each condition. It's 200 pages of solid gold, with clickable links!

- **Part 3:** *Bonus Resources!* Grab your free bonuses today, including digital downloads and step-by-step video tutorials, to learn how to increase your VA disability rating in less time—even if you've already filed or been denied.

Scan the QR code now to secure your instant *free* digital download of "Secondary Service Connection *Secrets!*"

CONCLUSION

It's hugely important to me to put this book out into the world. My life's work is to help as many veterans as possible, and I can't do so alone. I need *you* to help spread the message. We need to help each other to reach even more veterans and their families.

This book, my blog, the VA Claims Insider website, and the entire business were born out of my own frustration about being stuck and underrated for years. I felt alone. I struggled with undiagnosed mental health conditions, substance abuse, and marital issues. Everywhere I went, I felt I didn't belong. I wanted my identity back. I craved being part of a community with fellow brothers and sisters again. After I got myself straight, I knew that God had called me to *give veterans hope.*

It is my mission to guide you through the contents of this book so you can make a change. At VA Claims Insider, we always celebrate *life change*—including not only receiving financial compensation but also overcoming addictions; finding fulfilling jobs; building stronger marriages, families, and relationships; improving physical and mental health; and becoming part of a community again. Often, these life changes start when veterans finally apply for and receive VA benefits.

Prior to this book, there was no comprehensive resource that covered all the benefits available to veterans. Sure, there's plenty of information freely available at your fingertips, but information alone is not helpful, especially when it's disorganized and there's too much of it. What I have tried to do here is tell you only what you need to know and then contextualize it in a way that makes sense and allows you to take action.

Remember that this is an *action* book. Yes, my team and I have given you hundreds of different opportunities to receive compensation and discounts, but the most important thing we are giving you is permission to take action. There's one thing I'm sure of: if you don't take action, you won't get the result. Nobody is going to do this work for you. You need to take control of your own veteran benefits.

When we ask veterans in our community why they haven't tried to apply for benefits yet or why they gave up trying, the number one answer we hear is that they think they don't deserve the benefits: "I'm not disabled," or "Somebody has it worse than I do, and I don't want to take their benefits." Those are lies we tell ourselves that hold us back from taking action.

You served; you deserve. You served; you earned! You earned benefits. You may not be missing a limb. Heck, you may never have deployed! But you raised your hand. You took that oath of office, and you swore to support and defend the Constitution of the United States against all enemies, foreign and domestic. Very few people do that. That journey is special. You were a part of something bigger than yourself. Sometimes we don't realize the significance of our contribution until we're out, but the VA does—and it wants to acknowledge your service by helping you in your new civilian life and career. Take advantage of whatever in these pages applies to you. You earned it.

Thank you for letting me be a part of your journey. It's the highest honor of my life to serve the veteran community and give you hope. Now go open a claim already! I'll talk to you soon.

ACKNOWLEDGMENTS

Thank you to my Lord and Savior Jesus Christ, who died on the cross for my sins. You are the way and the truth and the life. I put my faith and life in your hands.

Many thanks to my wife, Laurel Reese, who is my partner and best friend. You're the calm to my storm. And your constant encouragement, patience, and insights made our movement and this book possible. I love you with all my heart.

Thanks to my three incredible children, Dylan, Everley, and Remington Reese, for your fun, your laughter, and the continued blessings you bring to my life. You're my world. I love you so much.

A big thank-you to the second edition editing and book launch team of Rob Nichols, Thirdy Rivera, and Beatrice Highsmith. This incredible gift of federal and state benefits for veterans would not have been possible without your countless hours researching, writing, and editing.

To Jane Borden, Libby Allen, Brannan Sirratt, Aleksandra Mendel, and the entire Scribe writing team, seriously, thank you. Without your constant presence, writing skills, content guidance, and program management, this book would never have been written. You gave life to this most important project.

ABOUT THE AUTHOR

Brian Reese is one of the world's leading experts in veteran benefits, having helped millions of veterans secure their financial future since 2013. A former active duty air force officer, Brian deployed to Afghanistan in support of Operation Enduring Freedom. He is a distinguished graduate of management of the United States Air Force Academy and earned his MBA as a National Honor Scholar from the Spears School of Business at Oklahoma State University.

Made in the USA
Middletown, DE
09 August 2023

36443358R00248